Happy ...

Clarion Cotter

THE HIGH FLYER'S HANDBOOK

Did you know that as a business traveller you represent the lifeblood of the travel industry? (Profits would plummet without its lucrative corporate accounts.) So what better reason for making sure you get the red carpet treatment you truly deserve?

In *The High Flyer's Handbook* Marion Cotter shows you how, as a premium customer, you can be treated as a VIP on your travels. In a lively and humourous style, she gives you the inside track on how to:

- Get the best deals from airlines, hotels and travel agents
- Successfully combine business with pleasure on a trip
- Cut hold-ups and delays
- Get an upgrade on flights
- Avoid being ripped off in a foreign place
- Understand business etiquette around the world
- Cope as a female business traveller

and much more.

Packed with useful tips and advice, *The High Flyer's Handbook* shows you in no uncertain terms how to get the most out of your trips and enjoy yourself too. Don't take off without it!

Published in association with the International Airline Passenger's Association (IAPA).

DUBAI DUTY FREE'S FINEST SURPRISE CONTINUES...

YOUR OPPORTUNITY TO WIN THE FINEST CARS AT THE WORLD'S FINEST DUTY FREE

DUBAI DUTY FREE'S FINEST SURPRISE NOW OFFERS YOU A CHOICE. TICKETS MAY BE PURCHASED FOR ONE OR BOTH CARS.

For each car, tickets are priced at Dhs 500/US $139 and limited to 1,000 bonafide travellers either departing, or transiting, through the Dubai International Airport.

The draw date and winning numbers will be published, and each participant will be advised.

The cars will be shipped to the winners address free of charge.

THE FINEST COLLECTION AT THE WORLD'S MOST ELEGANT DUTY FREE

For The World's Finest... **Fly Buy Dubai**

For further information please call Dubai (9714) 206-2433 or Fax (9714) 241 455

CONGRATULATIONS!
DUBAI DUTY FREE'S FINEST SURPRISE WINNERS

227th Winner
ABDULLA AL-BLAIHED
(Series # 227 – Ticket # 0756)
of the Saudi Arabia, winner of the
green metallic Porsche 928 GTS

228th Winner
RICHARD BRAY
(Series # 228 – Ticket # 0084)
of Dubai, UAE, winner of the
kashmir beige BMW 850 Ci

Why settle for a place to stay, when Cheval is a home from home?

Think about it.

Which would you really prefer? Simply a place to stay - or your own private apartment in Central London?

We offer the finest range of accommodation in Knightsbridge. Whether you're a business traveller or a leisure visitor, you'll find a Cheval apartment, house or maisonette a real home from home.

Every one is different. Each is individually styled, fitted and furnished to the highest international standard. All come complete with direct-dial telephone, weekday maid service, and car parking.

But the real difference is the freedom.

Freedom of lifestyle. To come and go when and where you want, to do precisely as you please. An informal business meeting? Invite your colleagues to a central, comfortable and private venue. An impromptu party? Simply call your friends.

Freedom of choice. A stylish night out? Some of London's finest restaurants and bistros are just around the corner. A relaxing evening at home? Every apartment has a luxury kitchen and colour TV with video. A fitness session? Every rental includes free membership of a local private health and leisure centre.

But there's more. We provide dedicated and professional management. Valet and baby-sitting services. Fax and telex facilities. Everything you need really to make the most of your stay in the capital.

Which is why our reputation is worldwide, and why so many of our guests stay with us time and again.

For full details, simply call, fax or write to our international reservation service. We'll send you a brochure by return.

CHEVAL APARTMENTS LIMITED
140 Brompton Road,
Knightsbridge,
London SW3 1HY.
Tel: 071-225 3325
Fax: 071-581 2869

CHEVAL APARTMENTS LIMITED
A home from home in London

A member of The Cheval Group
Cheval Apartments · Gloucester Park · Thorney Court

IAPA
INTERNATIONAL
AIRLINE
PASSENGERS
ASSOCIATION

THE HIGH FLYER'S HANDBOOK

THE DEFINITIVE GUIDE FOR TODAY'S BUSINESS TRAVELLER

MARION COTTER

KOGAN PAGE

Disclaimer
The author and publisher have made every effort to ensure that the information and advice contained in this handbook is accurate. However, they can take no responsibility for any loss, inconvenience, injury or other liability arising as a result of anyone using the book. Data and examples used to illustrate specific points in the book are intended – and should be used – as a general guide rather than an up-to-date source of information, since the travel business is, by definition, a fast-moving industry.

First published in 1993

Apart from any fair dealing for the purposes of research or private study, or criticism or review, as permitted under the Copyright, Designs and Patents Act, 1988, this publication may only be reproduced, stored or transmitted, in any form or by any means, with the prior permission in writing of the publishers, or in the case of reprographic reproduction in accordance with the terms of licences issued by the Copyright Licensing Agency. Enquiries concerning reproduction outside those terms should be sent to the publishers at the undermentioned address:

Kogan Page Limited
120 Pentonville Road
London N1 9JN

©Marion Cotter 1993

British Library Cataloguing in Publication Data

A CIP record for this book is available from the British Library.

ISBN 0 7494 1075 2

Typeset by DP Photosetting, Aylesbury, Bucks
Printed and bound in Great Britain by
Clays Ltd, St Ives plc

FOR THE BEST IN CHAUFFEUR DRIVE SERVICE...GUARANTEED

If you're looking for air conditioned Jaguars, Limousines and Executive Micro Buses all with the latest registrations, there is only one number to call first. All our cars are professionally driven & immaculately presented for your corporate and personal use. Phone us first. We guarantee to get it right first time every time.

CHAUFFEUR DRIVE AND SELF-DRIVE

081-960 1357   **081-770 7762**
FAX 081-964 3268   FAX 081-661 7403

Boardroom Services
(A Division of F.S.E.I.), 11 Mayfield Court,
6-8 Egmont Rd, Sutton SM2 5JN

SLOANE SQUARE/CHELSEA

Elegant Edwardian house comprising seven individually-designed apartments, including delightful Penthouse; fully fitted kitchens, luxury bathrooms, daily maid service, TV, direct-dial 'phone, fax, lift.

Excellent location – 2 minutes walk Sloane Square underground station, 5 minutes walk Harrods and the interesting Chelsea locality.

For further information and reservations please call Christine Smith
(0) 932 336668 phone   (0) 932 336165 fax

☐ Contents

Acknowledgements   8

About the Author   9

About IAPA   10

Introduction – Why You Are a VIP   11

1 The Flying Business   17
How the airline business works

2 Air Fares and Agents   34
The inside track on deals, discounts and dodges

3 Planning your Trip   50
Everything to do before you go

4 At the Airport   62
Minimizing the hassles on take-off and touchdown

5 Flying in Style   83
Making the most of airline perks

6 Getting About on Arrival   102
Going by car, bus and train

7 Hotels and the Red Carpet Treatment   115
Getting most room for your money

8 Staying Safe   133
Perils in the air and on the ground

SAVE 50%
long distance international fax & telephone users

HOME OR AWAY – AROUND THE WORLD*

Using a new US-based system with the latest technology in call-processing, enjoy fast, clear connections and **save 20-50% on all long distance international calls.**

NO LANGUAGE PROBLEMS
NO LOCAL TAXES OR HEFTY HOTEL SURCHARGES
NO SPECIAL EQUIPMENT REQUIRED

Can be used from **any touch-tone phone** (payphone, private, business, hotel, fax or mobile). Offers unprecedented mobility, convenience and savings to:

RESIDENT COMPANIES   **BUSINESS TRAVELLERS**
PRIVATE USERS   **TOURISTS**

A no-nonsense system which offers users confidence to save continuously throughout the world

SAVE WITH CONFIDENCE WITH DTC INTERNATIONAL
FACILITY AVAILABLE NOW!

For easy-to-use instructions & an application form call your nearest office...

UK	(44 71) 376 7881	USA	(516) 441 9696
Australia	(61 76) 35 64 65	Germany	(49 471) 979 410
S. Arabia	(966 1) 462 8000	France	(33 35) 30 65 56
U.A.E.	(97 14) 45 23 50	Greece	(30 1) 778 3698
Kuwait	(965) 240 1600	Africa	(234 1) 96 61 39
Bahrain	(97 3) 21 48 83		(234 1) 96 54 55
Lebanon	(961 1) 89 78 81	Far East	(85 2) 549 78 28

...or call our Head Office on 44 71 724 8115
APPLICATIONS FOR SALES AGENCIES WORLDWIDE ARE WELCOMED

*except Cuba and N. Korea

9	**After-hours Fun** *Having a good time in the AIDS era*	150
10	**Money** *Spending it and safeguarding it*	159
11	**In the Pink** *Staying healthy on your travels*	175
12	**The Female Factor** *Survival tactics for today's woman traveller*	188
13	**Doing it Right** *Business etiquette around the world*	201
14	**Business Holidays** *Sidetrips, incentives and corporate freebies*	213
	Appendix – Sources of Further Information	222
	Index	234
	Index of advertisers	240

TARGUS COMPUTERFASHION

We've Raised The Industry Standards... Again.

Workstation

Computer/Printer Compartment

Luggage Compartment

Accordion File Section

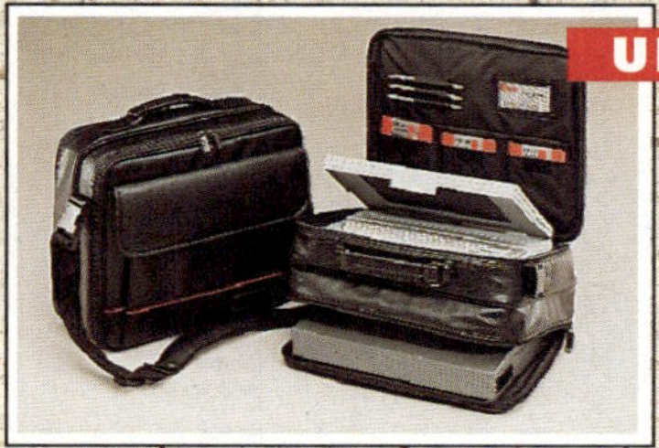

UNIVERSAL NOTEBOOK CASE

is designed for all models of notebook computers and is made of an innovative new material that is both stylish and durable. The case offers two padded compartments that measure 11"x13"x2.3" each. The padded computer compartment features disk pockets, pen and business card holders and two straps to secure the computer. The other padded compartment comes with adjustable dividers to fit power-supplies, A.C. adaptors, external disk drives or keypads. These dividers can be removed to accommodate a personal printer or to be used as a briefcase. The case also features a detachable shoulder strap and two external pockets that will hold standard file folders.

THE BUSINESS TRAVELER

is the ultimate case for the traveling executive. The result of years of consumer testing, this luxurious full-grain leather case combines four functional sections; a zip-down workstation, a padded note-book and printer compartment, a fully-lined and padded luggage section and an accordion file section. The Business Traveler is available in two versions-standard or cellular and is sized to fit under an airline seat or in an overhead compartment.
New and innovative features include an ergonomically-designed padded shoulder strap, reinforced-oversized handle, see-through mesh accessory pouches and pockets for both a cellular phone and electronic organizer. The Business Traveler, like all Targus brand products, is covered by our lifetime replacement warranty. Targus, the tradition continues.

Targus Benelux B.V.
P.O. box 108, NL-5070 AC Udenhout, Holland.
Tel: +31(0)4241 - 4445, Fax: +31(0)4241 - 3185.

TARGUS
A TRADITION OF EXCELLENCE

☐ Acknowledgements

Many thanks to Patrick Walsh, who helped get this project off the ground, and to Pauline Goodwin and the production team at Kogan Page. Others who played a part include Joanna Pegum, Alex McWhirter of *Business Traveller*, and the many people in the airline and hotel business prepared to share their knowledge and expertise. Very special thanks must go to Ben Etherton for his valuable comments on the book's script and format as a whole.

Additional research — Joanna Pegum
Specialist contributors — Alex McWhirter, Philip Ray
Crime and safety adviser — Ben Etherton

☐ About the Author

Marion Cotter has been writing about business travel for the last six years. She has freelanced on the subject for *The Times, Sunday Times, The Guardian, Daily Telegraph* and *Financial Times*, and is a regular contributor to *Executive Travel* magazine and other titles. She is also a director of The Word Association, a London-based company producing newsletters and corporate literature.

Born in Cardiff and a graduate of London University, Marion is widely travelled and is a veteran of business trips, good and bad. Not averse to the champagne treatment, she has to make do with rather less at times.

☐ About IAPA

The International Airline Passengers Association has over 30 years experience in understanding and meeting the needs of frequent business travellers. Today IAPA has offices worldwide and a membership of over 110,000.

Members enjoy a range of savings from up to 40 per cent on hotel bills at over 4,000 luxury hotels worldwide and up to 30 per cent savings on car hire with Hertz, Avis, Interrent National Europcar and Tilden. The WorldWide Personal Accident Insurance Programme also offers members up to £1,000,000 accident insurance protection 365 days a year.

Priority Pass, the largest independent optional airport lounge access programme in the world, enables members to gain entry to over 50 VIP lounges at major international airports worldwide, irrespective of class of travel, airline flown or membership of an airline club.

Other member benefits include a unique Bag-Guard® luggage protection and retrieval service and free card protection scheme. There are also special privileges for members at strategically located business centres in the major cities of the world.

IAPA Service Offices are manned by multi-lingual staff seven days a week for assistance with travel problems.

If you would like to join or would like more information, please call (UK) 44 London (81) 681 6555. Alternatively, see IAPA's address listed in the appendix (page 222).

Introduction
☐ Why You Are a VIP

Business travel is big business. Globally, it runs up a bill of some $450 billion a year – over one-third of that spent in Britain and the US alone.

Travel and entertainment costs are the third highest overhead for many businesses. Corporate travel mops up nearly half of all spending on air travel, and makes up a hefty slice of travel and tourism as a whole – an economic powerhouse that ranks as the world's largest industry and employs 1 in 15 workers around the globe.

Unrelenting recession has, of course, taken its toll on corporate travel spending in the last three years. Downgrading is still the name of the game as travellers tighten their belts another notch and shop around for better deals. Many company seniors who some years back might have luxuriated upfront in first class are now squeezed at the back of the plane – where it's hard to find a spare seat these days.

Cost-clipping cutbacks

Research by the International Air Transport Association (IATA) shows that nearly 30 per cent of companies trimmed their travel sails in the first half of 1993, with over a quarter reducing the number of trips made. Industry insiders predict the cutbacks will continue long after the economic upturn gathers pace, with many firms adopting long-term cost-clipping strategies. Like it or not, the devil-may-care days of the high-spending '80s are gone.

Global recovery will come none too soon for the world's airlines, whose much-publicized losses since 1990 are now running in the double-digit billions. Hotels, too, have taken a hammering as customers shorten trips, axe budgets or simply stay at home. Two-thirds of US companies, according to American Express, now require their employees to take the lowest logical fare.

But for all its troubles, business travel remains a formidable force. More than three million business class travellers will fly on Europe's top five air routes during 1993, building a profitable pillar for an EC industry generating 1 per cent of the Community's gross domestic product and employing some 700,000 people. The number of business journeys through UK airports is predicted to total nearly 30 million by the turn of the century.

Revenue from corporate travellers remains the industry's bedrock. Without it, many air carriers, hotels and car hire firms would see their profits quite simply wiped out. It's a telling fact that an airline can make money on the flagship London–New York route without a single passenger in first or economy, providing its business class cabin is full.

Premium passengers

For the travel industry, then, business travellers still have Big Bucks written all over them. Even trimmed of the fat, corporate accounts remain the lifeblood of the airline and hotel world, not to mention scores of travel agencies. Tour groups and families flying on Apex tickets may provide much of the bread and butter, but full-fare paying executive globetrotters lay on the jam. Lashings of it.

In short, today's expense-account corporate nomads are the travel industry's VIPs. Airlines and hotels alike readily unfurl the red carpet for the customers who provide the mainstay of their business and the cream of their profits. Often chauffeured to and from the airport in gleaming limousines, they can choose their seat weeks before they travel, relax in private airline lounges before take-off, and enjoy the champagne treatment the minute they step on board. First in line for upgrades in the air, they are often shown to the best room in the house.

Other side of the coin

Spending power is not the only reason these premium travellers merit the seemingly lavish rewards heaped upon them. While colleagues back at the office like to think business trips are a blank cheque to live it up at the firm's expense, seasoned globetrotters know full well that going abroad on business has a downside, as well as a glamorous edge.

Putting on a winning performance after 12 sleepless hours next to a bawling toddler is not exactly a breeze. What's more, most trips are to less-than-divine destinations. Today's contract-hunting traveller is more likely to be heading for the factories of the Ruhr and the industrial heartland of Russia than for some Pacific island playground. And more than a few are relieved to say farewell to Frankfurt and so long to St Louis when all they've seen of the city is the inside of a bank or a steel plant.

JA.

"I've got two hours in Brussels between flights. Is there somewhere quiet where we can actually work?"

©1992 Diners Club International Ltd.

Diners Club® says "yes" in more than 175 countries around the world. And with Diners Club, "yes" means more than global acceptance. It also means you're welcome in 47 exclusive Diners Club airport and business lounges in major cities around the world. It's something other cards just don't offer. So why take chances? Take Diners Club.

DINERS CLUB. THE RIGHT ANSWER IN ANY LANGUAGE.℠

See the Diners Club Airport and Business/Member Lounge listing in the Travel Tips section.

With more firms trying to shoehorn trips that might once have taken a week into a matter of days, pleasures have been superseded by pressures yet more. Flying from London to the States just for the night, or jetting around the world in a week is no longer uncommon as companies tighten the spending reins and scrutinize costs. Time-pressed travellers are more likely to be dashing for the last flight home than checking in for a night of pampered luxury at some five-star foreign pad.

All the more reason, then, why today's executive high flyers – roving ambassadors for their firms, as well as premium customers to the industry – earn the right to business trips second to none. As a corporate traveller, you have prestige and spending power. Don't be afraid to trade on it. You should expect – and get – the best the business travel industry can offer. Whether you are catching a plane, booking into a hotel, renting a car or planning a sidetrip, this book aims to show you how to do just that.

TAILPIECES

- According to the US Travel Data Center, today's average business traveller is male, 39, married and as likely or not to be a college graduate – or at least, that was the picture in 1991.

- Mr Average is also a pretty clued-up customer. According to Official Airline Guides, he has plenty in common with Clint Eastwood's cheroot-chewing cowboy – a self-reliant, hard bargaining, sceptical operator who becomes more hard-bitten with experience.

- How do corporate travellers kill time in their hotel at night? According to the same OAG survey, industrious Brits burn the midnight oil while their continental cousins party. While 68 per cent of the Latins are out on the town, some 80 per cent of the British work diligently away in their rooms. Germans are busy pumping iron in the gym.

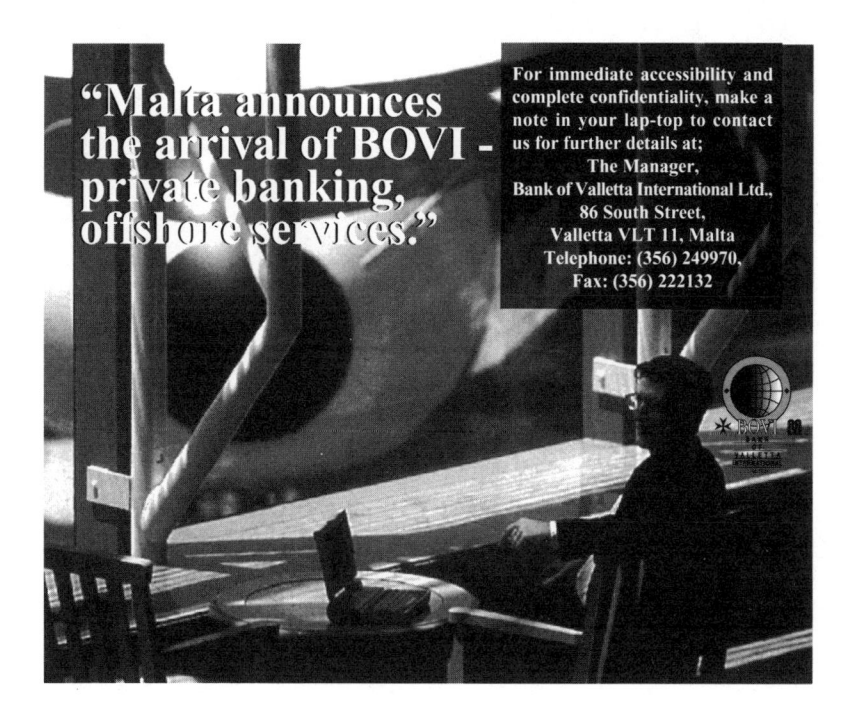

"Malta announces the arrival of BOVI - private banking, offshore services."

For immediate accessibility and complete confidentiality, make a note in your lap-top to contact us for further details at;
The Manager,
Bank of Valletta International Ltd.,
86 South Street,
Valletta VLT 11, Malta
Telephone: (356) 249970,
Fax: (356) 222132

1
☐ The Flying Business

Airlines are rarely out of the headlines. News of their price wars, quarrels, investments and mid-air dramas makes compulsive reading even for armchair travellers.

Frequent flyers who board B747s at the drop of a hat need to know a little more, however. Some insight into how the flying business actually works can prove valuable ammunition in not only making informed air travel decisions, but in dealing with those who work in the industry.

What are the all-too-common reasons behind delays? Why are flights so often overbooked? What does deregulation actually mean? And how are carriers gearing up to meet the demands of the 21st century? Serious corporate travellers should make a point of knowing at least some of the answers.

FLYING INTO THE RED

Airlines have flown through some stormy weather of late. Biting recession has pushed up their global losses to more than $11 billion since 1990 – more than their accumulated profits in the industry's entire history.

Hit by a dramatic fall in revenue, many have been forced to lay off staff, cut salaries, cancel aircraft orders, axe unprofitable routes and discount tickets on an unprecedented scale simply to stay in business. Faced with a trading downturn of nightmare proportions, even the fittest have struggled to stay in the black.

US airlines have figured prominently among the loss-makers. Some of the industry's biggest names have gone to the wall – among them Pan Am and Eastern – with stablemates TWA and Continental forced to file for bankruptcy protection. Even American Airlines turned in losses of more than $900 million in 1992, forcing it to cut staff levels, sell off assets and prune back fleet orders.

British Airways absorbed stricken fellow UK carrier Dan-Air – the latest in a string of European casualties – for the nominal sum of £1, plus an inherited debt burden of some £35 million. Surprise chinks of light came from a few small airlines such as British Midland, which posted record results in the first three months of 1993.

Critics blame this industry-wide sea of losses on poor decision-making by airline management, over-ambitious expansion plans, suicidal ticket discounting and a failure to make prudent cutbacks in time. Unions, governments and suppliers have also taken the rap for standing by while the industry nosedived deeper into the red.

Aerial dogfights

Passengers are unquestionably the winners as carriers struggling to get back into the black lock horns in a round of aerial battles, turning flagship routes like the North Atlantic into a fares free-for-all as each tries to price the other out of business. The result is that many are pricing themselves out of business, as revenue takes a battering despite rising passenger counts.

Airlines are now waging a war of extras to keep their premium-fare passengers at the front of the plane. Cutting costs network-wide to ensure they are still flying is the other big priority.

MERGERS AND MEGA-CARRIERS

Air carriers have been forging a series of multi-national alliances in a bid to stave off the competitive blast of their bigger rivals. A string of landmark business deals has seen some of the world's heavyweights interlocking to create a new breed of flying giants, knocking some small carriers out of the ring altogether.

Airline Amazons

In the US, the air travel market is now dominated by just three giant carriers. American, United and Delta each operate huge hub-and-spoke networks designed to consolidate their operations and rationalize costs in a fiercely price-sensitive marketplace. In the meantime, smaller carriers like People Express, Braniff and Air Europe have been squeezed out of business.

The scramble to strike up alliances and global airbridges is much in evidence in Europe, where pundits now predict the financial collapse of some well-known names and the emergence of four or five all-powerful carriers by the turn of the century.

GO FOR GOLD

Ballantine's
GOLD SEAL

British Airways – already the world's biggest international carrier – has been out on a buying spree, purchasing stakes in American carrier USAir and Qantas of Australia. It is also a founder partner in Air Russia, due to take to the skies in 1994. Air France has bought into Czech carrier CSA and taken a major stake in Belgium's Sabena, while Alitalia has bought shares in Malev of Hungary.

Global link-ups

KLM, SAS, Swissair and Austrian have meanwhile discussed linking up in a fully-fledged merger to form an airline even bigger than British Airways. KLM has already invested heavily in US carrier Northwest, paving the way for an integration of the two airlines' networks.

Small regional carriers have also been active on the partnership front. Crossair, which links London and Zurich via London City Airport, is part-owned by Swissair, while tiny CityFlyer Express has the backing of British Airways. Air UK feeds traffic from some 20 UK airports into Schiphol, thus becoming near-indispensable to KLM.

What do all the mergers and marketing tie-ups mean for the flying public? One-stop check-ins to a multitude of destinations are one key benefit – something British Airways now offers from the UK to more than 200 domestic US points through its tie-in with USAir. Others include greater access to business class lounges and – by merging frequent flyer programmes – better loyalty benefits. Discounts and special deals on each other's networks, and easier transfers are other spin-offs.

Mega monsters

It's not all good news, however. While the new breed of mega-carriers claim their economies of scale should reduce costs and bring lower fares for the traveller, critics claim they could ultimately turn into unresponsive monoliths that strangle competition. Only time will tell.

HUB-AND-SPOKE NETWORKS

Huge hub-and-spoke systems – now spreading from the US to Europe – have become vital to the game plans of the mega-carriers. By feeding flights in and out of a central hub airport, airlines can link points on which direct flights would be unprofitable, and consolidate traffic for their major longhaul routes.

Hub systems can double or treble journey times for travellers on some

HOTELINK INTERNATIONAL

GUIDEBOOK - THE HOTEL DIRECTORY ON DISK

Problems finding and booking good hotels around the world? Then you need HoteLink's GuideBook disk the quick and easy way to find over 5,000 quality hotels world wide.

GUIDEBOOK CONTAINS

- comprehensive information on more than 5,000 hotels world-wide majoring on Europe and the U.S.
- useful data where available on the style and size of each hotel, its price, sports and conference facilities, nearby airports, phone/fax number and address.
- many smaller independent properties, offering more of the local character than some of the larger chains.

A BOOKING FACILITY TOO!

- Once a suitable hotel has been chosen, those with a modem can make a booking request directly from the computer via` the disk's inbuilt "E-mail" facility.

COMPUTER REQUIREMENTS:

- GuideBook will run on any DOS based (IBM compatible) PC
- 8 MB of disk space required
- GuideBook is supplied on 3.5" disk
- Uses simple keyboard commands - ideal for even the most non-computer literate

INTRODUCTORY PRICE

- only £99 (£119 inc. VAT & p&p)
- to order just mail or fax us your completed form below.

I would like a copy of GuideBook at

£99 (£119 inc.VAT & p&p).

Mr / Mrs / Miss / Ms ....

Position ....

Company ....

Address ....

....

Tel: .... Fax: ....

I enclose a cheque for .... Payable to Hotelink International Ltd.

or please debit my credit card :**Access** ☐ **Visa** ☐ **Master Card** ☐

Card No.: .... Expiry Date: ....

routes, forcing them to go from A to B via C. They also enable certain carriers to dominate flight frequencies at key airports. Atlanta is synonomous with Delta, for instance, Dallas with American and Chicago with United. Northwest is a key player in Boston, and TWA in St Louis.

Each of these vast aerial junctions – some strained to capacity at peak hours – has its strong selling points. Each carrier invests heavily in its major hubs, pruning on-line connection times and boasting smooth and speedy transfers.

Europe's major airports are also expanding as international air traffic hubs, and pushing hard to win more lucrative transfer traffic. One-third of Amsterdam's yearly 16 million passengers are now in transit, while neighbouring Brussels hopes to become the hub of a network serving 75 airports in the next few years.

DEREGULATION

International aviation is still governed largely by bilateral agreements between governments, which dictate the routes that can be flown by the airlines of each country.

Regulation on an international scale has traditionally been reflected at national level, with most governments keen to protect their state-owned airline. This system began breaking down in 1978 when America's Carter administration deregulated the domestic US airline business overnight, throwing it open to unrestricted competition.

Good news or bad?

While some experts have slammed US deregulation as a commercial disaster (of the 176 new carriers launched as a result, only 1 still survived in 1992), passengers have had a field-day. Air fares have dropped sharply, and nine out of ten travellers now fly on discounted fares. Analysts calculate that deregulation has resulted in annual savings of more than £10 billion a year for the flying public.

Europe has shunned the Big Bang approach of the US. Although the so-called Third Package of air transport measures which took effect in January 1993 has gone some way towards creating free competition, it will be 1997 before any European airline can fly on any route within the Community.

While EC airlines can now set their own fares, the European Commission can still investigate any felt to be too high, or low enough to be deemed predatory. And while a British airline already flying from

London to Paris can fly on to Lyon or Nice, for instance, there are limits on the traffic it can pick up on the all-French sector.

The ultimate prize in deregulation will be an 'open skies' regime between the US and Europe. Airlines on both sides of the Atlantic are now calling for greater freedom, though much will depend on the outcome of the 1994 bilateral agreement between the UK and US.

Two factors seem certain to delay the reality of a fully-fledged deregulated marketplace – physical restraints on expansion at busy major airports, and the fact that most EC airlines remain subsidized, and thus reluctant to give freedom of the skies more than lukewarm support.

THE CONGESTION MENACE

Crowded skies and congested airports are not only hampering deregulation, but costing carriers a fortune. New runways and terminals are simply not being built fast enough to cope with growth in air traffic.

Major airlines are reckoned to foot a yearly bill of over $100 million each in wasted fuel, holding time and take-off delays. The cost to the US airline industry as a whole is said to be close to $5 billion, with another $1.5 billion being written off in western Europe.

British Airways burns up over 60,000 tonnes of extra fuel every year because of traffic hold-ups at Heathrow and Gatwick alone, with taxiing delays devouring a further 21,000 tonnes. Lufthansa's planes were held up more than 27,000 hours on the ground and in the air in 1992 – a total of three years in waiting time that cost the airline DM140 million.

Untangling spaghetti skies

Association of European Airlines figures show that one in six flights is currently delayed for 15 minutes or more. With airports such as Heathrow and Frankfurt running at virtually 100 per cent capacity at peak times, and other key gateway airports not far behind, the problem is not going to go away overnight. Urgent action is now needed to untangle spaghetti skies.

Brussels-based EuroControl has been charged with co-ordinating Europe's diverse multi-state air traffic control networks. A task force known as EATCHIP is now looking at ways to optimize use of Europe's airspace through improved radar and communications.

Nearly £600 million is being ploughed into upgrading Britain's overstretched air traffic control (ATC) system to help meet the traffic pressures of the '90s. Air space above southern England is being marshalled into one-way 'sky tunnels' designed to allow up to 30 per cent more traffic to be handled in the area by 1995, and a new £200 million ATC centre will open by the following year.

Massaging schedules

In the meantime, airline timetables are being discreetly rewritten with a built-in delay factor, to help reduce passengers' increasing frustration at arriving at their destination late. A survey published in *Executive Travel* magazine comparing schedules from the ABC World Airways Guide revealed that passengers flying Viscounts, Vanguards and Tridents 20 years ago could expect to reach their destination several minutes faster than those flying new-generation jets today.

AIRLINE PERFORMANCE

If you're taking a domestic flight with any of the top ten US airlines, you can check out its on-time arrival record first. America's Department of Transportation (DOT) publishes a monthly Air Travel Consumer Report, detailing not just a carrier's punctuality, but its rates of mishandled baggage, oversales and consumer complaints.

The data can be called up by travel agents using one of the big computer reservation systems. Flights are assigned a number between 0 and 9 to show the percentage of on-time arrivals achieved in the previous month. Figures for February 1993, for instance, show Delta at the bottom of the timekeeping league, with just under 71 per cent of flights arriving on time. Alaska, by contrast, mustered an 88 per cent on-time rating.

DOT data should be treated as an indicator rather than an infallible guide, since it does not take into account cancellations or mechanical delays, nor the fact that cold-weather carriers may be more delay-prone in winter than others.

European airlines to make their punctuality ratings known include SAS, which posted an on-time performance rating of over 92 per cent on all international flights in April 1993 – making the airline number two in Europe in punctuality terms.

TOMORROW'S AIRPORTS

With worldwide passenger counts growing by leaps and bounds, airports already creaking at the seams are doomed to become perpetual building sites over the next decade. Investment in start-to-finish automation at leading gateways promises to ultimately replace short-term hell with a smoother passage for 21st-century globetrotters.

More combined ticket/boarding passes, off-terminal check-ins and fast-track immigration channels are already speeding things up for business travellers. Carriers such as SAS, Lufthansa, Swissair and Cathay Pacific allow passengers to check in before they even leave for the airport, either by phone or by using city-centre counters. Kerbside check-ins, already commonplace in the States, are spreading to Europe, while pre-flight seat allocation is a near-standard perk.

British Airways runs a check-in desk at Heathrow airport's Hertz car hire depot, and plans to set up mobile check-in facilities at airport car parks, terminal kerbsides and even underground stations in the next few years. The carrier is also testing palm-top computers which allow staff to check in passengers waiting in line.

Smarter tickets

Smart airline tickets are also cutting waiting time on the ground. Automatic ticket and boarding passes (ATBs) with a built-in magnetic strip which are simply swiped through credit-card style machines are now shaving check-in times, cutting some 45 minutes off the time needed to check in a fully laden B747.

Technology which 'reads' a traveller's hand pattern against an encoded identity card is being trialled in the US, where immigration has traditionally been a slow shuffle. Already successfully tested on the inmates of a Georgia jail, the system is now being used on a group of frequent flyers at New York's JFK and Newark airports. A similar system has been tested at Amsterdam's Schiphol Airport.

Gatwick airport and Heathrow's terminal 4 now offer fast track channels for checked-in first and business class passengers, providing dedicated lines at security, passport control, duty-free stores and bureaux de change. The aim is to trim 30 minutes off the time needed to make shorthaul flights, and more for those travelling longhaul.

High-tech newcomers

State-of-the-art airports are now handling more passengers than ever in less time. Denver's new showpiece airport – occupying 53 square miles – is designed to handle simultaneous take-offs and landings on four of its six runways, while Singapore's $650 million second terminal will allow Changi airport to handle 24 million passengers a year by 1995. A high-speed Skytrain links the new complex to terminal 1.

Elsewhere in the Pacific Rim, Japan's new Kansai airport – built to relieve pressure on both Tokyo and Osaka – should open in late 1994 in what ranks as one of Asia's most ambitious ever building projects. Located in Osaka Bay, the airport will boast over 40 aircraft parking bays, a four-tier passenger terminal and a double-decked, six-lane highway link to the mainland. Hong Kong's badly needed successor to Kai Tak airport should meanwhile be open by 1997.

In Europe, both London Stansted and Munich 2 have been hailed as built-for-tomorrow gems of new technology. Futuristic Stansted handles only a fraction of the eight million passengers a year it was designed for, making it a dream to use compared with crowded rival Heathrow, where a fifth terminal should open by 2002. Schiphol's impressive new west terminal provides welcome new capacity, plus saunas, a casino and a wealth of open-plan retailing. A business centre will open there in 1995.

Twenty-first century jets

Aircraft manufacturers are also preparing to blast into the 21st century with a fleet of new-age aircraft capable of flying more passengers than ever in record time. Turn-of-the-century travellers could be stepping on board 600-seater superliners complete with noise-free cabins, piano lounges, live entertainers and even flying conference rooms. Concorde could give way to supersonic aircraft flying between London and Tokyo in five hours by the year 2005, while monster jumbos carrying up to 1,000 passengers could be commonplace ten years later.

ON BOARD TODAY

Smoke-free flights

Airlines have also been cleaning up the air their customers breathe. Smokers have become the *bêtes noires* of international air travel as more and more flights are designated smoke-free.

Smoking is already banned on domestic flights within the US and Canada (unless more than six hours long), Australia, Saudi Arabia, France and Scandinavia. Other countries are expected to follow suit, and an EC-wide ban now looks a distinct possibility. Some transatlantic and transpacific flights now ban smoking, and Aer Lingus has banned cigarettes on flights between Ireland and the UK.

Industry watchdog ICAO, the International Civil Aviation Organization, has voted for a blanket smoking ban on all international flights by

July 1996 or earlier. In the meantime, US airlines are now required to provide a non-smoking seat for any passenger who wants one, enlarging the smoke-free section of aircraft cabins if need be.

Given a free hand, most carriers would prefer to ban smoking outright. Cigarettes pose an obvious on-board fire hazard, and cabin crew dislike working in a smoke-filled atmosphere for long periods. Smoking raises the cost of maintaining air filtration systems and even smokers, research shows, often favour fug-free flights.

These arguments predictably carry little weight with pro-smoking lobbying groups like FOREST, which publishes a 40-page guide to smoker-friendly airlines for those desperate for a puff.

In-flight entertainment

Killing time in the clouds with a good old-fashioned paperback could soon be decidedly passé. Some 20 major airlines now provide individual screens and a glut of video entertainment for their front-cabin passengers.

Air travellers now cross continents in subsonic movie houses whose galaxy of screened attractions could put even Hollywood in the shade. They can watch anything from thrillers and spaghetti westerns to comedy, cartoons, TV soaps and vintage film classics, not to mention same-day satellite news bulletins – with reports of any air crashes hastily edited out. Those who don't fancy a film can flick through audio channels carrying anything from Bach to Japanese pop.

Calling planet earth

In-flight communications have also come a long way. Credit-card telephones are now commonplace, and every inter-continental United passenger can expect a personal phone fitted to their seat by 1995. Singapore Airlines has introduced the world's first air cabin fax machines, while telefax units that take incoming calls are just around the corner. By the end of the decade, business class passengers will use their seat-back screen consoles to order duty-frees, check out share prices, book hire cars and even send flowers to the in-laws.

Japan Airlines now carries portable massage machines (unlike Virgin, which provides a live masseur), Lauda Air stores Apple Mac PowerBook computers, while Emirates favours electronic typewriters. Those who would sooner escape from the tyranny of faxes and phones, or simply detest flickering screens, chattering keyboards and mindless muzak will soon be able to don headphones playing nothing but blissful canned silence.

Having spent up to $2 million per aircraft kitting out their fleets with the latest in technology, airlines are, not surprisingly, keen to see it pay off. As a result, mail-order shopping designed to encourage passengers to spend, spend, spend is rapidly gaining ground. United, American and Northwest are among the US carriers now developing armchair shopping in the sky in a big way.

The problem with some of the mind-boggling array of in-flight gadgetry now installed is that it doesn't work. Channel-zapping under-12s, digitally illiterate grandparents and all-fingers-and-thumbs businesspeople can sometimes leave the circuitry as dead as a dodo. On older jets in particular, high-tech toys can often give low-tech satisfaction.

The flying gourmet

Frequent flyers who get more hot dinners in the air than they do at home, are fond of slating airline food as overhyped, overcooked and overambitious. They'll probably tell you that the only difference between the meals served in first and economy is that the former's menu is sprinkled with French and the coffee comes in a china cup.

Despite such derision, most airline passengers love to get their tucker. Killing the boredom factor at 30,000 feet means food takes on a disproportionate importance, and thus often merits more fuss and ceremony than in the poshest restaurant on the ground.

Pre-cooked, chilled, then re-heated on board, airline food is often bland at best and inedible at worst. Bullet-proof rolls, cremated steaks, limp salads and aerated sponges covered in swirls of shaving-cream topping are all too often *plat du jour*. Under-10s who munch their way through a burger, jelly and ice cream often get the tastiest-looking meal trays.

Superstar chefs

Airlines are, admittedly, taking more steps to prevent their food giving passengers terminal boredom. Gourmet chefs now put their names to signature dishes that would grace the menus of top Paris restaurants, while a host of dietary options – vegan, low cholesterol, low fat and gluten-free – now cater for virtually every taste and regime. You could be offered fresh chocolate chip cookies baked in-flight by American, freshly-made sushi by JAL, and even a low-fat emu steak by Qantas.

Virgin features specials created by superstar chef Raymond Blanc, while Lauda Air serves up *haute cuisine* dishes prepared by one of

Vienna's top restaurants. Saudia has even devised special meals for blind travellers, complete with menus in braille.

More is also being done for flying vegetarians. Meat-free eaters once handed platters resembling yesterday's lawn clippings now enjoy delights such as stuffed mushroom caps and artichoke hearts sautéed in garlic butter. Organic foods are spreading fast, and menus rotated more often to help ensure frequent flyers plying the same route week after week don't tire of the same fare.

After a decade of plying front-cabin passengers with brandies, truffles and calorific desserts, airlines have also jumped aboard the health bandwagon, trading sauce-laden steaks for sculpted courgettes. All-in-one slimline suppers can now be served straight after take-off for those who would sooner forgo the full works in favour of work or sleep.

THE SMALLPRINT

Losing your ticket

Getting a refund on a lost air ticket can take literally months. Some local agents will simply re-issue a new single flight coupon, charge you the appropriate value, and expect you to get a refund on the unused portions of the original ticket on your return home. Because of currency fluctuations, you will inevitably pay more for the new one than you receive back for the old one.

To obtain a refund, you will need to fill out an indemnity form. Many airlines hold these for six months or more before paying up, to ensure the original ticket is not used. Some are reluctant to make refunds even on fully-refundable tickets if you fail to turn up for the flight. Credit cards are useful when paying for tickets, since a thief cannot get a cash refund.

Overbooked flights

Airlines routinely overbook their scheduled flights by 20–30 per cent to offset the numbers of no-show passengers. The Association of European Airlines says its members lose a million seats every year through no-shows, though passengers who fail to check in for their original flight admittedly usually travel later on another.

Modern computer technology enables airlines to forecast the likely level of no-shows on a given flight with reasonable accuracy. The result is that, in practice, only small numbers of passengers are actually 'bumped', or denied boarding. British Airways, for instance, claims the figure is only 0.05 per cent, against a typical no-show rate of 15 per cent or more. In the US, less than 0.78 passengers per thousand flying with American, Delta and Northwest were left without a seat in 1992.

Penalties imposed on no-show passengers would, of course, help banish the practice of overbooking at a stroke. The problem is that no carrier wants to make itself unpopular by penalizing customers who might then simply switch airlines. Instead, business class fares are set at a level which effectively allows for no-shows, letting ticketholders cancel or change their bookings freely in return for paying more.

Passengers who add to the problem by making multiple flight bookings are, however, being firmly weeded out. Airline computers are now wise to the trick, and will immediately flash a warning to alert the reservations clerk that a booking is already held in that name.

Denied boarding compensation

Carriers caught out when virtually every booked passenger turns up for a flight usually call for volunteers to step down and take a later flight, in return for generous compensation – usually cash or free travel. Denied Boarding Compensation (DBC) levels depend on the carrier and the delay involved.

No compensation is mandatory if you get to your destination within an hour of the originally scheduled time, but you should expect the equivalent of at least $360, where the delay is four hours or more. The airline should also meet the cost of getting a message to your destination, plus meals, refreshments and overnight accommodation where necessary. Some may be prepared to refund the cost of the ticket or endorse it to another airline, if a delay is long.

Charter flights are not covered, and in the US neither are scheduled flights on planes holding fewer than 60 passengers. Carriers are required to give passengers a statement detailing their rights, and their policy on boarding priority, if asked.

Outside the EC and US, compensation is at the discretion of the carrier – and some pay nothing at all. A pocket flight guide will be useful for checking out alternative flights on-the-spot, while a good travel insurance policy will contain provision for delays.

LUGGAGE ALLOWANCES

Airline luggage limits can vary not only from country to country, but from carrier to carrier. The class you are flying and the aircraft you are using also count, and your allowance on a roomy B747 is unlikely to be matched on a small commuter plane. The mood of the check-in clerk can be another factor determining just how much you can take. While one will wave your excess trappings through with a smile, another will play it strictly by the book.

Pieces or weight?

While some airlines dictate luggage limits by weight, others simply set a ceiling of two (or even three) pieces. You're generally better off with the latter system, since although pieces are also subject to an upper weight limit, it's usually too high – around 32kg per piece – to worry about. Two cases of 32kg (70lb) each add up to a lot more luggage than the otherwise all-in weight limits of 20kg in economy, 30kg in business class and 40kg in first recommended by IATA. Outer dimensions are also limited, but can add up to a generous 62 inches or more each, or 106 inches together.

The piece method is applied on most domestic US, transpacific, transatlantic and US–South America routes. Weight is generally the standard elsewhere, though the piece system looks likely to become universal before too long. You can see which method your airline uses by checking the smallprint on your ticket.

Matters can become complicated on multi-sector and round-the-world trips, since the luggage ceiling on one leg of the journey may be much lower than on another. While this might not worry travellers habitually living out of a holdall, colleagues with bags of heavy samples in tow can occasionally come unstuck.

CARRY-ON BAGS

Hand baggage rules have become a fiasco in recent years. So many passengers now try to take all their bags as carry-ons that barely an inch of locker space flies empty. With airports offering an ever-increasing array of retail stores, customers are now boarding their flight laden with everything from T-shirts to toys.

Carry-on baggage – limited to one piece per person in most cases – must strictly speaking be small enough to fit under the seat in front, which usually means an all-round measurement of no more than 45 inches. Other items permitted include a handbag, coat, umbrella, camera, reading material and duty-free goods. Business class passengers can generally take a briefcase, and some carriers turn a blind eye to garment bags as well.

Business and first class passengers get the most leeway, and most US airlines allow two pieces in all classes. European carriers tend to be the strictest. Hazardous items you must not take on board include aerosols, corrosives, flammables, explosives, radioactives and compressed gases.

Discretionary rules

As with hold luggage, the disparity in hand luggage rules can make interlining tricky. Anyone travelling on, say, a business class ticket from London to Sydney, then taking a domestic hop in economy on a smaller plane, will be expected to jettison some of their hand luggage en route. The problem is that rules are often discretionary, so what applies on one day won't necessarily apply the next.

Business travellers are frequent offenders when it comes to flouting the hand luggage rules. So numerous are the culprits that some airports now operate a sticker system, banning any stickerless carry-ons from being taken past security controls. Some Spanish airports have installed X-ray machines that reject bags beyond a certain size, obliging their owners to check them in on the spot.

CLAIMS, COMPLAINTS AND COMPENSATION

Airlines have strict liability limits when it comes to compensating passengers for lost bags and other eventualities. Present limits for lost, damaged or delayed baggage for US domestic flights are $1,250 per passenger on all aircraft with more than 60 seats. Carriers will only pay the depreciated cost of any item lost or damaged, though some offer 'excess valuation coverage', which increases their liability.

In the UK, airline liability is currently limited to £13.65 for each kilo of luggage lost – not bad if you have lost a case full of socks and hankies, but poor compensation for a kilo of camcorder or Armani suit. What's more, most carriers will not accept liability for valuables such as money, jewellery and documents, or for fragile or perishable goods.

If your bag is delayed, the airline should reimburse you for reasonable out-of-pocket expenses. Most US airlines will offer to pay half the cost of new clothes, providing you produce receipts. Don't rely simply on airline handouts, however, should your bags go astray. Carrier compensation is not over generous, and adequate insurance is vital.

A carrier's conditions of carriage are listed on the inside cover of the ticket. You can request copies of the full contract by post. Under the Warsaw Convention, airlines have a limited liability of $75,000 per passenger in most cases for death or personal injury.

Filing a claim

Before letting off steam, note that:

- You'll need to give dates, flight numbers and airport names. Photocopy your ticket or baggage stubs if sending the originals.
- You're unlikely to get a personal reply from the chairman. Most complaints are dealt with by the customer relations manager.
- Your travel agent may be willing to take up a complaint or claim on your behalf. In Britain, the Air Transport Users Committee takes up complaints against carriers on behalf of customers.

Airlines are now giving in-flight and counter crew more power to deal with complaints and put things right on the spot. British Airways research shows that 80 per cent of customers will come back if something goes wrong, providing it is satisfactorily dealt with, as against only 35 per cent who will return otherwise. Senior cabin crew members have now been given more authority to appease disgruntled passengers – whether with an apology, a gift or a bouquet of flowers the next day.

TAILPIECES

- The world's first scheduled international air service left London for Paris in August 1919 with a cargo of clotted cream, fresh grouse and passengers. Pan Am launched the first transatlantic service in 1939 on Yankee Clipper, whose mod cons included sleeping berths and a bridal suite. Supersonic Concorde services took off in January 1976, enabling westbound travellers to beat the sun – arriving earlier than they took off.

- An EC taskforce has been set up to integrate Europe's unwieldy air traffic control systems. Not before time, since the region currently boasts 31 separate systems using computers from 18 different manufacturers, 22 operating systems and 33 different programming languages.

2
☐ Air Fares and Agents

Air fares are an unholy muddle. Even travel professionals have trouble plotting a course through the ever-thickening tangle of ticketing rules, regulations and anomalies – leaving their hapless customers at even more of a loss. Learning something about the types of fares on the market and the hush-hush tricks of the ticketing trade can pay huge dividends, since few passengers sitting side by side on a plane ever pay the same for their seat.

Dedicated discount hunters also need to know how to de-code their airline ticket, how travel agents and bucket shops work, and what hazards to watch out for when buying bargain-basement air seats.

AIR FARES AND DEREGULATION

Air travellers hoping to welcome in a new dawn of low-cost European air fares in 1993 have so far been disappointed. The much-trumpeted open skies policy of the new EC Single Market has to date been something of a damp squib.

The picture is patchy, with countries like the UK, Holland and Sweden embracing the concept more willingly than others. Nonetheless, consumers who previously had little or no choice in many European countries now have an increasing number of fare options.

British Midland, the UK's second largest scheduled airline, has campaigned hard for lower fares and greater liberalization. Its policy of undercutting the business class tariffs of major flag carriers has seen fares fall dramatically on routes such as Heathrow–Paris and Heathrow–Amsterdam, where its rivals have been forced to follow suit.

Elsewhere in the world, air fare liberalization has given business travellers an unprecedented range of price options and products. In the US and Australia, where the domestic airline business is fully deregulated, air tickets now cost less than the long-distance bus fare.

Not all the news is good, however. Since liberalization enables airlines

BEAUFORT HOUSE
KNIGHTSBRIDGE

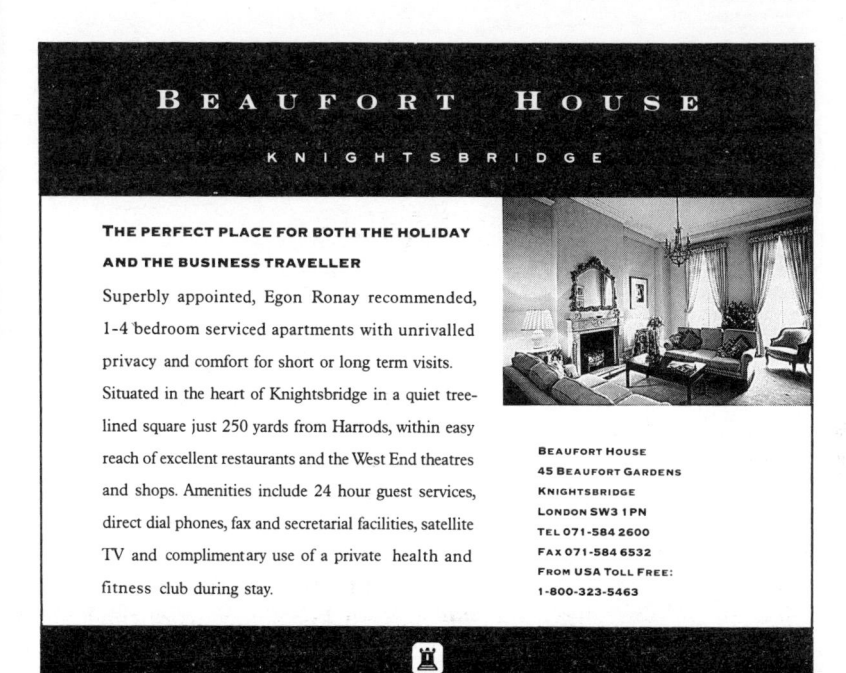

THE PERFECT PLACE FOR BOTH THE HOLIDAY AND THE BUSINESS TRAVELLER

Superbly appointed, Egon Ronay recommended, 1-4 bedroom serviced apartments with unrivalled privacy and comfort for short or long term visits. Situated in the heart of Knightsbridge in a quiet tree-lined square just 250 yards from Harrods, within easy reach of excellent restaurants and the West End theatres and shops. Amenities include 24 hour guest services, direct dial phones, fax and secretarial facilities, satellite TV and complimentary use of a private health and fitness club during stay.

BEAUFORT HOUSE
45 BEAUFORT GARDENS
KNIGHTSBRIDGE
LONDON SW3 1PN
TEL 071-584 2600
FAX 071-584 6532
FROM USA TOLL FREE:
1-800-323-5463

---

to price tickets in line with market forces, the onus is now on consumers to get the best deal. Business travellers can actually lose out on routes like the North Atlantic, where there is a yawning disparity (see Table 1) between the cost of flying in first and flying economy. There's no other route in the world where a first class ticket costs more than 15 times the price of a discount deal at the back of the plane.

Deregulation has spawned far more air fares than existed hitherto. Continually adjusted to take account of supply and demand, they can often change several times a day. If load factors are low on certain routes, for instance, allocations of discounted seats increase. When the opposite happens, the reverse applies.

How fare deals work

Generally speaking, a first class seat costs 50–100 per cent more than one in business class. The latter costs 50–250 per cent more than full-fare economy, which in turn costs several times more than the excursion tariff. The differences are not so marked on shorthaul routes. Within Europe, for example, business class costs 10–20 per cent more than economy, which in turn costs double or treble the excursion fare rate.

Table 1 — London–New York: fare's fair?

Concorde	£5030
First class	£3870
Business class	£2122
Economy class (full fare)	£756
Apex (seasonal)	£259 to £419
Discount (seasonal)	£200 to £300

Since longhaul business class fares are determined largely by what the market will bear rather than quality of service, executives flying on well-patronized business routes like London to New York, Chicago or Tokyo pay roughly twice the price per mile than their counterparts flying less popular routes to, say, Johannesburg, Mexico City and Singapore (see Table 2).

On European shorthaul routes, business class pricing is related to the volume of competition. At the time of writing, the flexible business class fare on the competitive London–Paris route (440 miles round-trip) costs £240 or 54.5 pence per mile. Conversely, on the less competitive Frankfurt–Brussels run (380 miles round-trip), executives must pay no less than £322 or 84.7 pence per mile.

Fares are costly if the route in question is a monopoly service. For example, Norwich–Amsterdam (300 miles round-trip) is flown solely by Air UK. As a result, the carrier gets away with charging East Anglian executives a whopping £276 – or 92 pence per mile.

Table 2 — What you pay per mile

Routing (ex-London)	Round-trip (miles)	Round-trip fare (business class)	Cost per mile (pence)
Chicago	7,900	£2,586	32.7
New York	6,916	£2,122	30.7
Tokyo	12,440	£3,179	25.5
Bahrain	6,308	£1,562	24.8
Mexico City	11,086	£2,126	19.2
Singapore	13,486	£2,208	16.4
Johannesburg	11,280	£1,835	16.3
Sydney	21,130	£3,061	14.5

MAIN PROMOTIONAL FARES

Most promotional fares come with restrictions of one sort and another, which vary from airline to airline and route to route. Off-peak fares are often cheap, but involve flying at unpopular times. Standby fares – strictly for those who dare take the risk – are also bargains for the brave. (All examples quoted here are correct at the time of writing.)

Apex

Probably the most popular promotional deal. On most routes, the Apex – or advance purchase – tariff is the lowest available. Passengers must book between 7 and 30 days ahead (the time limit varies from route to route) and must usually stay a Saturday night. Apex fares are almost always for economy travel.

Pex

Bookable until near departure time. Saturday night stay restrictions usually apply.

Eurobudget

Available on selected routes within Europe and offering a modest saving on the business class fare. London–Vienna costs £414 on Eurobudget and £482 on business class, while Amsterdam–Zurich costs Dfl 1,141 and Dfl 1,268 respectively.

Airpass

Multi-sector fares, mainly for use on domestic services but normally sold to non-residents, can offer substantial savings. For example, a Singaporean could fly Paris–Stockholm–Brussels–Paris for a total fare of £238 using an Air France/Sabena pass, whereas a European resident would have to pay over £1,000 for the same flights. Likewise, a Briton would pay £270 for a United Airlines New York–Chicago–Denver–Seattle–Los Angeles routing, while an American would pay £910 for the same flights.

Two-for-one offers

Increasingly common on both longhaul and shorthaul routes, especially for first and business class tickets. Singapore Airlines (SIA) currently offers two first or business class tickets for the price of one on its Manchester–Singapore route. Malaysia Airlines (MAS) has a similar offer for passengers flying London–Kuala Lumpur that enables two people to fly in first for less than the cost of flying in business. While the first class fare for two works out at £4,255, two business class tickets on the same flight would cost £4,416.

Round-the-world (RTW) fares

These provide the best value for long-distance flying in first and business. The joint British Airways/United RTW fare costs £3,844 in first and £2,471 in business and covers global destinations such as Hong Kong, Taipei, Tokyo, Osaka, Los Angeles, Chicago and New York – yet a simple return fare to many of these cities would cost the same or even more. London–Los Angeles, for example, costs £4,358 return in first and £3,254 in business, while London–Tokyo costs £4,986 and £3,179 respectively.

Three-day excursion

A shorthaul fare pioneered by British Midland, offering savings of 10–30 per cent on normal fares. It is sold on this carrier's UK domestic flights and those to mainland Europe, especially Amsterdam, Brussels, Frankfurt and Paris.

Discount tickets

Often bought through 'bucket shops', discount tickets are available to a greater or lesser extent on most airlines and routes. The golden rule is that while a national airline rarely, if ever, discounts fares on home ground, carriers with less market identity, fewer flights and less attractive schedules or services will be much more likely to.

While British Airways for example adheres mainly to published tariffs in the UK, it is keener to wheel and deal overseas. Air New Zealand is a major discounter on the London–Los Angeles route because it doesn't fly daily and because many consumers don't realize it operates on the route. It's a similar case with SIA's transatlantic flights between Brussels, Frankfurt and New York. Dubai-based Emirates uses price as a marketing weapon to entice Europeans flying to the Far East to travel via the Gulf.

AIR FARES AND AGENTS ■ 39

TRICKS OF THE TRADE

Round-the-world (RTW) savings

The cost of an RTW ticket can vary enormously depending on where it's purchased. Let's take the case of an executive circling the globe more than once a year to visit the company's branch offices. By buying a ticket in Hong Kong, he or she can fly first class for roughly the same price as a business class ticket would cost in Europe or the US.

The Hong Kong price of a British Airways/Qantas/United RTW fare in first would be £3,424, while the same ticket in business would cost £3,342 in London, £3,693 in Zurich and £3,320 in New York.

Back-to-back ticketing

This offers savings when regular travellers fly between strong and weak currency countries. For instance, a Zurich–London one-way business class ticket costs £344, while a London–Zurich one-way ticket costs £182. Regular travellers flying Zurich–London arrange to buy all their tickets – still fully flexible, fully refundable and valid for one year – in the UK, a practice which saves £240 on every return flight.

Coast-to-coast savings

US Airpasses come in handy for cut-price flying between the East and West coasts. TWA charges £183 for a simple 5,000-mile round-trip flight between New York and Los Angeles, which is less than the regular fare for a 700-mile domestic flight in Europe. US Airpasses must be bought outside North America.

Cross-border ticketing

Shifting currency values and different market conditions can provide savings when tickets are purchased in another country. Amsterdam, for instance, acts as a cut-price gateway for travellers from northern Germany.

Amsterdam–Hong Kong costs £1,840 on the discount market as against Düsseldorf–Hong Kong, which costs £2,783. Amsterdam–Tokyo is readily available in Holland at the discounted rate of £2,107 compared to Düsseldorf-Tokyo, which costs £3,625 in Germany. Residents of Swiss Ticino can also make good savings by purchasing their tickets in lire rather than Swiss francs and flying from, say, Milan Malpensa (under 30 miles from the Swiss border) rather than Lugano. Milan–New York costs £1,498 return in business class as against Lugano–New York via Zurich, which would cost £1,966.

Regardless of the savings, many destinations can be reached more easily by flying via an airport in a third country. Someone in Manchester flying to Singapore, for instance, encounters less hassle changing planes in Amsterdam than in London Heathrow, where a change of terminal is required. Likewise, some destinations in Thailand, Malaysia and Indonesia can be accessed more easily via Singapore than via Bangkok, Kuala Lumpur or Jakarta.

Hidden-city ticketing

This is a ticketing method for only the most experienced traveller, which involves a travel agent issuing a ticket to a destination he or she doesn't intend to visit.

For example, an executive booking a business class ticket from London to Dallas can save £500 if that ticket is routed on to Mexico City. That's because a London–Mexico City business class return costs £2,126 as against £2,650 for London–Dallas. On arrival in the US, the traveller detaches the Dallas–Mexico City–Dallas flight coupons and cancels the flight bookings made between those two cities.

Be forewarned, however, that hidden-city ticketing violates any airline's conditions of carriage. If the ruse is uncovered, airline staff will deny boarding. While the International Airline Passengers Assocation (IAPA) is realistic enough to accept that such ticketing practices take place, it does not condone them.

BUYING A DISCOUNTED TICKET

While discounted tickets are now widely available, laws of supply and demand mean they can be bought more readily on some routes, and from some airlines, than others. They are less common on inter-European routes, for instance, than on the North Atlantic ones. The cheapest fares – often for flights with the most stops – are often to be had from less reputable and Third World carriers. Aeroflot is often accused of dumping cheap seats on the market simply to accrue hard currency.

Generally speaking, the cheaper the ticket, the greater the restrictions and penalties. Don't expect to qualify for refunds, transfers, upgrades or frequent flyer points with a bargain-basement air fare. Surcharges may apply at weekends or other peak travel times.

Take care when buying cut-price tickets from a bucket shop. Some are issued through partner agencies in other countries to cash in on currency fluctuations, while others are strictly non-transferable/non refundable.

Before you buy

To avoid coming unstuck, you should:

- Check the details carefully before booking. Make sure you know the carriers, routing and connection times involved.
- Ask what restrictions apply. These may dictate a minimum length of stay, prevent you changing travel dates, or stop you switching to another carrier in case of delay.
- Avoid paying in full until you collect the ticket. If time pressures or distance preclude picking it up in person, offer to pay a deposit equivalent to a cancellation fee, and the balance on receipt.
- Check with the airline concerned that you do indeed have confirmed seats on the flights booked, before collecting your ticket.
- See that flight numbers, dates and all other details are correct on the ticket. Is there a flight coupon for each sector? The status box against each flight should be marked OK, or with the letters NK or KK.
- Stick to shops that take credit cards, which afford consumers some protection, such as those bonded by ABTA (the Assocation of British Travel Agents). More reputable establishments will also have an IATA licence. Look for the appropriate stickers in the window.

READING AN AIRLINE TICKET

The seemingly complex jigsaw of boxes, letters and codes on your ticket reveals the type of fare you have paid, the ticket's validity and the way it has been paid for.

It should contain a flight coupon for every sector of your journey. Cities are denoted by a three-letter code – LGW for London Gatwick, JFK for New York's Kennedy airport and CDG for Paris Charles de Gaulle, for instance. Less obvious are codes like YYZ for Toronto and YMX for Montreal Mirabel.

Fares are shown in the appropriate fare box in the left-hand corner. Forms of payment are denoted by CC for credit cards and CHQ for cheque. Baggage entitlements and ticket validity restrictions are also shown. Look under the 'Fare/class basis' box to see what class you are travelling – C or J for business, E for economy and F for first. The letters

Common fare codes

A	– first class discounted	F	– first class	R	– supersonic
AB	– advance purchase	J	– business class premium	RT	– round trip
		K	– economy/ discounted	W	– economy premium
B	– budget/instant saver	OW	– one way	Y	– economy fare
C	– club class	P	– first class premium	OJ	– open jaw
D	– business class discounted			RW	– round the world
E	– excursion fare	PX	– Pex fare	UU	– standby
		Q	– no stopover		

OK show you have a confirmed flight; WL that you are waitlisted. All tickets should be date-stamped with the agent's validator. Common fare codes are shown in the box above.

HOW TRAVEL AGENTS WORK

Travel agents work today in much the same way as they did in the last century – albeit with computers rather than quill pens. Selling flights, tours and hotel nights, they receive a percentage of the bill from their principals – the airlines, tour operators and hotel chains concerned – in the form of commission.

The typical rate for an international airline ticket is 9 per cent, and 10 per cent for a package tour or hotel stay. Larger hotel chains now have centralized commission-tracking programmes which collect monies from across their network and forward payments to agents in a monthly cheque.

Split commission

These commission rates tended to be cast in stone until comparatively recently. Now, agencies specializing in corporate travel often split the commission with their clients or charge them at the net rate, billing them for an agreed monthly service fee instead. This ensures that extra effort spent trying to secure a lower fare does not dent the agent's profit, and takes into account the fact that the time taken to process an airline ticket costing $2,000 may be no more than for one costing $200.

Agents frequently get a panning for sloppy service, lack of professionalism and failure to give their customers value for money. Clerks often change jobs frequently, and sometimes have scarcely more training than the clients they are serving.

Tempting incentives

More importantly, they are often plied with tempting incentives – whether money, gifts or free travel – to sell the services of a particular airline or hotel chain. Clients are thus often offered what is in the agency's best interests, rather than in their own.

These problems are compounded by the fact that many agencies are now enslaved to new technology. Rather than pick up a tariff book, staff now merely access a lightning-fast computer reservation system (CRS) to select and book flights, hotels and car rental. Experience shows that rather than scroll through screen after screen of information, many take the easy way out and book the first suitable-looking service to pop up.

Doing this often fails to secure the best fare, as well as the best flight options. While autoquotes – the so-called logical fare for a given route – can be called up in seconds, they are official, rather than unofficial, tariffs. Better deals can often be had by shopping around or calling the carrier direct for details of special offers.

Management data

While agents are not surprisingly rattled by the barbs from their critics, they are keen to be seen as professionals whose specialist knowledge, purchasing muscle and state-of-the-art technology makes them anything but mere order-takers.

Powerful management information packages – some of them in danger of deluging clients with data – tot up and break down a client's travel spend in detail, while file-free reservation systems turn screens into electronic notebooks that do away with paperwork until a final itinerary is printed out.

Some systems can highlight any booking made that violates company travel policy, and show where savings might have been made given greater flexibility. Others can receive and monitor messages around the clock, alerting staff if a client's flight has been delayed or cancelled, so that individuals may be called before setting off. UK-based market leaders such as Thomas Cook Travel Management and Hogg Robinson have databases, updated daily, designed to offer clients the lowest legal scheduled air fares available.

Global alliances

Travel agents are also becoming more international. Many are hot on the acquisition trail, flexing greater global muscle through a flurry of takeovers, partnerships and alliances. Thomas Cook is now represented in 120 countries, while continental group Wagonlit, one of the world's biggest agency players, has nearly 1,700 outlets in 125 countries through partners and owned agencies.

Hogg Robinson meanwhile is a founding partner of Business Travel International, a network of corporate agencies with consolidated annual billings of more than $12 billion. Members include Chicago based IVI – the sixth largest agency in the US – DNATA in the Middle East and Nippon Travel Agency in Japan.

Smaller companies are also joining forces to build up their muscle in the marketplace. In Britain, NAITA – the 700-member National Association of Independent Travel Agents – offers corporate travellers a 24-hour worldwide helpline as well as several other useful services that compete with the major business travel houses.

Corporate travel agents at every level are striving to become more professional. Britain's Guild of Business Travel Agents, whose 40-odd members handle around 80 per cent of business air traffic in the UK, has been a leader in raising the industry's training levels.

All Guild members hold IATA licences, while newcomers are closely vetted before being admitted. The Guild employs parliamentary and technology consultants, and issues an annual hotel guide listing properties worldwide at which members offer corporate rates. The Guild of European Business Travel Agents, whose members include seven other national guilds, has a total turnover exceeding $10 billion and full-time representation in Brussels.

AGENTS AND EC LAW

EC law now requires organizers of packaged travel arrangements to take full responsibility for the proper performance of their contracts and provide financial security for their clients' money. They must therefore make provision for refunds and for the repatriation of travellers in the event of an insolvency.

The Directive defines a package as travel arrangements and events lasting longer than 24 hours, or which incorporate overnight accommodation, or which include two of the following: transport, accommodation and other tourist services. The UK is the first country in the EC to implement the Directive, which many travel agents say imposes unrealistic responsibilities on them and cannot be effectively enforced.

COMPUTER RESERVATION SYSTEMS

Thirty years ago, most travel agents operated manual reservations systems which today would look positively archaic. Telexes requesting space were sent off to the airlines concerned, and seats were crossed off on a wall chart or entered in a card index as they were sold.

A mixed blessing

Now, even the most intricate journey can be booked on a computer screen within seconds. Agents can even call up the seat configuration on a given aircraft, selecting a seat and booking special meals on the spot. But for all their impressive capabilities, computer reservation systems – CRSs – have proved something of a mixed blessing for the traveller.

Originally, each major airline operated its own CRS. Travel agents telephoned a central reservations office to check out fares and book flights. Things started to change in the late 1970s, when airlines began installing reservations terminals linked to their own systems in travel agency networks. It was not long before the thorny issue of computer bias became a growing concern.

An agent checking out flight availability on the busy New York–Los Angeles route, for instance, might have to scroll through up to 15 screens full of flight times and other information to check out all possibilities. To save time, most looked no farther than the first screen and made 80 per cent of their bookings on flights shown on that one alone.

Carriers sponsoring CRS systems not surprisingly began rigging their displays so that their own flights had priority on the all-important first screen, with those of the opposition appearing later or even eliminated altogether.

Dealing with CRS bias

Regulators on both sides of the Atlantic became alarmed by this abuse, which led to an increasing number of calls for unbiased CRSs. The big European and US-run systems are now obliged to present schedule information to their subscribers in an unbiased format. Flights must be shown in strict chronological order, starting with direct non-stop flights, then direct stopping flights, and finally connecting flights involving a change of aircraft.

Europe's two competing CRS mega-systems are each sponsored by a group of leading airlines. Galileo, whose shareholders include British Airways, KLM and Swissair, is installed in around 13,000 travel agencies worldwide and handles some 220 reservations messages a second. Its rival Amadeus, owned by Air France, Iberia and Lufthansa, has terminals in almost 18,000 locations and claims to generate ten million bookings a month.

While all the major airline CRSs handle hotel bookings, specialist hotel booking agencies do the same with their own computer systems. Utell International, for instance, handles well over two million bookings a year at more than 6,500 hotels in 140 countries.

Code-sharing

Despite the regulations governing CRS systems, there are still some ways in which carriers can give their flights a higher priority on travel agents' information screens – notably through the practice known as code-sharing. This is especially common between larger longhaul airlines and smaller feeder carriers.

For example, a passenger travelling from Dallas to Düsseldorf might book a flight shown as a through-KLM service, despite the fact that the major leg of the journey is on a Northwest aircraft, connecting with a KLM flight in Amsterdam. Airlines sometimes even code-share with themselves, allocating a through-flight number from, say, Stockholm to Dallas, even though the journey involves a change of aircraft in Chicago. The term 'change of gauge' denotes a flight where a change in aircraft type is necessary.

Government-imposed regulations do make it clear that any code-sharing flights or change of aircraft must be identified on the agent's screen display, and that flights with the shortest overall journey time must be shown first. Having said that, it's still wise to check. Those classed as 'direct' can sometimes involve two connecting flights.

BUCKET SHOPS

Discount ticket houses, or bucket shops, sprang up in the 1970s. Many countries had laws at the time forbidding the sale of air tickets at less than government-approved rates. Since the airlines still needed to sell off surplus seats at whatever price they could get, a shadowy network of bucket shop traders – a term originally applied to shady share-dealing shops in the US – mushroomed to market them at prices which were strictly illegal.

These unlicensed and unbonded agents – often sleazy back-room operations attracting criminal elements – were not surprisingly highly unpopular with established travel agencies, which were generally denied access to discounted deals and obliged to sell fares at the officially-approved rates.

Matters have changed considerably over the past decade, however. The role of bucket shops has diminished as airlines have been given more freedom to set their fares without government interference, and IATA appointed agencies have had more access to cut-price fares. Most major travel agency chains now have special fares units skilled at hunting out the bargains – either at a lower price or free of Apex restrictions.

The role of consolidators – wholesalers in discounted fares – remains important, since airlines still need to dispose of blocks of seats that would otherwise fly out empty. Since most of the big scheduled carriers fly only two-thirds full, consolidators – many of them with their own agency networks – provide a practical and efficient sales channel.

CHOOSING A TRAVEL AGENT

Whatever an agency group's high-tech hardware or global credentials, it is only as good as its local office. Quality service on the doorstep will be more valuable in the long run than a high-profile name over the door.

When choosing an agency, bypass High Street retail chains majoring in mass-market holidays, in favour of a business travel specialist – preferably one that belongs to the appropriate Guild of Business Travel Agents. Bear in mind that few will stay on their toes unless regular performance checks are made, either through occasional price checks or annual user-satisfaction surveys among the firm's frequent flyers.

What to look for

The best agents will offer:

- **A genuine round-the-clock service**, backed by a 24-hour emergency number. Some may also have airport representatives.
- **A nominated individual to run your account**.
- **Good national and international coverage** through affiliates or branches.
- **Access to low fares and other savings**. You can judge how good they are by getting some quotes yourself.

- **Speed and flexibility**. That means being able to provide instant worldwide confirmation of bookings, satellite ticket printing, a free messenger service, direct telephone link to your office, and the ability to change itineraries at short notice. An agent not on line to the big airline CRS systems is not worth considering.
- **A broad service range**. This may include insurance, visa and currency services, or a trade fair and conference desk.
- **Specialist know-how**. That means good destination knowledge and the ability to plot a practised route through the labyrinth of international air fares.
- **The muscle to open doors** – whether to airport VIP lounges, flight upgrades or airline frequent flyer perks.
- **A sensible fee structure** – perhaps with a shared commission agreement on heavily used air routes.
- **Loyal staff**. An agency that hangs on to its employees is often a winner – and gives better personal service.

TRAVEL JARGON

If you're dealing regularly with travel professionals, you'll need to be *au fait* with some of the industry's jargon, such as:

- **Maximum permitted mileage (MPM)**. Rules dictating the stopovers you can make on your ticket without incurring any extra charge.
- **Bumping**. The practice of denying a seat to passengers who hold valid tickets to travel on an overbooked flight.
- **Denied boarding compensation (DBC)**. The cash you are offered for being bumped.
- **Open jaw tickets**. Those which enable you to fly out to one point and return from another without backtracking.
- **Fifth freedom flights**. Those operated by a carrier based in one country that fly passengers between two others – such as an Air India flight between New York and London. Sixth and seventh freedom flights are variations of the same principle.
- **Offline carrier**. An airline which does not operate flights into a particular country, but maintains a sales presence there.
- **IATA**. The International Air Transport Association represents more than 100 of the world's international scheduled airlines. Traditionally involved in fare-fixing, IATA sets the consumer protection standards for the agencies it appoints to sell air tickets.

❑ **ICAO**. Based in Montreal, the International Civil Aviation Organization sets standards for air traffic control, safety, air navigation and other matters.

TAILPIECES

- Three of the world's top five international scheduled airlines are European. British Airways leads the way, carrying over 20 million passengers a year. Coming next are Lufthansa, American Airlines, Air France and United.

- A friend was explaining to the hotel doorman why air fares are generally dearer per mile on shorthaul routes than on longhaul ones. 'But why', he asked after a moment's thought, 'can't the planes on short routes just fly around a bit longer?'

3
☐ Planning Your Trip

Intrepid travellers setting off for the other side of the world 100 years ago probably spent months preparing for their journey. Today's frequent flyers often have only hours.

Booking flights at breakfast time to leave London for Paris at lunchtime, New York by three or Tokyo before dinner now barely raises an eyebrow. Today's savvy traveller not surprisingly keeps an overnight case and a spare passport handy at the office.

Assuming the pace is not quite so manic, however, several things need to be accomplished to ensure a hassle-free trip.

PASSPORTS AND VISAS

One passport may be good enough for most people, but have you thought about a second? If you can demonstrate that an extra passport is needed for your work – enabling you to travel on one while visas are issued on another – it's usually not a problem.

A second passport will also get round the problem of sensitive stamps. Those from South Africa, Israel, Northern Cyprus or Cuba may deny you entry to another country, or at least make life difficult at the airport. Make a point of getting any potentially troublesome stamps on a loose-leaf sheet that is simply stapled into your passport during your stay.

While mass tourism has made visa-free travel common in many parts of the world, visas are still required in several countries. Although the lengthy waits at consulates working a three-hour day have been reduced, few as yet issue computerized stamps on the spot.

Some countries demand more than a simple signed form and some photographs. Business visitors to Nigeria and the Soviet Union normally need a letter from their sponsors; others may require vaccination certificates, airline tickets, proof of accommodation or evidence of an AIDS test. Some countries issue single-entry visas of short duration, while others provide one that lasts indefinitely. Make sure you know which you're getting.

Since postal applications can take weeks – worsened by the fact that visa departments close for their own national holidays as well as your own – most travel agents employ couriers to speed paperwork to and fro. Check that your passport still has at least six months to run – you may be refused a stamp if the expiry date is looming. Likewise, keep a spare page or two in case your plans change and you need a visa renewed *en route*.

On receipt of your visa, check:

- Its validity. Will it hold for more than one entry? Can it be extended? Is it likely to run out while you're away?
- Its restrictions. I arrived on holiday in Hawaii, once, to be told my US visa was only valid for business.

If you are refused a visa for any reason, make sure a note to that effect is not indelibly stamped in your passport. It will almost certainly put paid to any future attempts to travel to that country.

Currency declarations are still required in some countries – among them, Algeria. These declarations may need details of cameras, jewellery and any other valuables in your possession, in addition to cash. Note that bank receipts may be checked against the form on departure, making it unwise to engage in black-market currency deals.

Taking on a second nationality is not impossible, should the need arise. Those in the know say a decent law firm in Costa Rica or the Dominican Republic should be able to do the business for you – all quite legitimately – for a reasonable consideration.

YOUR ITINERARY

Make sure your travel agent gives you a detailed print-out of flights, accommodation bookings and other relevant details, together with a note of latest check-in times and a 24-hour number you can call in emergencies.

Get your timing right. Arriving anywhere on a public holiday will probably mean losing an otherwise productive day. Make sure you don't arrive in Arab countries during the holy month of Ramadan, when all-day fasting disrupts office life.

Bear in mind that discounted airline seats won't give you the flexibility of a full-fare ticket. You may end up having to pay a heavy premium to change a restricted ticket, should you need an extra day somewhere at short notice.

TRAVEL INSURANCE

One in three travellers fail to take out adequate insurance for their trips, according to the international travel group Wexas. As a result, they risk coming badly unstuck.

Failing to take out adequate medical cover has bankrupted many of those who find themselves looking at the sharp end of a scalpel in some unlikely part of the world. Around 1 in 15 travellers make a claim against their insurance policy, with medical expenses gobbling up half the money paid out.

Don't assume you are automatically fully covered for accidents, illness, cancellation or major financial loss by your firm's travel policy. Comprehensive cover is sometimes reserved for upper-echelon management, or only activated on a trip-by-trip basis. This can often be overlooked when plans are made or changed in a hurry.

Business travellers seeking year-round cover for the many minor and major dramas that can strike unexpectedly now have ample choice. Market leaders in the travel insurance field include Europ Assistance, which claims to be the biggest in the business, running 42 operational centres around the world. French-based GESA Assistance claims to be the oldest, and has 22 offices worldwide. Rival Mondial Assistance likewise provides packages for numerous large corporate clients.

Larger travel agents often offer their own schemes, while credit and charge card companies have leapt on the bandwagon in a big way in recent years. Diners Club operates a Travellercare Worldwide package, while American Express offers a choice of plans. Several airline loyalty programmes, including British Airways Executive Club, also offer wide-ranging cover. IAPA has introduced an IAPACare policy to complement its worldwide personal accident programme.

Round-the-clock cover

What should you look for? The best business travel policies offer a round-the-clock emergency service covering not simply medical expenses and hospital care, but assistance with transport, accommodation, legal costs, emergency cash, and transmission of messages. A 24-hour telephone helpline is a must – preferably one that will even spring to your aid if you're 3,000 miles from home and realize you've left the cat locked in the kitchen.

While repatriation by air in the event of a medical emergency is often promised, some firms are less than keen to exercise this option. With an emergency airlift by air ambulance from the US to the UK costing up to

British Homes-London Flats Ltd.
UK PROPERTY IS OUR ONLY BUSINESS

LUXURY APARTMENT RENTALS short/long term in prime London areas. Include maid service. Reduce hotel/restaurant costs without sacrificing luxury.

UK RELOCATIONS for business and professional people. A variety of properties and services available through our daily involvement with estate agents, property developers and management companies in the UK.

COUNTRY COTTAGES, CASTLES AND ESTATES, a select group of Britain's finest properties.

UK Toll Free 0800 824475   USA Tel: 516-883-2717/5540   Fax: 516-944-5267

£25,000, and a scheduled air stretcher repatriation from the Arab Gulf to Europe running up a bill as high as £10,000, don't bank on the company concerned pulling out all the stops.

Even seemingly reputable operators can pack their policies with get-out clauses that protect them from paying up eight times out of ten. Cover offered by credit and charge card groups is sometimes intended as secondary insurance only, so there's no pay-out unless you have no other form of cover. There's no substitute for reading the small print.

Choosing the right policy

Don't go for the cheapest offer on the market. When your bags have been rifled in Bogota, or you are waiting to see a costly consultant in Singapore, you'll regret not shelling out a little more for gold-plated cover. Keep your policy details or plastic member's card with you at all times, and remember to check:

- **The claims ceiling**. You'll need £1 million plus for medical care if your travel includes the US.
- **The excess clause**. This will preclude many small claims.
- **The exclusions**. These could include injuries from not only daredevil sports like hang-gliding, but those such as motorcycling. AIDS may be excluded, even if caught from contaminated blood.
- **The limitations**. You are unlikely to be covered for walking around with £5,000 cash in your pocket. Similarly, the ceiling for replacement of single items may not buy you a new laptop.
- **The emergency cover**. This should include air repatriation, in-house doctors and a 24-hour helpline manned by multi-lingual staff.

- **The legal assistance**. You may well need on-the-spot advice if you are involved in, or cause, an accident.
- **The age limit**. Separate terms and conditions may apply for anyone over 65.

MAKING THE BOOKINGS

Studies show that 3 out of 4 business travellers leave their travel bookings to a secretary or PA. Since few have any formal training in the field, they will need to be thoroughly briefed.

What class of air travel do you use? Does your company have carrier preferences? What about alternative times/dates if your first choice flights are full? Do you like a window seat, vegetarian meals or a smoke-free cabin? Will a hire car be needed? Are you entitled to free airport transfers or any other airline perk? Do any short-term fare offers apply? What's your budget for accommodation? How will you settle the bill? Do you need foreign currency?

Keep a few handy reference guides in the office, such as:

- **Official Airline Guides (OAG) pocket flight guide**. This miniature bible, updated monthly, contains details of flights to and from just about everywhere. OAG also produces desk-top books and data on disks.
- *ABC World Airways Guide* corporate edition. Aimed specifically at business travellers, PAs and travel planners, this monthly guide claims to be a 'one-stop shop' for frequent flyers. It includes data on 450,000 flight schedules and connections, plus other useful information.

Alternatively, information can be accessed on IBM-compatible ABC Travel Disks, which enable users to print out personalized itineraries. The pocket-sized Executive Flight Planners make a useful companion to both systems. Other guides include:

- *A Question of Class*. Published in the UK by Hogg Robinson, this provides a breakdown of the services offered by every major airline, down to seat pitch, meals, and advance seat selection.
- Copies of *Executive Travel* or *Business Traveller* **magazine**. Both monthlies – available on subscription – contain a mine of topical information on all aspects of corporate travel.

Reconfirming tickets

If in doubt, do it. Although flights in Europe and North America technically no longer need to be reconfirmed, it's better to be safe than sorry – especially if you are flying on a discounted ticket. Always reconfirm in the Third World, preferably by fax. Having a piece of paper to wave at the check-in clerk will be a lot better than your word against theirs.

BROCHURE-SPEAK

Since costly fully-flexible flights may not be necessary for every trip, you'll almost certainly want to take advantage of fly-drive deals, short break offers and other travel packages at times. That means getting to grips with travel brochures.

While some travel agents now supply the natty electronic kind, complete with virtual reality images to gaze at on your PC, most still make do with the racked variety – and poetic licence flourishes once brochure writers reach for their purple quills. Their legendary powers of exaggeration led to a 30 per cent rise in complaints to Britain's Advertising Standards Authority in 1992.

Being skilled at interpreting the cliché-ridden jargon of brochure-speak is a must. A brief guide follows, with translations in brackets:

- **Convenient for the airport.** (Watch out for B747 tyre marks on the roof.)
- **Sophisticated five-star address.** (You'll need a mortgage for the bar bill.)
- **Just opening.** (Well, it might be by the time you get there.)
- **Newly renovated.** (The cement mixers are just leaving.)
- **In the bustling heart of town.** (Deafening sirens all night.)
- **Futuristic-looking.** (High-rise concrete egg-box.)
- **A big hit with conference groups.** (They'll be wearing Go-for-It hats at breakfast.)

WHAT TO TAKE

Gadgets

The days of staggering home from a two-week trip with a knee-high pile of papers and call reports are now gone. Take the right portable gadgetry along, and you can fire off bulletins from anywhere between Bangkok and Bridgetown to keep the office in touch.

High-tech travellers can snap up anything from natty digital diaries no bigger than a cigarette packet to computerized travel guides, videophones, portable karaoke machines and electronic bibles these days. Laptop PCs and faxes (handy for avoiding extortionate hotel charges) are some of the top-selling lines now turning many a bulging executive briefcase into a mobile gadget store.

Gadget junkies should remember that what feels featherlight in the shop can be a tiresome burden on the road, especially when spare batteries and mains adaptors are needed. Minimize the weight, rather than maximize the power, to ensure your new toy isn't left to gather dust.

Flying with laptops

Most carriers permit laptops to be used in-flight, seeing them more as a potential irritation to others than a danger to cockpit navigational aids, providing the plane has reached cruising altitude. However, it's wise to check first if you are banking on doing a day's work over the Pacific. United, American, Virgin, Lufthansa and Swissair staff often ban portable CD players, while British Airways dislikes them being used below 10,000 feet.

Not all handy gadgets run on all-singing, all-dancing microchips. Other useful travel companions include lightweight steam irons, inflatable neck pillows for the flight, fold-up miniature clothes lines, and door guards that prevent people from entering your room. Even DIY dental kits complete with spatula, cement and mixing tray for impromptu fillings are on sale for those who like being prepared for the worst.

Habla Usted Inglés?

Do invest in a phrase book if you are heading for a foreign-language country. While most airport and hotel employees speak some English these days, the same cannot be said of cab drivers, room staff and secretaries.

Berlitz, Linguaphone and other organizations produce tapes, CDs, videos and books for those keen to conquer another tongue. Even tele-language courses are now available for executive high flyers too busy for evening classes. Failing that, pocket-sized electronic dictionaries and translators will help you get by in restaurants or filling stations.

Take plenty of business cards (they will vanish like hot cakes in the Far East), and have them printed on the back in Chinese, Japanese or Arabic if appropriate. This can often be done within an hour or so at your destination.

Flying suits

Veteran globetrotters agree that you'll be happier dressed for comfort, rather than cachet, in the air. A tracksuit and a pair of comfy shoes is probably the ideal flying suit from a practical point of view. The downside is that turning up at the airport in a sweatshirt, baggy trousers and trainers won't do you any favours in the upgrade stakes. Airline staff like to bestow their favours on those who look the part.

PACKING YOUR CASE

Keep a checklist of everything you need on a business trip. It's astonishingly easy (speaking as someone who buys an umbrella on every other trip) to leave for foreign shores without the most obvious basics. Carry travel-sized toiletries (try re-using empty hotel shampoo bottles) and take clothes you can mix and match. With a basic suit, an extra jacket and some spare shirts or tops, you've effectively got half a dozen different outfits.

Golden rules

- Travel light. Your bags will gain a pound in weight for every yard you carry them. If you can't travel light, travel small.
- Stick to hand luggage where possible (but see p31). Stowed luggage gets lost and delayed.
- Choose a garment bag in preference to a case or holdall to keep clothes in better shape. Choosing non-iron shirts and non-crushable fabrics will also help.
- Keep valuables, ticket wallet and anything breakable in your carry-on bag. Remember fountain pens and over-filled bottles can leak in pressurized aircraft cabins.
- Put shoes and bulky items at the bottom of your bag. Use socks and underwear to fill up corners, to create a fairly level surface. Jewellery and small items can be used to fill up shoes, which won't mark your clothes if kept in plastic bags. Make sure delicate items are well-padded.
- Turn jackets inside out to make creasing less obvious. Try interfolding your clothes to soften the folds, or using sheets of tissue or plastic paper between the layers. Alternatively, pack your clothes in dry-cleaning bags.
- Remember underpacking is as bad as overpacking. Use the inner

suitcase straps to prevent things sliding around, or pad out the case with a bath towel. (Yours, not the hotel's.)
- Unpack as soon as you arrive. Clothes that sit in your suitcase for three days will look decidely worse for wear.
- Try hanging clothes in a steamy bathroom to soften the creases. It may save you paying to have them pressed.
- Cut down on unnecessary appliances. Most good hotels now provide hairdryers, and will supply an iron on request.

CHOOSING LUGGAGE

Anyone who has watched airport baggage handlers at work will realize the importance of a sturdy set of luggage. What isn't thrown on to trolleys, flung on to conveyor belts or rammed into containers usually gets left standing on the tarmac in all weathers.

Having worked out how much you can take (see pp30–2) you must decide which type of luggage best suits your needs. Rigid aluminium or leather cases can be strong and hardwearing, but heavy to carry. Semi-soft cases with a rigid frame will bounce back into shape if knocked, but offer limited protection. Colourful soft-sided holdalls made from ballistic nylon are both lightweight and tough, but do little to prevent contents from being crushed. Garment bags designed to hold a suit or dress at full length are another useful option.

Travelling light

Going for lightness is usually the best policy. The new breed of hard-sided suitcases from Carlton, Delsey, Samsonite and others are made of high-tech materials that are both batter-proof and lightweight. Since you may only have 20kg to play with if travelling economy, you don't want a case that weighs half that before you start packing. Garment bags should be designed to grip the hangers in place, and allow you to detach them as needed to hang clothes directly in the wardrobe.

Features best avoided include wheels, buckles and pull-out handles that can be easily knocked and damaged. While cases designed to be up-ended and wheeled along poodle-style are fine if you hate lifting weights, they can also make an unbearable din on metal moving pavements. Holdalls with one handle – or two that lock together – are better than those with a pair, since bags will inevitably be tossed around using just one.

Security also comes into the equation. Swish designer luggage in matching monogrammed leather may do great things for your image, but

Reduce business travel costs

Recover VAT on European business expenditure

- **travel and accommodation**
- **business entertaining**
- **exhibition and conference expenses**
- **consultancy & lawyers' fees**

Call on Cash Back, the world's leading VAT recovery people - WE DO THE REST. Representation in over 20 countries.
(Recovery varies country by country)

CASH BACK

Cash Back Consultancy (UK) Ltd. 20 St Dunstan's Hill, London EC3R 8HL. Tel: 071 626 3262. Fax: 071 626 0384.

It's easy to claim your VAT back.

Cash Back recovers VAT paid on business expenditure incurred throughout Europe

- travel and accommodation
- business entertaining
- exhibition and conference expenses
- consultancy & lawyers' fees

Call on us, the world's leading VAT recovery people – WE DO THE REST. Representation in over 20 countries.

CASH BACK

Cash Back Consultancy (UK) Ltd, 20 St. Dunstans Hill, London EC3R 8HL
Tel: 071 626 3262   Fax: 071 626 0384

could be a ready-made target for thieves. While there's no need to travel with a battered old box, you'll be safer with something that doesn't make you look like the richest kid in town.

Much the same goes for briefcases. Anyone sporting a polished Italian attaché case, with the obligatory laptop and mobile phone nestled inside, will be more at risk than either media trendies with their aluminium film-crew type cases, or tweedy intellectuals with their pre-war vintage Gladstone bags.

Combination locks are the hardest to pick, though a padlock is preferable if you tend to forget the code. Extra straps can deter opportunist thieves, as well as help you identify your bag quickly from the dozens of grey and brown suitcases disgorged on to the airport carousel.

Tie-on airline tags are easily torn off in transit. Opt instead for a permanent label in a leather or plastic sleeve, bearing your name and – since the details are less helpful to potential burglars – a business address or telephone number. Reserve your home address for a label stuck inside the case. IAPA members receive plastic tags carrying only their name, membership number and an airline communication code which enables the bag to be tracked down easily if lost.

COMPLAINING

Things are certain to go wrong sooner or later on your travels – and demanding satisfaction is an art. Losing your temper in parts of Asia and the Far East is not simply uncool, but totally counter-productive. Tact and diplomacy will achieve a good deal more when it comes to getting your way. Wherever you are:

- Don't complain to the wrong person. Reducing the front-desk clerk to tears might vent your feelings, but will achieve little else.
- Don't dig yourself into a hole without a fallback position. Basically, you are negotiating.
- Win sympathy. Disappointment often gets a better hearing than anger.
- Don't let the other person lose face. You'll simply make an enemy.
- Know what makes your case unique. The manager concerned won't want to concede what 20 others will demand ten minutes later.
- Decide what you'll settle for. An upgrade or a full-scale refund?

TAILPIECES

- What kind of packer are you? Suitcase manufacturer Samsonite has come up with stuffers, rummagers and the self-assured. Stuffers cram everything into bulging suitcases, and take an assortment of carriers and bags for good measure. Rummagers hate to unpack on arrival, preferring to forage in search of socks, ties and shirts. The self-assured (wouldn't you know it?) dress and pack immaculately. Unfortunately they make up less than a quarter of the total.

- National tastes vary greatly. Britons spend less on luggage than any nationality in Europe, going for conservative styles and drab colours. High-spending Continentals favour flashier shades and styles, and are big fans of briefcases with shoulder straps.

- Passports in Britain date back to the 1400s. Until the reign of King Charles II, they were actually signed personally by the monarch. All-French text was replaced by English in the 1800s, and photographs added in 1915. Much to their chagrin, patriotic Brits are now being issued with regulation computer-printed Euro-passports.

4
☐ At the Airport

Waiting around at airports is one of the most frustrating aspects of international air travel – and the bad news is, it's getting worse. Turn-up-and-take-off air travel remains a pipe dream as lengthier security checks and growing air traffic congestion conspire to test sorely the patience of the battle-weary business traveller. And that's just the start.

PARKING YOUR CAR

Airport parking charges can be punitive. Don't make the mistake of the chap who arrived back at Heathrow after a month-long holiday in Florida, only to discover he had mistakenly left his car in the short-term carpark. The bill came to more than the cost of his vacation.

Rates in the handy short-term carpark can be six times higher than those in the less convenient long-term parking lot – enough of a difference to hire a chauffeured limo and arrive in style in the first place. To confuse matters, Heathrow also has a third option – business parking lots that charge somewhere between the two, and guarantee to get time-pressed executives back to the terminal inside 15 minutes.

Car park security

Often deserted after dark, airport carparks can also be less than safe. Detachable CD and tape players should be locked in the boot, and anything bearing a visible home address – a tailor-made lead for thieves looking for an empty house – removed from the back seat or dashboard. Keep a note of the zone and row your car is left in, on your receipt.

Valet parking is the quickest, if most expensive, option. Now becoming common at major gateways, it's also useful for anyone who dislikes being dropped in empty long-term car parks late at night. Passengers simply drop their car at the kerbside and retrieve it with a phone call on their return, and can usually have it cleaned and serviced while they are away. Air Canada offers the service at Toronto and Vancouver, while British Airways, among others, provides it at Heathrow.

Risk-takers can of course merely drop their car at an airport hotel and take the courtesy bus to the terminal. Latecomers feeling even more reckless can risk the wrath of the law by dropping their car outside the terminal door and merely dashing for the flight. The downside will be the bill for tow-away fees, parking fine and daily storage charges waiting at the police car pound on their return.

CHECKING IN

You can minimize hold-ups at the check-in counter by observing a few simple rules:

- Choose the right queue. Get behind a fellow executive with just a briefcase or suit carrier in tow, rather than the family with kids, trolleys and bulging ticket wallets.
- Switch lines if the clerk goes off to sort out queries. You're probably behind someone rearranging their entire round-the-world itinerary.
- Remember, queuing etiquette differs from country to country. In Italy, you'll get nowhere without some pushing and shoving. In Germany, you'll be sternly sent to the back of the line for doing the same.
- Try an empty business class counter even if you're flying economy. The clerk may be quite happy to check you in.
- Get a pre-assigned seat, so you can arrive later. This should be no problem on most business class tickets.
- See if your airline offers a city-centre, telephone or off-airport check-in service. That way, you need only stop to collect your boarding card.
- Make do with hand luggage if your trip is less than a week. Do you really need enough underwear to start a lingerie stall?
- See if there's a check-in desk for hand-luggage passengers only. Alternatively, check whether you can go straight to the gate or business lounge.
- Check whether your carrier offers a kerbside check-in. You may even be able to drop your bags there before returning your rental car, to save carrying them back on the courtesy bus. Wait to see that your bags are correctly tagged, though.

City-centre airports

Another way to cut down check-in times is to use a city-centre airport. Tiny London City Airport in the heart of Docklands is only 6 miles from the capital's banking centre (compared to Heathrow's 16, Gatwick's 28 and Stansted's 32), and accepts passengers up to 10 minutes before take-off. You're unlikely to ever see a queue, and the distance between check-in desks and boarding gates is just 75 yards. The airport handled only 186,000 passengers in 1992 – a fraction of the number it was built for.

The world's other four city-centre business airports are Belfast City, Berlin Tempelhof – just 3 miles from the city's former eastern sector – Stockholm Bromma, 20 miles closer to town than bigger Arlanda, and Toronto Island. German carrier Conti-Flug links London City with Tempelhof twice a day using BAe 146 jets.

EXCESS LUGGAGE

Assuming you already know your luggage entitlements (see p30), you're unlikely to tempt fate by risking the prospect of sky-high excess bag charges. These have traditionally been calculated as a percentage of the first-class fare – a rule dating back to the days of DC-3s, when every kilo mattered – with the result that, in some cases, taking 20kg of excess luggage both ways could end up costing more than your air ticket itself.

The growing tendency of airlines to adopt a pieces-per-passenger rule has helped, since it not only permits more weight to start with, but applies a flat-rate charge to excess bags. This, of course, may work against you if your extra bag weighs just a few kilos.

Shipping your spare kilos as unaccompanied baggage is the cheapest option, since the cost is not only half that of the regular air-freight rate, but as much as 20 times less than excess baggage rates. The disadvantage is that this can involve time-consuming paperwork. Finding an excess baggage broker – a firm that buys up space from the airlines, and sells it on at a reasonable rate – is another option.

Avoiding hefty charges

In brief, your options are to:

- Use your charm. Much depends on the mood of the check-in clerk. It's not uncommon for one unfortunate to be charged the full whack while someone at the next desk gets off scot-free.
- Try a second counter. Not all counter staff will follow the rules to the letter. If the plane's not full, chances are they will not be scrutinizing weights too closely anyway.

- Ask a fellow passenger if they would mind checking in your extra kilos. Remember, though, that this breaks strict security rules.
- Do some impromptu re-packing. Spare shoes, papers and books can often be squeezed into your hand luggage.
- Use the post, find an excess luggage broker or buy whatever it is, new at your destination instead.

Departure taxes

These are taxing times. If you have ever wondered just who is footing the bill for all the slick new security and other state-of-the-art airport facilities, it's you. Air travellers are collectively coughing up millions of pounds a year for the purpose.

French airports levy around FF15 per ticket – not bad when you think that three million or more people fly the London–Paris route every year. While most charges are disguised in the cost of the ticket, you'll be asked for a cash payment when leaving Sydney, Hong Kong, Tokyo, Vancouver (where it's termed an airport improvement tax) and several other cities.

Films

Not all X-ray units are as film-friendly as you might suppose. Many Third World airports use old machines which shine a continuous beam of X-rays that can leave your film fogged or sporting a venetian-blind effect. Those in Russia, Vietnam and China are singled out for criticism in many guides. According to Kodak, lead-lined bags sold specially for the purpose offer no protection against high-dosage X-rays as they are not thick enough. Films most at risk are high-speed (eg 400 ASA) colour print films. Don't worry about newer machines – the X-ray burst lasts for just six-thousandths of a second. Processed films are not at risk.

Airport eating

Airports are no place for gourmet dining, but fine for some fast eats. Food critic Egon Ronay has helped improve standards immeasurably at London Gatwick, where even UHT milk has now gone for good.

Since you can't drag your suitcase along the self-service cafeteria queue while balancing a tray, and are not supposed to leave it unattended, try padlocking it to the chair while you stand in line. Otherwise, ask someone else to keep an eye on it for you.

AIRLINE LOUNGES

Nothing takes the sting out of waiting around at an airport as much as an invitation to an airline business lounge. The best have comfortable sofas, TV corners, well-stocked magazine racks and a free help-yourself bar laden with everything from coffee and nibbles to champagne on ice. The newest have credit card phones, work stations, plug-in points for portable PCs and faxes, and a range of business services. Some even have showers and generous supplies of toiletries. A few are so ritzy it's a wonder passengers ever want to leave to get on the plane.

More and more lounges also offer conference rooms – sometimes rented by the hour – for executives flying in from different destinations. In others, you'll find check-in desks, message-drop or cheque-cashing facilities, and push-button screens to monitor your frequent flyer mileage account or check out financial news. Invaluable when you are in transit, arriving early or grounded by a delay, these lounges are also invariably free of squawking toddlers. Some also admit guests.

However, not every airport lounge is the kind of place you would cheerfully check into for a week. One or two are gloomy, windowless waiting rooms done out in shades of brown, while others are almost sterile in their bid to look businesslike. Some are badly signposted and tucked away down obscure corridors. Those with the panoramic views and wall-to-wall comforts are the exception rather than the rule.

Peak time pressures

Lounges are also fast becoming a victim of their own success. Many are so popular that they can feel like miniature departure areas at peak times. Airport authorities are battling to keep up with airline demands for bigger and better sites, and British Airways Executive Club has been forced to restrict member access in recent years. Since all those at London Gatwick are 'landside' (as opposed to 'airside' – near the runways), passengers relaxing over a Scotch still face a ten-minute hike past passport control and security before reaching their departure gate.

Not all carriers extend an unconditional welcome to their business class passengers, either. Those without their own facility may make use of a common-user lounge, paying the operator a monthly fee. Since every visit costs money, they are not always keen to over-stretch themselves in the hospitality department. Smaller lounges may keep limited opening hours, or even shut up shop between flights.

Anyone flying to their destination with one flag carrier and returning with another – easy if you intend catching the first and last flights of the day – may also find that while they have paid the full return business class fare, they are eligible to use an airport lounge going one way but not the other.

Europe's lounge battle is centred on Heathrow, whose havens for high-flying lounge lizards would win a five-star rating on Park Lane. Virgin's latest creation offers unmatched amenities plus plenty of visual pizazz. British Airways' three-suite lounge pavilion is also a showpiece, while its 400-seater Club Europe lounge – largest of its type in Europe – has a duty-free shop and car rental desk. American's Admiral's Club lounge has back massage chairs, reading room and showers.

Getting into a lounge

The main ways to get through the doors every time you fly are to:

- Fly business or first class. Many carriers allow all premium-fare ticket holders use of their business lounges.
- Join an airline's frequent flyer programme. While the rules vary, this often guarantees entry providing you chalk up a certain level of mileage each year. Some schemes have reciprocal arrangements with other carriers, too.
- Pay to join a lounge club, such as Delta's Crown Club – currently $150 a year. Check before paying up that the airline offers facilities at the airports you use most often, and that you won't need to travel business class – or even use that carrier – every time.
- Join IAPA's optional lounge scheme. Members pay $60 a year, plus $21 each time they use an airport lounge. They have a choice of 54 worldwide. The scheme allows members to use lounges irrespective of the class travelled or club membership.
- Use your charm. Saying you're a guest of another passenger, a friend of the managing director or a key overseas customer may work if the lounge is half empty and the receptionist is feeling friendly. Some carriers are more relaxed than others about bending the rules.
- Carry a Diners Club card. Members enjoy use of lounges at more than 30 airports around the world, many equipped with work stations, meeting rooms, fax machines, photocopiers and secretarial services.

Doing business

Meeting facilities are available at numerous US airports (JFK being an excellent example), while Thomas Cook runs a network of business centres at a number of UK airports. The Heathrow complex offers work stations, a choice of conference rooms, secretarial services and a panoramic lounge.

DUTY-FREE SHOPPING

Killing time at the world's big duty-free stores doesn't come cheap. As anyone with a cobwebbed collection of obscure liqueurs at home can testify, it's amazing what you can buy when you're bored.

Most travellers can't resist a duty-free bargain or two. A survey undertaken by IAPA found that 84 per cent of members always or often succumbed to the temptation to shop, with only 2 per cent resolutely refraining.

Duty-free sales totalled $15,000 million worldwide in 1990 – a frenzy of buying worth almost as much as the national debt of some smaller countries. With almost half that sum spent in Europe, it's not surprisingly a key source of revenue for EC airports. Without it, the average cost of an airline ticket would rise by around $20, since airports would be forced to raise their landing and other charges instead.

Britain's airport operator BAA, whose shopfloor turnover puts it on a par with the country's top retailers, generates more than £400 million in shopfloor sales a year. With more than 180 retail outlets at Gatwick and Heathrow alone, income from shoppers is poised to become its biggest source of revenue in the near future.

What do people buy? Spirits and tobacco are not surprisingly the big sellers. Books are another favourite, with newsagent W H Smith selling more than 2.5 million titles a year at its UK airport stores. At Heathrow, where a third of all international passengers buy before they fly, shoppers snap up over two million bottles of Scotch a year, and a bottle of Johnny Walker Red Label every two minutes.

Airport buying habits look set to change radically by 1999, however, when intra-EC sales of duty-free goods are finally phased out. From then, only passengers departing on flights outside the Community will be able to snap up their quota of booty. Surplus duty-free stores will give way to more speciality shops as other merchandise replaces the cheap gin and cut-price cigarettes.

Bargain hunting

Research shows that most airport shopping is boredom buying rather than bargain-hunting – which is just as well, since duty-free buys are not always the snips they're cracked up to be. While you'll find anything from smoked salmon and Pavarotti to T-shirts and diaphanous undies on sale these days, you may well end up paying more for them than you would in your local High Street. Goods sold free of duty are not, needless to say, sold free of profit.

Dubious bargains include spirits bought in Scandinavia – except, perhaps, Copenhagen – and gin bought to take to America, since it's usually cheaper there. Buyers of caviar at Moscow's Sheremetyevo Airport will find the same jars at knock-down prices in the city's markets.

Duty-free can also be cheaper on the plane – particularly if you fly with lesser-known Third World carriers, who often undercut the big airport duty-free meccas. Airlines are now trying hard to get in on the shopping act, reasoning that bored captive customers are even more likely to reach for their plastic in the clouds than on the ground. The traditional trolley of prime-brand spirits and cigarettes is now laden with watches, CDs, electronic games and lots more. Catalogue buying is fast gaining ground with American and other carriers.

Buying as you land

Most passengers would love to do duty-free shopping on arrival. There would then be no cumbersome bags to lug around the world, no danger of bottles breaking in-flight, fewer fire risks and less of a weight penalty for airlines. *Flight International* magazine has calculated that it actually costs carriers 6.5 million gallons of fuel each year merely to fly the stuff around. For the moment, however, the choice is slender. Airports where you can spend as you land include Reykjavik, Sydney, Moscow, St Petersburg, Kuala Lumpur and Singapore.

So where are the best bargains? Amsterdam, Singapore, Dubai and Bahrain repeatedly come out top in passenger polls, with other top scorers including Copenhagen, Abu Dhabi, Zurich and Paris Charles de Gaulle. Heathrow and Gatwick are also competitive, pledging to undercut UK High Street prices by up to half.

Make sure any electronic gadgets you buy don't become expensive white elephants by checking that when you get home:

- You won't be liable for duty.
- The voltage is compatible.
- The repairs warranty will be valid.

Reclaiming VAT

Heathrow and other airports have VAT refund desks in the main departure lounge where foreign residents leaving the country can exchange vouchers issued by tax-free shops during their stay for cash. These must first be validated at the Customs counter.

FLIGHT DELAYS

Nothing is more frustrating than to find that just as you are ready to board, your take-off time goes on hold.

Delay factors can vary enormously among competing airports. According to IATA, 16 European and 7 Asia/Pacific gateways are now heavily congested, or will be by the year 2000. London Gatwick operates at 90 per cent of its capacity during the summer months, and other airports nearing their flight handling ceilings include Frankfurt, Milan–Linate, Geneva, Athens, Dublin, Madrid and Hong Kong.

A 1992 study of six UK airports found see-sawing standards of punctuality. Average arrival/departure delays were 22 minutes at Gatwick, 16 at Manchester and 12 at Heathrow. Flights to the US suffered an average 19-minute hold-up. Gatwick showed an average 8-minute delay for flights to and from New York, while Luton kept its passengers waiting 57 minutes for Channel-hopping flights to Paris.

US airports also turn in varying departure delays. Figures for February 1993 show that while 83 per cent of departures were on time at Dallas Fort Worth, Denver managed just 75 per cent on-time take-offs. Canada's most delay-prone airport in March '93 was Montreal Dorval.

Being bumped

Airline overbooking practices mean that sooner or later you may be denied a seat on a flight for which you hold a confirmed reservation and even a boarding card. This often happens at the departure gate, when airline staff will call for volunteers to stand down in lieu of a cash offer. To minimize the chances of any inconvenience, you should:

- ❑ Confirm your reservation and get to the airport on time. Stand-by passengers may well be waiting for unclaimed seats.
- ❑ Avoid being a no-show, or failing to cancel bookings made on other flights. You may be the one needing that seat next time.
- ❑ Wait till the carrier makes a substantial offer – including a firm reservation for another flight – before being tempted to stand down.
- ❑ Check that you will be getting free meals, transport to another airport and any other essentials. Your pay-off may otherwise vanish on necessities.

Carlos №1 Place

MAYFAIR LONDON

A HOME YOU CAN TREAT LIKE A HOTEL

THE 11 SELF-CONTAINED APARTMENTS, RANGING FROM 1 TO 4 BEDROOMS ARE LUXURIOUSLY FURNISHED AND FULLY EQUIPPED. IDEALLY LOCATED FOR LONDON'S FOREMOST BUSINESS DISTRICTS, STORES, THEATRES AND RESTAURANTS.

DAILY MAID SERVICE • 24 HOUR PORTERAGE • COMPREHENSIVE SECURITY
AIR CONDITIONING • LIFT SERVICE

"The very best in serviced accommodation"

071-753 0744

1 CARLOS PLACE, MAYFAIR, LONDON W1Y 5AE FAX: 071 753 0731

- Be assertive. Some airlines only offer amenities to passengers who insist.
- Remember, excess passengers are not always seated on a first-come basis. Boarding priorities can differ. Tell staff if you have an important deadline to meet, since the airline is obliged to help – even if by another carrier.

CONNECTING FLIGHTS

Some arriving passengers see little more of a gateway airport than the transit lounge. Facilities vary widely, as does the time needed to make a connection without cutting things too fine.

Hard-to-beat airports for changing planes include Singapore, Amsterdam Schiphol, Zurich and Copenhagen. In the US, Atlanta's Hartsfield airport boasts the fastest transfer times and offers plenty of diversions to while away the hours.

London Heathrow is to have a custom-built £65 million new flight connections centre by late 1994 – a world first – designed to make life easier for the seven million plus passengers who transit the airport each year. It's hoped the complex will help wean traffic away from European rivals Schiphol, Frankfurt and Paris.

Minimum connecting times can vary from a speedy 25 to 30 minutes at Vienna and 40 to 50 at Schiphol to three hours or more at Bombay. Much depends on whether you are obliged to reclaim your baggage and clear Customs – an operation that can take two hours at many US airports – before proceeding on a domestic hop.

There's no doubt that if you have to change planes, you'll do it faster at a single-terminal airport. Walking from gate to gate takes a lot less time than finding a transfer bus or mile-long walkway at a multi-terminal airport. Since Los Angeles has nine terminals, JFK eight, Boston five, and Chicago and Houston four apiece, an inter-terminal bus stopping at each can devour precious time. While Schiphol now has two terminals, these are linked by moving pavements.

Smoother connections

- Choose an on-line connection – that is, with the same airline – rather than an interline one. The flight gates should be closer and staff are more likely to help if you're pressed for time.
- Travel with hand luggage only. Checked-in bags are more likely to go astray on connecting flights, and will have to be reclaimed if you need to clear Customs and Immigration.
- Tell the cabin crew if your incoming flight is perilously late. They can at least help ensure you're first off the plane.
- Try a less hectic gateway. Charlotte/Douglas in the southern US, for instance, is within a two-hour flight of more than half the US population and has a spacious international concourse.

Airport hotels

Killing time when you have several hours to wait between flights can be tedious – especially if you don't have the magic entry pass to a lounge. A five-hour gap is often too short a time to go into town, and too long to sit around comfortably.

Most airport hotels rent out rooms by the day, or even the hour – Sydney Airport Parkroyal being the first to launch the latter service Down Under. What's more, they usually provide free courtesy transport. If this does not run to a fixed schedule, you should find courtesy phones in the terminal building, enabling you to book a ride.

Bear in mind that some 'airport' hotels are actually a 20-minute drive away, and few are palaces. They don't walk off with many oscars for ambience or food, and are often functional hen-houses designed to provide little more than convenient dormitory space.

CLEARING CUSTOMS

Few people coming home from a business trip have plans for an extended stay in the Customs hall. Play your cards right, and you won't.

Most Customs officers are not too worried about the odd traveller sneaking past with an illicit flagon of vodka. Catching bigger fish – those who make a living out of ferrying drugs, guns, counterfeits or pornography around the world – are more pressing priorities.

At London Gatwick, 400 officers and sniffer-dog Bonky (there are two vacancies) work around the clock checking out passengers, luggage, cargo and crew. Busier Heathrow has a force of 1,000 Customs staff – though with planes landing every 90 seconds at peak times, they are stretched. Even Colombian drugs barons probably never see the quantities of narcotics uncovered by staff in an average year.

Twin channels – green if you have nothing to declare, red if you do – are fairly universal. Some European airports now have an additional blue one – effectively a green channel for those moving around the Community. Fatter EC duty-free allowances mean that Brits who till recently had to count every four-pack of lager bought on the Continent can now stagger home legally with enough cheap booze to sink the *Titanic*.

Customs are not over-generous when it comes to allowances on personal goods bought abroad. Those brought back into the EC may only total £36 at the time of writing before being liable for duty of at least 20 per cent. What's more, you can still be asked to cough up if they were bought on a previous trip any time in the last 20 years.

Brand new toys

Officers are on the lookout for shiny new toys – whether watches, cameras or laptops – as well the expensive suit you're wearing. Revenue smuggling is high on their hit list, and they'll know both which currencies cannot be brought back home, and whether your pound or dollar has been particularly buoyant in the country you've just been to.

Australian Customs will class you public enemy number one for trying to take an apple into the country, while those in Saudi Arabia may ban not simply girlie magazines, but those showing revealing paintings by the Old Masters. Other countries are particularly keen to find prohibited or restricted goods, whether antiques or crocodile skin handbags. US Customs are generally more rigorous than those in Europe.

Who gets stopped?

Just who do they stop, and why? Officers say they rely heavily on intuition, and that 'cold pulls' unearth far more serious smuggling attempts than tip-offs from contacts or police. Today's drug trafficker is more likely to wear a suit than to sport dreadlocks and denims, and no one is presumed a safe bet.

Don't be fooled into thinking that the near-deserted green channels at many airports are a licence for casual smuggling. Customs are shrewd at carrying out spot checks, and someone, somewhere will be keeping watch. Officers are more likely to stop, search, or invite to the interview room those who:

- Fly in from 'source countries' for drugs. That includes transit countries such as the Caribbean, West Africa and the Middle East. They will be more alert if you step off a flight from Karachi, Bogota or Bangkok than one from Toronto.
- Look nervous or ill at ease. Since even the innocent can feel like a felon walking past the steely gaze of Customs officers, the guilty feel even guiltier.
- Re-pack, fiddle with or rummage through their bags before going through.
- Have forgotten to take the wrappings off their brand new set of golf clubs.
- Give answers that don't add up. Officers will compare what they see with what they hear.

ALTERNATIVE ACCOMMODATION – SERVICED APARTMENTS
by Linda Coulthard, Draycott House

A serviced apartment offers a cost effective alternative to hotel accommodation. There are fifty or so quality establishments in London, ranging in size from just 7 apartments to 158. Prices vary over an equally wide range, depending on size, location and, in some cases, season.

Apartment blocks vary in the length of lets they are permitted to make by law. Some can accept bookings of a day or two whilst others may have a minimum of 22 or even 90 days. Value Added Tax rates vary with the length of stay; business travellers can often obtain refunds of this tax but should obtain advice from their company or apartment manager.

Booking procedures vary but in general a deposit will be required in advance to secure a reservation; note that credit cards are accepted at many establishments but not all.

Most apartments have daily maid service from Monday to Friday and offer the range of services found in hotels, i.e. laundry service, chauffeur drive cars etc. Some have private gardens and even garage parking. Check whether children are welcome and if cots and highchairs are supplied.

Most establishments will do their best to ensure guests have everything they require, from welcome packs to personal fax machines, to arranging temporary secretarial services or even a cook, but do confirm whether these are extra charges and, indeed, exactly what is included in the rental charge.

Always check telephone meter charges which vary enormously – from 12p to 55p per unit! For business or for pleasure, a stay in a serviced apartment offers a friendly welcome, security and the comforts of your own home away from home.

Draycott House Limited, 10 Draycott Avenue, Chelsea, London SW3 3AA
Telephone: 071-584 4659   Fax: 071-225 3694

"We *are very grateful to you all for the welcome and kindness you gave to us during our stay at Draycott House. It made our transitional period all the more manageable (and perhaps less traumatic). The children are missing you, so don't be surprised if we pop in!"*

Over the years, many of our guests have written to Draycott House to endorse these sentiments.

Caught between homes, they have found in this delightful apartment block a true home-from-home in the heart of Chelsea.

Draycott House offers the family on the move an oasis of calm, supported by a sensible range of modern amenities.

Apartments are available with one, two or three bedrooms. Prices start at £715 (excluding VAT) per week, with a minimum booking period of five days. For further details contact:

Offering its guests a unique combination of cosseting comfort, total discretion, meticulous management and genuinely warm hospitality, Draycott House is the smallest DeLuxe-category serviced apartments to appear in Egon Ronay's Cellnet Guide 1993.

DRAYCOTT HOUSE, 10 DRAYCOTT AVENUE, CHELSEA, LONDON SW3 3AA
Tel: +44 (0)71 584 4659 Fax: +44 (0)71 225 3694

LINDA COULTHARD, GENERAL MANAGER,
DRAYCOTT HOUSE, 10 DRAYCOTT AVENUE, CHELSEA, LONDON SW3 3AA.

TELEPHONE 071-584 4659 OR FAX: 071-225 3694.

Clever Customs

Whether you pick the green channel – for those who have managed to curb their shopping excesses – or the red, you should:

- Keep a list of your purchases, with receipts and preferably serial numbers for expensive goods. That way, you can prove it if your gleaming Nikon camera really came from the local High Street.
- Never, ever, carry goods through for anyone you don't know. Drug smugglers resort to all manner of subterfuges to get their booty past official eyes.
- Know the rules. Lists of banned items and limits on duty-free goods are posted clearly for anyone suffering from temporary amnesia.
- Remember it's up to you to declare your hand, not wait to be caught. If you're unsure whether your new laptop or antique Buddha is liable for duty, ask.
- Steer clear of Gatwick's Bonky. If a four-legged Customs officer stops to investigate your case, you'd better pray he just lifts his leg and waters it.

What happens if you're caught? You'll end up paying far more than the value of the duty you sought to evade, and – if you are daft enough to try bringing prohibited items into the country – could easily end up in court.

Determined smugglers do not, of course, simply stop at their suitcase. Dozens of 'swallowers and stuffers' attempt to conceal their hoard in the most unlikely places – sometimes risking death, as for example a heroin-filled condom bursts in their stomach. Should you take leave of your senses and try the same, you could find yourself being escorted somewhere like Gatwick's notorious Emit room, where unspeakable things take place involving transparent lavatories and rubber gloves.

Some people, of course, are still hell-bent on outwitting the law. Common ruses – not that you would copy them, naturally – include:

- Making sure new designer gear looks suitably worn and crumpled.
- Persuading someone else to carry the offending item.
- Carrying small items in a duty-free carrier rather than hiding it in a suitcase.
- Swopping the label on a new Hong Kong suit with one from another bought from a chain store at home.
- Getting a pre-dated receipt – bearing in mind Customs may ask to see stamps from previous trips.
- Getting a receipt of lower value – not forgetting that officers keep databanks on prices around the world.

LOST OR DAMAGED LUGGAGE

Research shows that airline passengers are almost as scared of losing their bags as they are of their plane crashing – and not without reason. Minus luggage, you risk having nothing to change into, nothing to show clients and nothing to present to your hosts.

Airline luggage loss rates can vary considerably. According to IATA, 7 bags in every 1,000 go astray every day, though only 2 per cent of those stay lost. Missing bags are now logged on to electronic filing systems, and can usually be traced in minutes, no matter where. Air Canada quotes its mishandled baggage rate as 4.5 bags per 1,000, while Lufthansa admits to 8.6 – or 237,000 pieces lost out of 61 million items flown in 1992. Of those, 7,250 ominously never turned up.

The golden rules

Checked bags are reconciled with the passenger manifest before a flight leaves to try and ensure bags can't leave without their owner. However, no system is watertight. Don't pack anything you can't manage without for 24 hours, and:

- Stick to the published minimum check-in and flight connecting times for checked luggage. Your suitcase may have to travel a quarter of a mile to reach the aircraft.
- Remove the tags from your last trip.
- Make sure your case is properly labelled. Don't rely on airline paper tags – one tug, and they're gone.
- Don't advertise your home address on the outside of the case. It could tell thieves the whereabouts of your empty home.
- Don't assume suitcase locks are tamper-proof. Padlocks and combination locks are the hardest to pick.
- Keep duty-free bottles in your carry-on bags, unless you fancy clothes marinaded in Glenfiddich.
- Don't pack anything that can spill, stain, dent or smash. The same goes for cash and million-dollar contracts. Make sure your insurance covers you for valuables such as photographic gear.
- Keep a list of the contents of your suitcase, together with important receipts.
- Think twice about investing in expensive designer luggage. Something less ostentatious may be less tempting to thieves.
- Make sure someone else doesn't pick up your bag by mistake by making it instantly recognizable. Brightly coloured pompoms, stickers

and straps may not be the height of chic, but they'll do the trick.
- Don't overpack. Locks can sometimes spring apart in transit.

Pilferage problems

Pilferage rates vary greatly at airports around the world. A hard core of baggage handlers – sometimes using X-ray equipment to identify valuable goods – are often found to be on the fiddle. London's Heathrow airport has at times won the nickname Thiefrow for this very reason. Hidden cameras now help identify the culprits.

If you suspect your bags have been pilfered, check them on the spot. Any theft will be much harder to prove once you're home. Report anything missing or damaged at once to airline staff, and fill out claim forms before leaving the airport. Be sure to hang on to your ticket and baggage stubs – you'll need them to prove the bags were checked in.

Most airlines will deliver mislaid baggage straight to your address free of charge, and pay for any repairs. Bear in mind that misdirected luggage is routinely opened, and that any illegal goods are likely to result in a friendly visit from police. Most bags turn up eventually, so the airline is unlikely to declare them finally lost for up to six months.

Airlines will pay out a sum to cover emergency supplies while your bag is being found, which increases the longer it is mislaid. This will be more if you are away from home, or can demonstrate that you need a DJ for the night. Compensation is not exactly generous, so make sure your bags are adequately insured.

Astonishingly, a good deal of lost airport luggage is never reclaimed. Among Gatwick's more bizarre unclaimed items was a full-sized concert harp – eventually sold off to a dealer after fruitless attempts to find the owner. Regular auctions are held to sell off unclaimed goods, while drugs usually go up in smoke.

PORTERS

Few airports either post official porterage rates or – as is the case at Heathrow – ensure the price is boldly pinned to the porter's top pocket.

Porters will usually charge whatever they can get away with – and they're guaranteed to look indignant at anything much less than a $10 note these days. If you hate arguments afterwards, agree a price before you set off or seek advice from the information desk. Otherwise, keep a supply of $1 bills handy, pay what you feel is fair and ignore any howls of protest.

Alternatively, find a trolley – bearing in mind that they don't always come free, either. You'll need dollar bills at the ready at many US airports, where trolleys need to be rented. Some – as in Miami – have to be relinquished, moreover, right outside the baggage hall. Trolleys at Third World airports – where you could be lucky to find one with wheels on – are often commandeered by unofficial minders seeking tips from passengers wanting to use them. Keep some small change handy for the purpose.

Even if your trolley is free and unencumbered, that doesn't mean you'll be able to steer it the 20 or so yards to the cab rank or carpark without serious injury. Airport trolleys are notorious for being impossible to get on an escalator, incapable of braking, and liable to tip up or swivel 90 degrees the minute you balance one too many duty-free cartons on top. More than 200 a day are carted off for repairs at Heathrow.

CHANGING MONEY

Not surprisingly, airport bureaux de change often have a poor reputation. Don't expect the best rate in town – they are catering for captive customers. Passengers can easily be ripped off in soft-currency countries, where exchange rates are often not widely known. Watch out for out-of-date banknotes.

BRIBES

Don't be surprised to see some passengers handing over their passports with cigarettes or notes in parts of the Third World, where bribes (normally referred to as 'fines') are sometimes needed to steer a path past rampant officialdom. Problems are compounded when a visitor fails to realize a bribe is being sought, and becomes more and more exasperated. The result can be arguments and intransigence.

Airports like Bombay ('baksheesh all the way' in the words of one friend) and Lagos (most travellers' least favourite airport) are two where you may well come up against this. See Chapter 10.

LEFT LUGGAGE

Many airports no longer have luggage lockers or left luggage stores for security reasons. This can be a nuisance if you have hours to kill and can't check your bags in for the flight. Whatever happens, don't leave them unattended – you may find the bomb squad waiting on your return.

Leaving your bag in an airline business lounge may be an option, providing you are entitled to use it. This will depend on its location (landside or airside), and the helpfulness of staff. While the cloakroom area will not be supervised, it's unlikely to be a target for casual thieves.

MEETERS AND GREETERS

If, like me, you instinctively scan the array of boards bearing passenger names outside the arrivals hall, you'll know that there's nothing quite like being personally met on arrival.

Every airport has its meeters and greeters – firms who will arrange limo transport into town, hand-deliver documents or currency, transfer passengers between terminals or even arrange a champagne welcome on the spot. Most bigger business travel agents can arrange to book their services anywhere in the world, any time, while Diners Club members can book a 24-hour chauffered pick-up at most airports in the US. In Lagos, Wagonlit can arrange to meet clients airside (a privilege normally reserved for superstars and VIPs) and whisk them safely to their hotel.

Limousine transport (cheaper if pre-booked) and other ground services can, of course, be arranged on the spot. A limo with driver can often be cost-effective if shared by three or four people, and will usually be charged by the hour. If you don't see an appropriate-looking desk, check at the information counter.

GETTING INTO TOWN

Arm yourself with a guidebook such as Thomas Cook's *Airports Guide International* (£8.95), which lists all public transport links at 90 gateways around the world. As well as giving cab fares, it also details car-parking, car hire and other facilities.

Public transport

Business travellers often needlessly shun airport public transport, spending a fortune on long taxi rides as a result. Schiphol, Zurich and London Gatwick have excellent train services into town, even though the latter is deplorably expensive. Montreal's Mirabel airport and Tokyo's Narita are both so far out of town that the cost of taking a cab (more than

AT THE AIRPORT ■ 81

$150 at Narita – reckoned to be the world's costliest airport cab ride) is prohibitive.

At Washington National and Boston, you can ride into town by speedy subway for peanuts. Boston even has a water taxi service that takes 7 minutes and gives you a spectacular view of the harbour en route. Chicago O'Hare and Atlanta Hartsfield both have good mass transit systems, while JFK's best option is the bus service into Grand Central. London Heathrow, already linked to London's West End by tube, should have a £300 million non-stop rail link to Paddington station by 1997.

Airport limousine bus services are generally the best option in the US, since, while they may make half a dozen stops, they'll drop you right at the hotel door.

Taxis

While you should have few worries taking a metered cab into town, bear in mind that airports are a breeding ground for taxi touts out to make some fast bucks on the side. You should therefore:

- Take only official cabs. Sharing with a fellow traveller can cut the cost.
- Check to see whether fare guidelines are posted in the terminal, or whether a pre-paid voucher system (offered at airports such as Bombay) is available.
- Check for free courtesy transport if staying at an airport hotel.
- Try snatching an incoming cab on the departures level if the queue at arrivals looks huge. Although strictly not allowed, it may save a lengthy wait.
- Remember that drivers who have waited hours for a fare will not be keen to take you to nearby suburbs. Be ready to hand over three or four times the amount on the meter.

Helicopters

Choppers are another option at airports such as Tokyo, Bangkok and JFK – though the view can be better than the time saving. At Kennedy, you'll probably have to change terminals first – itself a major undertaking – before finding the right check-in counter, and waiting up to 15 minutes for the next departure. After a scenic but noisy ride to Manhattan, you'll be dropped at the East 34th Street heliport, and still need to get a taxi to your hotel.

TAILPIECES

- Busiest airport in the world is Chicago O'Hare, used by 64 million passengers in 1992. Next came LA, with 47 million, followed by London Heathrow – still the busiest in the international stakes – with a passenger count of 45 million. New York's JFK, ninth in the league table, handled 28 million.

- What's the world's best airport? In *Business Traveller* magazine's 1992 reader poll, plaudits went to Atlanta Hartsfield (best in North America), Singapore's Changi (best for passport control, luggage retrieval and Customs clearance), and Amsterdam (best for duty-frees). New York's JFK had the distinction of being voted worst on Customs, luggage and passport counts.

- What do Leo, Chester, Jodie, Shunny and Jack have in common? They're all 'operational animals' on the sniffer beat at Heathrow.

5
☐ Flying in Style

Knowing how the flying business works is one thing. Knowing how to travel in style whenever you fly is another. If there is kudos attached to sitting at the front of the plane, there's still more in knowing how to get there even when the firm's budget won't pay.

Savvy travellers make a point of checking out what's on offer in all three cabins, and learning the factors guaranteed to make most difference to their in-flight comfort. They'll know how to take advantage of frequent flyer perks, how to maximize the chances of an upgrade and even when to hire a private jet – getting more for their dollars, pounds or D-Marks every time they fly.

WHAT DO AIR TRAVELLERS WANT?

Airlines sink millions of dollars a year into promoting the virtues of large seats, fine food and solicitous cabin crew. Yet research shows that what matters most to their business passengers is simply getting from A to B at the right time.

Advert after glossy advert depicts the shameless pampering full-fare passengers can expect in-flight, with besuited frequent flyers – wearing smiles whose glow can only be described as post-coital – being tucked in and offered a refill of Bollinger by a stewardess with cover-girl looks. Outsiders could be forgiven for thinking that their only worries are the label on their champagne and the attentiveness of their (preferably female) flight attendant.

Food and drink do matter, of course, when you are holding a ticket that costs ten times the price of those in economy, and have little to do for five hours but eat your heart out. Even the seen-it-all traveller who feigns disinterest would no doubt be seriously miffed if the champers and roast quail turned into a soup and sandwich.

But it's basics that matter most to frequent flyers. Survey after survey shows that arriving punctually, safely and at the right time of day come top of the list of factors influencing the way they spend their money. In-flight cosseting is the icing on the cake.

PICKING A WINNER

A look at the league table of award-winners in business and travel magazine reader polls is one way of telling which airlines are giving customers what they want.

US carriers, whose style and innovation once set the pace for the industry as a whole, are conspicuously absent from the ranks these days. While American Airlines is a notable exception, many have been forced by market pressures to jettison service frills in favour of bargain basement fares and frequent flyer perks.

Business Traveller readers voted British Airways the top airline of 1992, naming Virgin the best carrier for longhaul business class. American was named best carrier in North America, while Swissair was voted best for punctuality. Alitalia won the unenviable title of worst timekeeper, with Iberia, TWA, Air India and Garuda following suit.

Executive Travel readers named Virgin Atlantic airline of the year for the third time running in 1993, piling another half-dozen awards on the carrier for service in specific sectors. Cathay Pacific and Singapore Airlines were runners-up for the main award, with British Airways taking the prize for best frequent flyer programme.

Euromoney, whose readers voted BA, Singapore Airlines and Swissair tops in the sky, invited readers to vote for their least favourite airlines as well. Topping the 'most disappointing' league came Continental (something of a blow, in light of the carrier's much-trumpeted launch of BusinessFirst class), followed by China Air, Aeroflot, Alitalia and TWA.

Such polls are, of course, relative. Third World flying veterans who are more familiar with a rattling Viscount than a sleek transatlantic business class cabin will confirm that being served a soggy steak or second-rate movie is nothing to the rigours of putting up with sheep, assorted spare passengers and primus stoves going full blast to brew tea.

BUSINESS CLASS

The battle for your custom

Never mind the accolades and column inches earned from the media – the proof of the product is in the flying. Business class (or 'J' class) passengers are being more fiercely courted than ever as airlines lay on a galaxy of gold-plated carrots to stop their premium-fare traffic defecting to the back of the plane. So numerous are the benefits on offer that some bosses would not unnaturally prefer to see fewer perks and more fare cuts.

KLM is credited with inventing business class air travel back in 1975 as a means of rewarding those paying higher fares for flexible tickets, but unable to justify flying first class. Since then, the concept has spread like wildfire. Whether it's called Premier or Prestige, Connoisseur or Club, Mabuhay or Amadeus, business class is now a vital source of revenue for more than 50 major carriers. Their advertising bill on British TV screens alone came to £14 million in the year to February 1993.

Many would say today's business class is simply yesterday's first in new clothes, and the standards now achieved certainly make the first class travel of old look positively punishing. While early passengers merely sat in a curtained-off cabin and enjoyed a fancier meal, today's business class flyer enjoys privileges and perks yesterday's first class veteran would have whistled for.

Start-to-finish perks

Astute carriers have taken on board the fact that global business class travel is not simply about being spoiled rotten in the air. Customer care now starts well before passengers stretch out in their reclining motorized seat with personal flip-up video screen and glass of bubbly. Gleaming limos collect them from their front door, while airport lounges provide private sanctuaries in which to relax before take-off.

Business class travellers enjoy a generous luggage allowance, dedicated check-in desk, and the chance to select their seat before they fly. They will be treated to some of the finest food airline chefs can muster, served course by course on porcelain rather than plastic, and a comfort kit packed with free toiletries. On landing, they'll enjoy priority disembarkation and luggage retrieval.

Other privileges

As if this is not enough, other giveaways, bonuses and benefits abound. More and more business class tickets now come hand in hand with vouchers for free future economy class travel or duty-free goods, discounted hotel rooms, free parking and generous frequent flyer programme perks. Passengers flying with a US carrier to the States from Europe are normally accorded first class seats for their onward flights.

As the traffic battles intensify, it's clear that business class is here to stay. Only a handful of carriers now fail to offer a dedicated service for their vital premium-fare corporate travellers.

What's on offer

Hardly a month goes by without one carrier or another revamping, rethinking or enhancing its business class product. Leading airlines are not only pounding down the added-value route with a wealth of frills and extras, but also coming up with some serious product innovation.

British Airways has sunk £100 million into improving its Club World, first and Concorde services in the carrier's biggest product rethink since the '80s. Added features include a fast-track channel to whisk passengers through airport formalities at Heathrow, new Club World seats with individual seat-back videos, bigger and better lounges – including some for use on arrival – and greater service choice in the air.

Club World passengers can sink back into recontoured seats (each with pivoted video screen) and decide whether to indulge in the classic lobster-and-champagne treatment or opt for a Well-Being programme, choosing healthier vegetarian fare and trying out exercise and relaxation techniques depicted in brochures and videos. They can tune into the sounds of waves and seagulls on a special audio channel, fuelling the feel-good factor with cold eye compresses, lip balm, face spray and rehydration gel to combat the effects of dry cabin air.

Continental has fused its North Atlantic first and business class cabins in BusinessFirst, branded as a first class service at a business class price. Space and configuration are now equal to Virgin's Upper class, and deep-reclining motorized seats are fitted with individual armrest videos. Passengers can choose between an all-in-one light meal or a leisurely dinner, enjoying free UK airport limo transfers, first class tickets on connecting US flights and the services of a hotel-style concierge on the ground. Continental hopes the changes will push its frequent traveller revenue up from single figures to nearer 40 per cent.

Hand-picked perks

Virgin offers a free in-flight massage and manicure, while other airlines are pushing hard on the value-added front. JAL's Executive class passengers can hand-pick perks from a list of business programme benefits that includes free gifts, business cards, airport transfers, duty free vouchers and hotel accommodation. Qantas passengers enjoy assorted discounts and benefits in its wide-ranging Connections programme, while Northwest has a portfolio of value-added extras.

U.S. Franchisors Offering
Master Franchising/Licensing Opportunities
All European Countries

(1) **Callanetics** The Shape of Success – Exercise Studios that make a difference to the lives of others. Leading Health and Fitness Studio. Franshisor will provide training and continuing support.

(2) **Water Doctors International** Has proven Track Record, servicing Auto Industry. Seeking qualified Licensees in Eurpoean and Asian countries. Recommended by Auto Manufacturers. Extensive Training given.

(3) **Pro Shred** The largest and most experienced provider of Mobile Shredding Services in North America. Excellent Marketing program.

(4) **Fast Food**
  (a) **Ho Lee Chow**
  Great Chinese Food – Delivered Fast and Fresh to customers. Training, Quality Control, Excellent Marketing, U.K. immediately available for Area Developer.
  (b) **Seawest Subs**
  Take out Sub Sandwiches, Salads – growth area of franchising – Support from experienced Food and Franchise Professionals.

(5) **Dr. Vinyl Mobile Repair and Reconditioning Service** for Home, Hotels, Offices, Automobiles, Restaurants. Full training and on going support.

(6) **Foliage Design Systems** Providing live plants, shrubs and relazed services to hotels, offices, institutions, commercial and private buildings.
Leads furnished. Extensive support from franchisor.

(7) **Kidsports** Health & Fitness Club – provides fun filled recreation/fitness/skill development with no emphasis on winning or losing – Poised for explosive growth.

We are Consultants for a range of U.S. franchisors in Services, Food, Retail and Automotive Products.

Please indicate your specific interest – substantial investment is required for Master Licenses.

Please contact: John Fitzgerald B.C.L., B.L., John Fitgerald & Associates, Management & Franchise Consultants, 6 Sullivan's Quay, Cork, Ireland.
Tel: + 353 21 963877   Fax: + 353 21 310273

More and more carriers are ripping out seats to give their longhaul business class passengers more space. Virgin and Continental provide a sweeping 55-inch seat pitch, while Sabena offers an even grander 62 inches. Lauda Air, SAS and others offer the option of roomy sleeper seats at a surcharge. A few, like Virgin, Iberia and Thai Airways, out-space the opposition with luxurious 2 × 2 B747 seating.

Swissair has relaunched its European business class product with roomier seats, extra legroom and lounge facilities at 25 airports, making the service available to all those paying the full economy fare. Lufthansa has relaunched its shorthaul product with added service enhancements, while fare-cutting British Midland has unveiled Diamond Euroclass on its prime continental routes. This offers dedicated lounges, five-course meals and a flight bonus scheme for frequent flyers.

Business class lounges

Access to an airline's airport lounges is another valued perk of business class travel. Many seasoned globetrotters would cheerfully forget many of the other benefits on offer to simply walk through the hallowed gates of an airline hospitality haven – whether a Captain's Club (Qantas), Silver Kris lounge (SIA) or Presidents Clubroom (Continental) – every time they fly.

British Airways can now claim to be the first airline to cosset passengers with the luxury lounge treatment on landing as well as departure. New arrivals lounges – an untried airline innovation – have opened at Heathrow and Gatwick, designed to offer those taking an overnight red-eye the chance to shower and freshen up before facing the rigours of the day. BA already operates a striking lounge pavilion, complete with showers and spa, at Heathrow's terminal 4.

While American carriers can be surprisingly stingy in the hospitality stakes (you can't even count on a free Coke at some US airport lounges), those in other parts of the world are happy to roll out the red carpet. The problem is getting access in the first place, since not every business class ticket holder automatically gets in. Air France and TWA are among the carriers who restrict usage largely to airline club members.

Belonging to the appropriate airline's frequent flyer programme is usually the answer. Silver and gold tier members of British Airways Executive Club, for instance, can use more than 100 dedicated lounges worldwide. Lounge clubs – like Delta's Crown Room scheme, costing $150 a year – are another avenue.

Choosing the best airline

Other things being equal (ie if fare offers or frequent flyer perks don't come into the picture), these factors will make all the difference to your trip as a business class passenger:

- **Legroom.** Look for the carrier giving you more inches for your mile. Tall travellers will feel cramped with a seat pitch much below 40 inches.
- **Lounge access.** With luck, your boarding class will guarantee entry.
- **Transfers.** Limos to whisk you to and from the airport will keep hassles to a minimum.
- **Cabin service.** Crew to passenger ratios can vary from 1:6 to 1:18.
- **Meal choice.** The best airlines let you choose between a five-course banquet or a quick supper and the chance to sleep.
- **Entertainment.** Individual video screens let you watch what you want, when you want.
- **Extras.** Anything from free economy tickets to complimentary hotel stays may be on offer.

GETTING AN UPGRADE

Clever travellers, of course, do not always need to buy a business class seat to travel in style. They book an economy seat and get an upgrade.

Although it's easier said than done, some passengers manage to wheedle an upgrade almost every time they travel. While airlines are steadfastly coy about discussing their policies on upgrading, it's worth knowing how to maximize your chances – especially since fewer people can now pay high business class fares each time they travel.

Upgrades are technically for those who have earned the requisite number of points through an airline's frequent flyer programme, are commercially important passengers, well-known figures or – due to overbooking – have been bumped out of economy. The truth, however, is that there are no hard and fast rules. Being upgraded to business or first can depend on the route, the load factor, and whether the check-in clerk has had a bad night.

Bear in mind that carriers will normally refuse to upgrade unless there are enough business class meals loaded on board, and that you're unlikely to talk your way to the front every time. To maximize your chances, you'll need to follow two tactical routes.

Before you travel

- **Join the airline's frequent flyer programme.** Collect the specified number of points, and you're entitled to an upgrade anyway. You'll

also be on the priority list for unearned, or goodwill upgrades.
- **Pay the full fare**. Some airlines routinely upgrade full-fare economy passengers to business, while others sometimes upgrade full-fare business class passengers to first. Choose BA, and you'll occasionally find yourself flying Concorde.
- **Use the right travel agent**. The best will have sufficient clout with some carriers to ensure their clients are first in line for an upgrade.
- **Strike an agreement**. Most carriers are receptive to volume deals from clients. Remember, you're in an age of wheeler-dealing.
- **Shop around**. Short-term and two-for-one ticket offers sometimes let you fly more cheaply in first than in business anyway. At the time of writing, you pay virtually the same to fly from London to New York using the Air France Concorde service from Paris, than flying first class direct from Britain.
- **Fly with a lean and hungry airline**. New carriers and foreign airlines are generally more obliging than a resident carrier with a ready-made client base.
- **Choose an airline that spoils full-fare economy passengers**. Try Virgin's Mid class, for example, and you'll be well away from the package holiday crowds.
- **Use your contacts**. Pulling strings will be easier if you know a key airline individual.

At the airport

- **Dress the part**. Unless you are Hollywood's latest darling, no one is going to whisk you to the front of the plane dressed in a T-shirt and jeans. Carry a briefcase – even if it only contains sunglasses and a Jackie Collins blockbuster.
- **Have a reason**. Your winning smile alone won't do. Do you fly with the airline often? Do you have a bad back? Are you too tall to fit in a tiny seat at the back? Do you have an important document to finish writing in-flight?
- **Look confident**. Anyone who is terminally timid will meet with less success than someone who looks as if they've done it a million times.
- **Keep trying**. If you get no joy from staff at the check-in desk or departure gate (whose first move will be to check your status in the computer), speak to the chief purser on board. He/she can upgrade on discretion.
- **Check in late**. If your pre-booked economy seat has been given away, you may find yourself moved upfront. On the other hand, you may find yourself waiting four hours for the next flight.

- **Turn up for a flight you know is** overbooked. You can then turn on a persuasively crestfallen face.
- **Try some good old-fashioned chutzpah.** A business card that starts with 'Sir', or a withering 'Don't you know who I am?', works wonders if you've got the nerve.

If all else fails, you can always try being inventive. The best story I've heard was that of a fellow journalist, who stopped at a little shop in Hong Kong years ago and bought a made-to-order rubber stamp. Ever since then, check-in clerks from Bali to Barbados have, he says, taken one look at his ticket and rushed to roll out the red carpet, decant the champers and whisk him off to the first class lounge.

The reason? Boldly emblazoning his tickets are the words: 'This passenger is of extreme commercial importance to the airline. Please do everything possible to ensure he enjoys his flight.' Simple, really.

FLYING FIRST CLASS

First class air travel has done a vanishing act in recent years. It has already disappeared on shorthaul European routes, and is in danger of becoming extinct on the North Atlantic and other sectors soon.

SAS scrapped its first class service in Europe some years ago. KLM, Lufthansa, Swissair and others have since followed suit, while British Airways has abolished the service on some longer routes. Cathay Pacific's B777s, now being built, will have no first class cabins at all, and those aboard other airlines are shrinking wholesale to make way for cheaper seats. KLM now has plans to scrap first class network-wide while American intends dropping it on the Atlantic.

First class travel has not surprisingly suffered badly in the recession. With a London–New York ticket in first costing up to 80 per cent more than a seat in business, firms whose top executives once flew in unfettered luxury have now down-classed dramatically – especially since airlines such as Virgin and Continental offer what is branded as a first class service at a business class price anyway. Others reserve first class travel for executives going straight to an important meeting after overnight flights, or flying tiring transpacific and Asia/Europe routes.

Habitués of first class travel – three out of four of them on business – tend to be captains of industry, diplomats, wealthy entrepreneurs, sportspeople or those in the entertainment world. Failing that, they are there on an upgrade – and it is the latter point that not only irritates genuine fare-paying passengers, but ensures that first class cabins generate little or no real revenue. The problem is that few people are now prepared to pay through the nose to sit in the nose of the aircraft.

Freebies at the front

Travel agents estimate that only one in ten first class passengers actually pay the full fare. Shell out the published price, and you could end up next to someone who has been handed a seat through a frequent flyer programme, talked their way into an upgrade, been offered one as a commercially important person or is simply an off-duty crew member.

While all this has destroyed some of the cachet of first class travel, airlines say it remains a viable and well patronized service on some routes. Flights into Lagos and Middle East Arab states are known to generate consistent high-revenue traffic, and thus look unlikely to lose first altogether.

Concorde travel continues to flourish among those who like to fly to New York, have three hours of meetings, and still be back in London by bedtime. The aircraft are now fitted with plusher seating, bigger overhead bins, and state-of-the-art audio systems. Other well-heeled execs fly to the Big Apple subsonic, and return on BA's first class Sleeper service. They can dine before take-off at JFK, before donning personal sleeper suits on board and snuggling down with duvet, pillow, and goodnight hot chocolate. The service also operates on other sectors.

What can other luxury-loving first class passengers – fare-paying or otherwise – expect to find? There should be oodles of space, dedicated loos (they're even gold-plated aboard Royal Brunei Airlines), a stretch-out sleeper seat, and freshly prepared food good enough to win an aerial Michelin star. Passengers and their bags should be last on, first off, and the cabin should feel more like a private jet than a busy B747. Back home, the pampered traveller will probably be plied with Christmas, birthday and even Valentine cards from the cap-doffing carrier.

NEW-LOOK ECONOMY

Virgin Atlantic chairman Richard Branson was apparently dissuaded from calling the carrier's economy service riff-raff in its early days. Unfortunately, it's a label all too many travel veterans would readily apply to the rear-cabin service offered by many airlines.

Economy in Europe has admittedly changed a lot since the early '80s, when catering often consisted of a cardboard picnic box. Now, fierce competition forces flight attendants to whip through the cabin with drinks and full-scale meals in barely 30 minutes of cruising time.

> # "BON VOYAGE!"
>
> Interlink Express hopes you enjoy your journey.
>   As one of the UK's largest Data, Parcel and Freight Carriers we understand the requirements for safe, efficient travel and delivery on time.
>   So, wish 'Bon Voyage' to your Data, Parcel and Freight and rest assured we will deliver, as promised.
>   For information call us on (0272) 426900.
>
> **YOU PROMISE. WE DELIVER.**
>
> By far and away the best value around. Locally, Nationally and Internationally.
>
> HEAD OFFICE: BRUNSWICK COURT, BRUNSWICK SQUARE, BRISTOL, BS2 8PE.

Pressure from one-class European airlines such as Transwede, Air UK and Crossair – who offer every passenger the roomy seats, free drinks and generous meals normally associated with front-end travel – has undoubtedly forced the rest of the pack to pull out the stops. British Midland, formerly Europe's leading one-class airline, abandoned the concept in '93 and now offers a traditional two-tier service.

Undoubtedly the most dynamic move to capture the custom of budget-strapped business travellers has been the launch of a new breed of full-fare economy service, aimed specifically at passengers relegated to the back of the plane by spending cuts but still paying considerably more for their seat than discount ticketholders.

Deluxe treatment

Virgin's Mid class, targeted at economy passengers travelling on business but unable to afford a seat at the front, does exactly that with a separate cabin and bigger seats. Other airlines copying the move include Taiwanese carrier Eva Air, which markets an Economy Deluxe service with better seats and personal videos, and Japanese carrier ANA, which provides extra legroom, amenity kits and a better meal.

Other airlines try and offer full-fare economy passengers better seating – in a B747 upper deck, for instance – while JAL has come up with a package of extras including lounge access at some airports and the chance to store mileage credits in the airine's frequent flyer scheme.

FREQUENT FLYER PROGRAMMES

More than 30 million people around the globe now belong to an airline frequent flyer programme. Invented back in 1981 by American Airlines – whose AAdvantage scheme now boasts a mind-boggling 16 million members – the concept has since become one of the industry's most successful ever innovations.

Free airline tickets, gifts and giveaways are just some of the perks showered upon signed-up members of frequent flyer programmes, who now get far more than just a ticket to ride every time they fly. Upgrades, discounts on car hire and hotel rooms, leisure breaks and spouse deals are all on offer – not to mention extras such as waitlisting priority, better baggage allowances and a guaranteed seat.

Members receive computerized statements, magazines detailing special offers and some dazzling introductory perks to entice them to sign up. And sign up they do. New members are rolling in at the rate of thousands a week, and two-thirds of US business travellers are reckoned to belong to at least one scheme. It's been estimated that nearly one thousand billion miles have been earned on the programmes since the idea first took off.

Designed to cement customer loyalty by rewarding passengers with points or 'miles' every time they fly, the schemes also offer tie-ins with hotel chains, car rental firms and other airline partners, enabling even passengers flying with other carriers to reap the benefits. Many also have elite categories – normally reserved for those who rack up 25,000 miles or more a year in the air – giving extra privileges.

Since taking America by storm, frequent flyer schemes have spread to Europe and, latterly, the Far East. Well aware that it makes little sense for travellers to dilute the perks and join more than two or three schemes, airlines are now hell-bent on signing members up as fast as possible.

Mileage madness

Not surprisingly, the schemes are hugely popular with their customers. A recent survey conducted by Official Airline Guides revealed that premium-fare passengers rated an airline's frequent flyer perks more highly than its lowest available fare. And therein lies the rub. Mileage madness – neatly summed up in this comic conversation from Simon Hoggart's book *America: A User's Guide* – has reached epidemic proportions.

You: How did you get here?
Your colleague: Oh, on United. I flew to Denver, picked up a connection to Anchorage, managed to get standby to San Francisco, and caught the red-eye to Miami.
You: But you started from Miami.
Your colleague: Yeah, but I'm hoping to take the family to Sydney this year. First class.

Corporate mileage junkies are now more concerned with maximizing their points than getting from A to B in the best way. Many gladly double or triple their journey times, pay full published fares when a cheap excursion ticket would do, and hatch all manner of techniques to fatten up their mileage account. Research suggests the schemes have now pushed up travel costs by more than $5 billion a year in the US as obsessive point-collectors travel on unnecessary full-fare tickets.

Blackout blues

With at least 1 passenger in 20 now reckoned to be on a frequent flyer freebie in the US, many carriers black out certain days and routes, limit free seat availability or impose shorter use-by deadlines to ensure they are not swamped by free riders. Even this ploy has backfired, since many members who religiously store up points to trade in for a major holiday now find it almost impossible to do so. Securing seats on the right date, route and flight can be a nightmare.

Another bone of contention is whether or not frequent flyer points are transferable. US airlines have waged an angry war against coupon brokers who buy up unwanted awards and then sell them on to eager buyers at a profit. Most strictly forbid the points to be sold, since the greater usage it precipitates upsets the economics of the schemes – designed for an uptake level of as little as 25 per cent.

Some airline insiders say members are now in a state of terminal confusion over the barrage of schemes, options and perks on offer – and if travellers feel frequent frustration, carriers certainly do. Many admit they would ditch the schemes like a shot if there was an easy way out, with some saying it's only a matter of time before they vanish.

Tax and other problems

Their hand could well be forced, since the other party taking more than passing interest is the tax inspector. While America's Inland Revenue Service has said it has no plans to crack down on frequent flyer awards, the European Commission has opted to investigate whether the benefits should be taxed. EC airlines are fuming at the news.

Bosses are also growing increasingly critical. A UK study commissioned by Wagonlit revealed widespread hostility towards the schemes from company decision-makers angered at the fact that while travellers reaped the rewards, their employers paid the bill. Travel bookers who arranged the flights also felt resentful of their globetrotting colleagues.

While most frequent flyers argue that the perks are a just reward for long days and weeks spent away from home, some firms are now cracking down hard with pre-travel audits to ensure staff have not paid more than necessary for their flights. Others offer to split the benefits between the firm and the traveller, banking points in a corporate mileage pool, and giving travellers half the cash value of the air fare saved. Companies such as Frequent Flyer Services manage and recapture miles accumulated by employees on company travel.

The reward options

Frequent flyer schemes are not identical in terms of the rewards they offer, the conditions they impose and the ease with which members can earn points and bonuses. Continental, whose OnePass system has won top awards from the readers of *Inside Flyer* magazine for many years, claims to offer the fastest route to the rewards.

While US schemes have gone down the free flights and upgrades route, others offer a range of awards. Virgin's Freeway scheme offers the chance to earn hot-air balloon rides, flying lessons and health club visits, arguing that the last thing many travel-weary executives want is yet more travel. Lufthansa's Miles and More offers a choice of 'fantasy awards', like rides on a veteran Junkers aircraft.

Scope for collecting awards can also vary according to the programme's participating partners – whether hotels, travel suppliers or non-competing airlines. At the time of writing, Virgin and British Midland offer reciprocal arrangements, while Swissair and SIA participate in Delta's scheme. Transavia participates in KLM's Flying Dutchman scheme.

Transfer options can also vary widely. While some airlines – KLM, Northwest and United, for instance – allow benefits to be transferred to anyone, Delta limits transfers to immediate family and dependants. Others extend the facility to friends and named individuals.

Joining the élite

The cream of the treats are reserved for the 2 per cent of members who achieve élite status – sometimes available by invitation only. Elite members of Air Canada's Aeroplan scheme need to have at least 55,000 miles in the bank, but gain use of first class lounges and other perks. SAS EuroBonus members must aspire to Royal Viking Gold level for the best rewards, while those in ANA's Goldpass scheme must wait to join the invitation-only Super Flyer level. British Airways Executive Club members must climb through silver and gold tiers to achieve premier status, reserved for VIP customers and captains of industry.

Frequent flyer programmes have spawned a string of copycats both among smaller carriers and hotel chains. Denmark's Maersk Air and Gatwick-based CityFlyer Express are two minnows to jump on the bandwagon, while East European carriers like Czech airline CSA have entered the fray. Marriott Miles allows hotel guests to collect miles with partner airlines such as BA, American, Continental and Northwest without leaving the ground, while Hilton's HHonors programme lets members choose between storing up hotel points or airline miles.

Anyone who takes frequent flyer programmes seriously would do well to subscribe to the US magazine *Inside Flyer*, published in Colorado Springs. Each issue is an unrivalled mine of information on all major programmes and promotions, detailing blackout dates and restrictions, and giving a breakdown of elite-level programmes, participating partners and hotel schemes. Publisher Randy Petersen reportedly belongs to nearly 30 different schemes and has banked more than five million airline miles.

CHOOSING A FREQUENT FLYER SCHEME

Don't forget there's no such thing as a free lunch. To earn upgrades and other perks in a frequent flyer programme, you will generally need to buy full-fare tickets and do some hard-nosed flying. Before signing up, remember that:

- There's little point joining more than a few schemes. Since it will take longer to earn awards, any benefits will be diluted.
- Award levels can vary from country to country. What your counterpart enjoys in the States may not be on offer in Europe.

- Restrictions vary widely. Are awards transferable? If so, to whom? Is there an unreasonable 'use-by' deadline for points? How extensive are blackouts?
- It helps to match your wanderlust with the right airline. If you fancy a trip to Rio, forget signing up with Alaska Airlines.
- Redemption procedures differ. You may need to request a mileage certificate, mail it to the carrier and then make reservations. Allow time.
- Everyone wants freebies to Hawaii and Disney World. You'll have much more luck getting free flights by steering clear of crowded holiday routes. LA–Honolulu is the most sought-after frequent flyer route.
- Weekend blackouts are common in peak season. You may need to travel midweek.
- Your free flights should be confirmed before you pay for the villa to go with them. Many people lose their holiday deposits by jumping the gun.
- Airline computers don't always get their sums right when calculating your mileage. Save your ticket stubs.
- Short journeys are often good mile-earners. To maximize your points at the expense of distance, time or convenience, try breaking your journey into shorter legs, or flying in a triangle rather than a straight line.
- Bonus points are often offered for getting friends to join. Invite them to sign up.
- Signing up with an airline when talk of mergers or takeovers is rife may leave you with miles to nowhere.

EXECUTIVE JETS

When it comes to rock-solid cachet, there's nothing to beat boarding a gleaming executive jet and flitting around the world with your own pair of wings.

Private jets have long been a sought-after status symbol among the rich and famous – whether pop stars, oil sheiks or cigar-chomping business barons. While some firms use them as a prestige plaything for whisking clients off on champagne junkets, few realize they can also be a cost-effective mode of transport for cash-conscious corporate travellers.

The truth is that executive jets can sometimes beat other forms of transport hands down. After all, time is money – and thousands of executive hours are wasted every year by managers kicking their heels

LAMBS APARTMENTS

Service apartments located in Knightsbridge, close to Harrods. Facilities include private kitchen and bathroom, welcome basket of tea/coffee, colour TV, use of sauna, electric door porter, six day maid service, private telephone.

Studio £86 per day £567 per week ★ Suite £125 per day £840 per week
All prices include VAT

Discounts are available for group bookings and long term tenancies

Please call or write for a brochure to:
21 Egerton Gardens, London SW3 2DF Tel: 071 589 6297 Fax 071 584 3302

---

in airport departure lounges everywhere between Denver and Delhi. The more they earn, the bigger the loss.

Business jets provide virtual door-to-door service. They depart when their passengers want to leave, and return directly the meeting is finished. They'll wait if it overruns, or if passengers get stuck in traffic. They can land at small airfields just miles from the factory gate, where red tape and air traffic delays are negligible.

Managers with a busy itinerary can thus cover far more ground in less time than those using scheduled aircraft. Five days' meetings can often be packed into three, and a few frayed tempers saved in the bargain. Added to that, clients will almost certainly be impressed.

Hush-hush security

Executive jets can also score on security counts. When many multinationals put an outright ban on scheduled air travel during the Gulf War, dozens of small jet charter firms did booming business, discreetly ferrying thousands of senior company executives around unnoticed. Places like Little Snoring Aerodrome, after all, are unlikely to be at the top of any terrorist hit lists.

Business and light aircraft account for 90 per cent of the world's 400,000 strong civil aviation fleet. Two-thirds of the world's *Fortune* 500 companies are thought to use them, particularly those in the banking, construction and oil sectors. Britain has more than 100 registered executive jets, together with nearly 6,000 single-engine planes used for business and pleasure.

New-generation business jets can fly non-stop between the capitals of Europe and the US, and will soon include supersonic models. All can be customized to suit the tastes and whims of their charterers – whether with beds, showers or logo-stamped napkins. They can be turned into flying flats, pleasure palaces or bug-free aerial boardrooms.

Avid executive jet users include the Sultan of Brunei, who has his own Jumbo. Other captains of industry stick to smaller craft, often taking Concorde to cross the Atlantic and having their own plane flown out to meet them on the tarmac. Users can hire anything from a helicopter to a B747, though most stick to medium sized turbo-props or smaller cabin-class aircraft.

While business jets don't come cheap, they come into their own on multi-city itineraries. Heathrow based MAM Aviation says that a London-based group of eight executives needing to travel to the Isle of Man, Edinburgh, Jersey and back to London – a typical bankers' itinerary – can do so in just a day. Using scheduled services, they would take two and a half. The group could also save money, spending around £3,900 + VAT to charter a turbo-prop King Air, against roughly £4,820 for scheduled air fares alone.

A two-day European itinerary would also show savings. Executives needing to visit Zaragoza, Turin, Munich and Basel before returning to London, could expect a bill of around £9,236, including their overnight stop. Going scheduled, they would spend around £920 per person – £7,360 for a group of eight – and spend £200 per head to cover each overnight stop with meals and transfers. That adds up to well over £10,000, without counting the crippling costs in wasted executive time.

Calculating the benefits

Before deciding whether to charter a jet, consider:

- **The cost of executive time**. A leading salesperson generating $10 million a year in sales is reckoned to be worth $5,000 an hour.
- **The importance of security**. Confidentiality is virtually assured in a private jet.
- **Convenience**. Business jets depart when you're ready. There's also little chance of luggage or valuable samples going astray, since they'll stay with you on board.
- **Insurance**. Some policies do specify that not more than six key staff can travel together. US schemes often exclude travel in single-engine planes or helicopters.

TAILPIECES

- Passengers' bottoms are getting bigger – official. Airlines are building their next-generation seats to fit an average per-person weight of 84kg (185lbs) – up from a leaner 77 (170lbs). Podgy flight attendants are shown no mercy, however. According to one newspaper report, United suspended over 1,000 cabin crew in '93 for getting too porky.

- Beware of ignoring the 'fasten seatbelt' sign when the call of nature is pressing. Turbulence can activate an airline toilet's vacuum pump. Combined with a sudden drop in altitude, it can literally suck you down the loo – as one chagrined Cathay Pacific passenger found out recently. It took three flight attendants to free his posterior.

- Airport visitors are evidently a thirsty lot. In an average year, Gatwick's catering outlets dispense a million pints of beer, 165,000 gallons of fizzy drinks and seven million cups of tea and coffee. The airport's Village Inn ranks as the world's busiest pub.

6
☐ Getting About on Arrival

If reaching your destination takes some doing, getting around it takes a whole lot more. You'll need to deal with unfamiliar transport systems, road signs and driving habits. You may have to bargain with cabbies who have never heard of meters, join a throng of traffic on the wrong side of the road, or make sense of bewildering-sounding addresses.

Away from the world of uniformed airport staff, multi-lingual signage and handy information desks, you're now fending for yourself. However you plan to get around, you'll need a little help.

RENTING A CAR

Having your own set of wheels can be an asset if you have a fair bit of ground to cover. At least 50 per cent of all frequent flyer trips are reckoned to include car hire, and slick computerized reservation systems now enable travellers to book anything from a Polo to a Porsche virtually anywhere in the world within minutes. Customers prepared to pay premium rates now enjoy instant recognition and paperless transactions at most major airports, where the route between road and runway has been radically shortened.

Those signing a master rental agreement with Hertz Number One Club Gold or Avis Preferred Service simply head for the airport rental location, look for their name in lights and go straight to the bay indicated to collect their vehicle. There, where keys and rental agreement should be waiting, they merely show their licence and drive off.

Other services now common include penalty-free one-way rentals, 24-hour breakdown cover, free mobile phone rental, complimentary vehicle delivery and collection, plus an impressive range of loyalty benefits through schemes operated with airline and hotel groups. Carpark staff can often provide computer-printed road directions, too.

Hertz, the largest and oldest car rental company, claims more vehicles, more locations – around 5,000 – and more customers worldwide than any of its rivals. The company is represented at all 700 rail stations in Switzerland, and ranks as market leader in several countries.

Avis – generally regarded as the world's number two – leads the field at airports. Frequent users can collect points in the company's Options scheme, which can be exchanged for a range of goods, car rental bookings and even flights. Points are stored in Avis's Wizard system, said to be the largest and most sophisticated reservation, billing and fleet management system in the industry.

Budget ranks as the world's largest franchise rental group, with a worldwide network of 3,200 locations in 110 countries. Europcar Interrent – number one in Germany – operates in nearly 90 countries and has a global fleet of more than 100,000 vehicles. EuroDollar is another big name on the European scene.

Simpler tariffs

Leading car rental groups have now simplified and streamlined their tariffs for the business user. Budget's Business Traveller programme offers rates inclusive of mileage, collision damage waiver, personal accident insurance and state taxes. Europcar Interrent's international Business Drive tariff is similarly fully inclusive. The company offers privileges for regular renters, and promises self-service machines soon for those in a hurry. Users will simply choose their car type from a screen menu, and proceed to a given bay to collect their vehicle.

Most major firms have tie-ins with international air carriers, offering lower rates to their customers. Hertz is the preferred car rental company for British Airways, signing up 50,000 rentals a year through the airline, and operating a BA check-in counter at its Heathrow location. Qantas offers discounts Down Under with Avis and Hertz through its Business Connections scheme.

Renting wheels for your stay need not necessarily mean a standard Golf or Scorpio. While lording it in a Roller will be prohibitive for most, some firms offer the option of two-wheeled transport. If the thought of streaking along with the wind in your hair is sorely tempting, try picking up a Honda or a Harley Davison for the day. Studs and leathers are optional.

Getting the best rate

Hire costs can vary by 50 per cent or more from country to country, due to differences in labour costs, re-sale values, local taxes and insurance.

They're high in Spain because of labour costs, in Sweden because of the relatively small market and in Italy because of rampant car theft.

In Britain – where, according to Budget, it costs 16 times less to hire a Sierra than to rent a photocopier, in terms of capital value – they are cheaper than anywhere in Europe. London's Heathrow airport remains the largest and most competitive single car rental location outside North America.

Cost versus convenience

While the market leaders offer corporate users the slickest range of services, they usually have rates to match. A survey published by *Business Traveller* in 1992 found Avis rates to be nearly four times higher than those offered by Alamo and Europcar for a one-day rental of the same grade car in some cases. Off-airport firms are invariably the cheapest for those who put cost before convenience.

There can also be a yawning gap between official and discounted rates. Such is the tangled web of deals, business tariffs and one-day specials that car hire rates are now almost as much of a monkey puzzle as air fares. Woe betide the renter who fails to pre-book or shop around, and ends up paying the full-blown 'walk up' rate at the hire counter.

While mileage-inclusive tariffs – rare till recently in mainland Europe – are fast becoming standard, not all hidden extras have been consigned to the bin. Collision damage waiver, personal accident insurance, 24-hour breakdown cover and other charges can still ensure that the rate you're quoted is not necessarily the one you pay. Moreover, prices are not always guaranteed in the relevant local currency.

The theft epidemic

Theft waivers and non-waiverable excesses in the event of an accident are now becoming widespread. A car theft epidemic in Italy, where EuroDollar says 8 per cent of its Naples-based fleet disappears every year, means theft waiver is a compulsory extra there. Renters who fail to pay up could be liable for the entire value of their vehicle.

Fly-drive packages are invariably good news, offering savings of 50 per cent and more over standard walk-up rental rates. Other airline deals proliferate, with carriers sometimes offering up to a week's free car hire to full-fare business class passengers. Rental groups also have tie-ins with the bigger travel agencies, offering preferred rates and upgrade vouchers to their bigger corporate customers.

Holiday and leisure deals are occasionally just the ticket for business travellers – and they're not just on offer at seaside resorts. Providing you can meet the hire restrictions, prices can fall dramatically for rentals of even three or four days.

Travel associations also offer business renters handsome savings. IAPA members get discounts of up to 30 per cent off Avis, Hertz and Europcar Interrent tariffs, in addition to upgrade coupons. Executive Club International members also enjoy substantial savings.

Getting the best rate

- Book ahead – even if it's only by a day. You could save 70 per cent or more on published rates.
- Push for the best deal if you have to rent on the spot. Persistence usually pays off.
- Hang on to your tickets or boarding pass, and see if you are eligible for an airport fly-drive package. Smaller airlines often have the keenest deals.
- Check out the extras. Collision damage and theft waivers, local taxes, personal accident cover and other charges may all be added to your basic bill.
- Beware of car phone rip-offs. While the handset may come free, you could pay through the nose for calls. Check out the rate.
- Remember, you get what you pay for. Smart uniforms, global reservation systems and slick booking systems don't come cheap.
- Try an off-airport operator if price is all-important. The savings may outweigh the inconvenience.
- Save even more by using a firm that rents out second-hand cars. In the States, you'll find them listed under names like Rent-a-Wreck, Ugly Duckling and Fender Bender. Remember, though, that old rattlers are gas guzzlers.
- Make sure clerks don't confuse miles with kilometres, if mileage is charged. It could work against you.

Having secured the best price, don't simply scan the smallprint on the agreement before roaring off – digest it. Pitfalls galore await drivers who fail to check for punitive excess clauses and other hidden nasties. Make sure any dents or scratches are noted on the hire form, and that you're clear about:

- **Breakdown cover.** You'll regret not having 24-hour cover when the fan belt goes at 2am on a foreign motorway.
- **Restrictions.** Some upmarket cars cannot be taken into countries

where car theft is rife. Rent a Mercedes, BMW or Saab in Switzerland, for instance, and you may be banned from taking it into Italy.
- **Insurance cover.** Don't be caught out with inadequate accident and emergency cover, or assume that hiring through a well-known company means you'll get cast-iron protection. In the US, where personal liability claims can read like computer print-outs, you can't be over-insured.
- **Insurance terminology.** Collision damage waiver (CDW) is a fee paid to absolve the driver of any personal cost in the event of a crash. Personal accident insurance (PAI) covers the driver against injury in an accident.

Finally, check out the state of the car. If the ashtrays are still full, the chances are no one has bothered to check essentials like oil, tyre pressure and treads, either.

ACCIDENTS AND BREAKDOWNS

Statistics prove that you are more likely to have a contretemps in a rented car than in your own. Normally sane drivers who take good care of their faithful Morris Minor at home like nothing better than to ram their foot on the floor when they're handed the keys of a gleaming new hire car with just a few hundred miles on the clock.

On top of that, the controls may be unfamiliar. You may be driving on the other side of the road, trying to decipher foreign-language road signs or be unfamiliar with the rules of the road. Scores of drivers come unstuck every day – whether wrecking the gearbox, ramming another vehicle or backing into walls. Others manage to run out of fuel, lock themselves out, lose their keys or end up with a flat battery.

Accidents and breakdowns can be a nightmare. More travellers die abroad on the road than from any other cause, and while accident rates in northern Europe are low, the same can't be said elsewhere (see Chapter 8). In Asia and Africa, you can lessen the risks by avoiding driving at night.

Accidents are the most critical test of a rental company's customer service levels. Although CDW and personal accident insurance should leave you fully covered, this is not always the case. Matters are dealt with differently in each country, and officials involved may not show the degree of fairness, justice and tolerance you might expect at home. You can expect to be rescued within the hour if you have round-the-clock breakdown cover from a reputable firm, but you may be in for a long wait if you don't.

Carry your insurance papers with you at all times, and make sure your policy covers garage repairs, accommodation and repatriation if driving your own vehicle. Make sure you have an elementary knowledge of accident procedures in the relevant country, since failure to stop or report a collision can entail a fine. Remember, too, that driving alone is itself inadvisable in some countries.

Collision dos and don'ts

- Take the names and addresses of any useful witnesses.
- Say as little as possible – unless to make it clear you feel someone else is to blame.
- Avoid saying you're sorry. It could be construed as an admission of guilt.
- Photograph the scene of the accident, if you have a camera handy.
- Avoid signing anything you don't understand.
- Contact a reputable solicitor through your national embassy, assistance programme or insurers, if need be.
- Inform your insurance company, and keep a copy of the letter.
- Remember that treatment at local hospitals in some countries can be more damaging than your injuries. Avoid submitting to blood tests unless you can vouch for the equipment.

Note that in the Middle East and certain other regions, road deaths are often unofficially settled by payment of blood money to the victim's relatives. Drivers may otherwise be detained or have their travel papers seized till a court settlement is reached. Logic does not always come into the picture, as a friend who lived in the Arabian Gulf learned to his cost one night after calling for a cab to take him to the airport.

While the taxi failed to show up, two burly policeman turned up on the doorstep half an hour later with handcuffs at the ready. The taxi had crashed on the way to collect him, they explained. He was therefore under arrest, since the accident would not have occurred but for his ill-timed call. Only a heated argument prevented them taking him into custody on the spot, followed by the promise of a goodwill cheque to the driver.

OTHER ROAD HAZARDS

Gold-plated insurance cover may not be all you need in the glove compartment when driving abroad. Some countries require international licences or other documentation, while others require drivers to carry red warning triangles, first aid kits and even fire extinguishers. UK drivers taking their car to the Continent need beambenders – re-usable clip-on lenses that prevent headlights from dazzling oncoming traffic.

Don't assume your only expense in getting from A to B will be petrol, either. Five EC countries, quite apart from the US, have motorway toll systems. In France, where drivers now pay £50 to get from the Channel to the Riviera, there are nearly 4,000 miles of toll-charging autoroutes and plans to build another 1,250. Private motorways are on the cards soon in Hungary, while Germany has announced plans to charge drivers for using its 7,000 miles of Autobahns. Italy currently charges Europe's highest road tolls, and Greece the lowest.

Legal clampdowns

Britain looks set to charge drivers using not simply national motorways, but main roads in the capital by the late '90s. Athens already restricts traffic by alternating the days when cars with odd and even number-plates can enter the city centre, while Los Angeles plans to restrict petrol-fuelled cars from entering parts of the metropolis by the turn of the century. Singapore charges drivers for city-centre entry permits during peak hours.

Drink-driving and parking laws are also getting tougher. Car drivers imbibe at their peril in Scandinavia, where they can be punished for having more than a drop of alcohol in their system. Other perils include tow-away fines and wheel clamps, now spreading like wildfire in many parts. Towed cars are not released till the fine is paid, and foreigners can be chased with vigour for unpaid sums even when back home. My father, who lives in Wales, was even sent a court summons (fortunately in error) from police 21,000 miles away in Melbourne.

TAKING TAXIS

Cab drivers can range from saints to sinners. Most travellers have horror stories about the kamikaze cabbie who nearly wrote them off in Mexico City or the one who saved their skin in deepest Ruritania. They vary from villains ready to take you for every cent, to dependable allies who almost become your best friend. They can have a fount of back-street knowledge or more trouble fathoming their way around than you do.

Cabs come in various guises. There are New York's yellow perils – the distinctive canary-coloured medallion cabs with the chequerboard stripe – London's quintessentially British black FX4s, and Bangkok's dreaded tuk-tuks, three-wheeled devils that sound like demented power drills.

Manila has its multi-coloured jeepneys, whose passengers are blasted with piped rock 'n' roll, while Istanbul has cabs guaranteed to have neither door handles, meters nor suspension.

Kamikaze cabbies ...

Hong Kong still has its wizened old rickshaw riders, while Honolulu has its pedal-pushing Waikiki blondes. Latin America has its would-be Nigel Mansells, who cannon through red lights and mount pavements to overtake. Havana provides cheap cabs for locals, and dollar-only ones for foreigners that charge three times the price. India is known for its entrepreneurs who automatically take the scenic route past their cousin's curio shop. And do they have a meter? Do they heck. A speedometer? No way. Some change? Not on your life.

Steering machines that can turn on a sixpence, London cab drivers are graduates of the so-called Knowledge, an advanced driving test that ensures they know the capital inside out. They are also guaranteed to know not just the latest test match score, but who's winning in the party political polls.

New York cabbies often don't know the Empire State from a sandwich bar – usually because they arrived the day before from Guatemala, or can only speak fluent Ukranian. Tokyo's taxi drivers can be as baffled by the city's obscure road naming system as you are, while those in Washington – where crashes average 75 a week – are under investigation by the city's crime squad. In Rome, cabs are harder to find than hen's teeth.

Shared taxis are a common sight in places such as Turkey, Israel and the United Arab Emirates. Well used by locals, they can be surprisingly speedy and cheap, and give the assurance of company on longer trips. Some airports even offer them, though an experiment at London Heathrow failed to win custom and was quickly shelved.

... or Russian roulette

While pirate cabs are usually the ones to avoid, taking one can occasionally make sense. Visitors to Moscow often by-pass overpriced official hotel cab ranks and hail a ride instead from the nearest corner. Having said that, they may find their driver – who probably speaks just five words of English – is soon frantically flagging down pedestrians to try and work out where their passenger wants to go to.

Don't take a cab in Tokyo, Taipei or Hong Kong without having the name of your destination written in oriental characters ready to hand to the driver. At Hong Kong's Kowloon hotel, they even have a computerized directory to do it for you, complete with mini-map and approximate cost. Try to avoid the mistake of one traveller, however, who handed the driver a hotel matchbox and told him to make haste. Forty minutes later, he was safely delivered to the gates of the match factory.

Rio has yet another problem – soaring inflation. Since cab meters cannot be adjusted fast enough to keep pace with rising prices, a chart stuck on the window shows what you actually have to pay. Major hotels have their own car fleets, offering guests a safer, if more costly, ride.

See Chapter 8 for further tips on taking taxis.

Fair's fare around the world

Fares around town can differ wildly. In a survey published by the Economist Intelligence Unit in June '93, cab fares around the world for a 3 kilometre trip ranged from £7.94 in Tokyo to just 36 pence in Bombay. The ride cost £5.25 in London, £2.58 in New York, £1.73 in Hong Kong and 89 pence in Prague.

Tips can also vary. Cabbies in London and Hong Kong settle for 10 per cent, while those in the US expect 15 per cent plus. They are not required in Tahiti, discouraged in Singapore, discretionary in Malaysia and included in the fare in Sweden. Drivers in Tokyo and Rome are happy if you merely round up the fare.

Hiring a cab and driver for the duration of your stay can be the best answer in places where driving standards defy description, signs are indecipherable or parking is a nightmare. The cost may be little more than that of renting a self-drive car, and your driver will not only know his way around, but probably prove to be a mine of information as well. He will be liable for any scrapes, at pains to ensure your safety, able to guard your luggage and probably willing to double as an interpreter.

If there's little choice but to take a dubious-looking cab, try to:

- Agree the price before getting in. If there's an argument later, it may turn unpleasant.
- Have the right money ready. It's a fair bet your driver won't have any change.
- Remember all dollar bills are the same colour. Don't hand over a $100 note by mistake when you're counting out cash in the dark.
- Ensure the driver doesn't pick up other passengers *en route*.
- Take the car's number and report it if there's a problem. Few drivers want any trouble with the law.

PUBLIC TRANSPORT

Buses and subway systems can be a cheap, clean and efficient way of getting around town once you know how. Your hotel should be able to supply a map and advise on whether they are deemed safe after dark. While it may be arduous trying to use foreign-language ticket machines or find out where to buy tokens first time around, it will be a breeze by the third day. Most visitors to London travel by tube, if only because traffic in the capital moves no faster now than it did in the days of horse-drawn buggies – averaging just 13 miles an hour.

Showpiece mass transit systems in Hong Kong and Singapore provide speedy, safe, air conditioned transport. Miami has a handy elevated monorail system, while even the much-maligned New York subway – now much cleaner than in the '80s – is considered fine by day. Buses ply north–south routes in Manhattan and offer views of the city at the same time.

Hong Kong's Star Ferry offers the cheapest and most scenic ride of the lot, still charging peanuts to cross one of the world's most stunning harbours nearly 100 years after it was launched. Ferries also abound in Istanbul, often beating the taxis struggling through traffic-choked streets.

Airport limousine bus services are common in the States, and call at most big hotels. Don't forget when ordering one from the front desk, however, that the word 'limo' can also mean a 40 foot stretched palace on wheels, complete with chauffeur, tinted windows and colour TV. I nearly ended up with a $200 bill at New York's Waldorf Astoria when the clerk mistakenly thought that's what I wanted to get out to Newark.

Europe's rail renaissance

Far from taking a back seat in the age of the jet, railways worldwide are experiencing a renaissance.

Five million European travellers are expected to switch from air to rail when the Channel Tunnel finally opens for business in 1994 – some 192 years after French engineer Albert Mathieu first proposed a link beneath the sea for horse-drawn traffic. High-speed Supertrains will see London well and truly plugged into the Continent with a network of EuroCity services.

Projected to carry 13 million people in its first two years of operation, the tunnel will speed rail travellers from Waterloo in the British capital to Gare du Nord in the heart of Paris in just three hours. Car drivers will be ferried beneath the sea on shuttles linking terminals in Folkestone and

Calais, promising motorway to motorway access in just over an hour.

The tunnel's new high-speed trains will race along at up to 300kph on the French side of the water. Providing nearly 800 seats, they will have telephones, dining cars, meeting rooms and on-board Immigration. Sleeper trains fitted out like mobile hotels will link several UK cities with every major European business capital. Hopping on a train from London to Brussels should be as simple as jumping on the 8.52 from Bradford to Leeds.

High-speed trains

Promising prices to rival those in the air, the trains will almost certainly corner a healthy slice of London–Paris air traffic, repeating a pattern already seen on high-speed rail corridors like Paris–Lyon, Stockholm–Gothenburg and Madrid–Seville. Travellers who habitually go by air could soon be flitting across Europe with an international rail pass, working on the train as they go.

Rail systems throughout Europe have been gearing up to meet the needs of executive travellers in a big way in recent years. First class passengers can now expect airline-style cabin service, office facilities and meals brought to their seat. Italy has its tilting Pendolino, speeding between Rome and Milan at up to 250kph, and offering frequent rail users access to special station lounges equipped with conference and meeting rooms, TVs, telephones, fax and telex.

France is a major player in the high-speed stakes, carrying 20 million passengers a year on prime inter-city routes. Rail chiefs moreover plan to spend £25 billion on a 3,000-mile national network by 2025. The system's much-lauded Euraffaires service provides business lounges at main stations, plus on-board conference suites, telephones, photocopiers and calculators. Staff will also book taxis to meet the train.

Germany is expanding its high-speed services through Berlin into the former Eastern bloc, with plans for a 2,000-mile network by 2010. Passengers boarding the country's slick InterCity Express trains have use of conference compartments, cordless telephones, luggage lockers and fax and copier machines. Headphones at every seat let passengers plug into Mozart or rock, while some even have seatback video screens.

Executive packages

Britain's InterCity network now promises users a faster, smoother ride. Business lounges have opened at main city stations, while executive tickets provide a convenient travel package with parking, meal vouchers and London tube tickets thrown in. Full-fare standard class ticketholders can use Silver Standard coaches, which offer a more work-conducive atmosphere and a steward dispensing free tea and coffee.

Swedish rail travellers will enjoy faster links with the Continent if the much-discussed Eurolink project, linking Sweden and Denmark by tunnel, gets the green light. Plans are well in hand to develop faster services in Austria, Denmark, Greece and Spain, while even Turkey is weighing up the cost of building a tunnel under the Bosphorus which would demolish journey times between Istanbul and Ankara by two-thirds.

On track across the Pond

Train services in the US – struggling to compete with bargain-basement air fares – have been much improved since Amtrak was formed in 1970. Though little used by business people except on busy urban corridors, they include 120mph Metroliners linking Boston, New York and Washington. Over the border in Canada, comfortable VIA trains compete with the airlines on sectors such as Montreal–Toronto. Travelling between the latter city to Vancouver, however, takes a slow, if scenic, three days.

In the Far East, Japan's bullet express Shinkansen trains have become a huge success on the busy Tokyo–Osaka corridor, ferrying 250,000 business passengers a day between the two cities. New prototype trains now being tested will eventually achieve speeds of up to 400kph.

Even Russia has its rail attractions. Trains can be a merciful alternative to domestic air travel with Aeroflot, whose questionable standards of food, comfort and in-flight service are legendary. Taking the overnight sleeper from Moscow to St Petersburg will be a memorable experience – even if your cabin is spartan, your tea undrinkable and your stewardess a graduate of the Rosa Klebb school. A few nips of local hooch should get you nicely off to sleep.

TAILPIECES

- Public transport in Budapest is fast, simple and cheap – but bear in mind that the English pronounciation of 'bus' denotes sexual frolics in Hungarian. You had better try asking for a 'boos' instead.

- Britain is the cheapest place in western Europe to rent a car, according to a 1993 study by Budget Rent A Car. It showed that the typical cost of hiring a Ford Escort for a week at an airport was £242, compared with more than £600 in Finland.

- New York City still has precisely the same number of licensed yellow cabs as it did in 1937 – 11,787 to be precise. That probably explains why they're never free.

7
Hotels and the Red Carpet Treatment

While a plane is a means to an end, a hotel can be an end in itself. More than just a place to hang your hat, it becomes a second home, a sanctuary and a substitute office while you're away. Its comforts, amenities and welcome can dictate much of the enjoyment you get from your trip.

Not everyone gets to check into a five-star pleasure palace every time they travel – but even a good hotel can feel like a great one when you get the red carpet treatment. Learn how to get the best room for your money, and you'll feel as if you're staying at the best place in town.

Making the most of your stay also means deciding on priorities – whether it's to be old-fashioned creature comforts, the latest in high-tech gadgetry or the ultimate in pampered luxury – as well as knowing how to deal with the thorny issue of surprise charges.

LEAN TIMES

Recession has hit the hotel industry hard. Hoteliers used to turning in handsome profits faced their leanest time in decades when a savage downturn in the world economy came hot on the heels of the calamitous Gulf War. Since then, many have gone to the wall as bookings have slumped and customers once happy to foot lavish bills have drawn in their spending horns.

Not all the news is bad, of course. While traditional markets have suffered, new ones have opened up. Growth has continued apace in the Pacific Rim, while new hotels have mushroomed in Russia and the former Soviet satellite states. In Moscow, business travellers used to the drab decor, grim furnishings and dire cuisine of pre-*perestroika* days are now greeted with mahogany and gold leaf, jacuzzi baths, deep-pile carpets and 24-hour satellite TV.

Cairo, Jakarta, Beijing and other gateway cities have also been recipients of large-scale hotel investment. Another dozen properties are to open in Singapore by 1995, while in Hong Kong nearly 3,000 more beds have come on stream since early '92. In New York, the latest Four Seasons property boasts rooms costing no less than $1 million apiece – the most expensive ever built there.

Customers now demand – and get – facilities unheard of ten years ago. Frequent guest programmes trading room bookings for future free stays and an array of other rewards have added a new twist to brand loyalty, while tariffs once cast in cement are now set in sand as wheeler dealing becomes the norm. The days of tempting executive clientele with little but bed and board are long gone.

Customers are the winners as hoteliers faced with filling an estimated 11 million rooms worldwide pile on lavish incentives to tempt their guests into staying on and coming back. Free transfers, breakfasts, room upgrades and shopping vouchers are just some of the perks on offer – and there's no sign of the giveaways letting up.

GETTING THE BEST RATE

Paying the published rate for your hotel room makes as much sense as shelling out the full-blown business class air fare when a cut-price excursion ticket will do. Only a fraction of hotel rooms – probably no more than 20 per cent industry-wide – are actually sold at their so-called 'rack' rate, with the remainder being discounted in some form or another.

Tough economic conditions coupled with a glut of rooms in many big cities have made a farce of published tariffs. In today's discount culture, rack rates merely serve as a benchmark from which to bargain – and guests who might have been shown the door three years ago for having the temerity to try are now foolish not to. Persistence should secure a reduction of 10 per cent at a stroke, and with luck, considerably more.

Cashing in on the discounts

While hotel chains are sensitive about the growing level of discounting – especially since the rates offered to one client may not be those offered to another – they are realistic enough to accept that no sane business traveller now simply hands over a cheque for the sum printed on the tariff card.

Many have reversed their practice of quoting rack rates on the phone and leaving callers to press for a cheaper deal. Now, their policy is to quote the lowest unrestricted corporate rate straight off, thus offering immediate discounts unasked. The logic is that guests swayed by an attractive initial rate may take a better room anyway, or plough back some of their savings on food and drink.

Westin's Best Rate programme allows reservation staff to offer the lowest available rate of the day for each room category, rather than non-negotiable rack and corporate rates. This not only saves reservations clerks from spending hours on the telephone running through a range of special deals, but ensures that no one quoted a price on the phone risks turning up at their hotel and finding a cheaper rate on the spot.

Avoiding rack rates

Business travel agents are also active on the discount front, offering not only reduced rates at several thousand properties worldwide, but – in the case of Thomas Cook Travel Management, for instance – promising to match any rate a client can find elsewhere. The company's hotel desk aims to help cash-conscious clients meet budget restraints by finding cheaper accommodation options.

Getting a lower rate is not simply a question of demanding money off. So numerous are the dodges, deals and discounts on offer that paying the best price often boils down to asking the right questions. What you end up paying may depend on the agency you use, the company you work for and the city you are based in – plus, of course, your skills at driving a hard bargain.

Discount club schemes

As well as cashing in on special rates where possible, it also makes sense to explore the many discount club schemes on the market. Hotel Express International, offers savings of 50 per cent at more than 3,000 hotels in 35 countries. International membership costs £75 – a fee the firm says should be recouped in the first two-night stay. Another scheme is offered by the Hotel Club with discounts of 25 per cent.

Anyone armed with a copy of *Half Price Europe*, sold by Entertainment Publications Inc, can also claim 50 per cent off their hotel bill at some 750 hotels listed. The discounts apply only to rooms which would otherwise remain empty, however – so there may be problems at peak times.

Executive Club International, managed by International Customer Loyalty Programmes plc, also offers a range of valuable price reductions. So too does European Travel Network (ETN), which markets a combined hotel discount/telephone card.

Maximising your discount

To maximize savings, you should:

- **Try your travel agent**. A good one should be able to halve the published rates at some properties. If yours can't, it may be time for a change.
- **Use your corporate clout**. Cut down the number of hotels used, and strike a volume deal with one well-patronized chain. Most are happy to negotiate favourable rates if the business is worthwhile.
- **Ask your airline**. Most carriers offer preferential rates with particular chains, and many have attractive stopover programmes offering bargain short-stay rates.
- **Get your local office to book**. Hotel managers often agree more favourable rates with local firms who regularly use their restaurants and meeting rooms.
- **Enquire about money-saving business packages**. Inter-Continental's Global Business Options programme, for instance, entitles customers paying corporate rates to choose from a range of free extras, including double loyalty scheme points or discounts on food and drink.
- **Ask about special deals**. Leisure and short-break rates, incentive rates, group rates or trade-show/conference rates may apply. Embassy staff are often offered privileged rates, while anyone staying ten days or more may be eligible for long-term rates.
- **Try a hotel booking agency**. While the major players like Utell work almost exclusively through the trade, others deal direct with travellers. Colorado-based Express Hotel Reservations claims to offer the lowest room rates in New York City and Los Angeles, with discounts of $20–75 a night.
- **Join IAPA**. Identify yourself as an IAPA member when making a reservation, and you're entitled to discounts of up to 30 per cent with over 4,000 leading hotels worldwide.
- **Carry a discount card**. The schemes run by Hotel Express International, ETN and Half Price Europe are outlined above.
- **Book ahead**. Marriott offers Apex-style savings of up to 50 per cent at its European properties for bookings made 14 or 21 days ahead. Cancellations and changes incur a penalty.
- **Travel in the summer**. July and August are traditionally slack times for business travel, and summer rate sales at city-centre hotels can wipe 50 per cent or more off accommodation bills.

- **Travel in winter.** December and January are also lean times for the hotel trade, and New Year deals proliferate.
- **Travel at weekends.** Rates at business hotels often fall dramatically at the end of the week. With more rates being offered on a per-room rather than a per-person basis, partners can often stay free.
- **Stay at a brand new hotel.** Bargain 'soft opening' rates are often offered for up to six months while minor works are finished, and a client base is built up.
- **Turn up late.** Arrive without a booking after 6pm, and the hotel will often be more than happy to discount rooms that otherwise stand a ten-to-one chance of staying empty.
- **Ask for an on-the-spot corporate rate** – typically 10 per cent below rack rates. A business card or briefcase is often all that's needed to secure it.
- **Tell the hotel your budget.** If it's a quiet night, it might even buy the best room in the house. Don't be coy about negotiating.
- **Ask for the minimum rate**, and request an upgrade instead. It will only cost the hotel goodwill, and you could well end up in a superior room or suite.

HOTEL LOYALTY SCHEMES

Paying a lower room rate is only half the battle when it comes to getting first-rate value for money at your hotel. The next challenge is to make sure you enjoy five-star treatment when you walk through the door.

The simplest way to enjoy preferential service is to join a hotel loyalty club. Often allied to the frequent flyer programmes operated by leading airlines, these have flourished in the last eight years as a ploy for luring corporate globetrotters back time and time again. Four out of five travellers in the US are reckoned to belong to at least one scheme, and some five million are now signed-up members of Marriott's Honored Guest Awards programme.

Cardholders flashing their member's card can generally enjoy free upgrades, priority bookings, guaranteed rooms, late check-outs and assorted discounts and gifts. They can earn complimentary stays or cheap weekend breaks by collecting points for every room night booked, and often enjoy preferred rates and other privileges. Many can even convert their points to air miles without ever leaving the ground.

Other common benefits include express check-ins/check-outs, free newspapers and cheque-cashing privileges, together with reciprocal perks from non-competing chains. Club membership should also ensure recognition at the front desk – though some cardholders maintain that with numbers swelling steadily, staff give their shiny bit of plastic a cursory glance before proceeding to treat them much like anyone else.

Loyalty schemes benefit the big hotel chains as much as their clientele, enabling them to identify – and thus court – their vital repeat guests. Although upmarket chains such as Mandarin Oriental and the Savoy Group have so far resisted the temptation to single out brand-loyal travellers for reward programmes, other groups do so in a big way. Oberoi, Four Seasons/Regent and Forte Crest are among the latest to jump aboard the bandwagon.

Optional air miles

Air miles are a big favourite with guests. Members of Westin's Premier scheme earn 500 frequent flyer miles with the airline of their choice every time they stay. Those staying with Shangri-La and Pan Pacific – partners in Passages, the frequent flyer programme run by Cathay Pacific, Singapore Airlines and Malaysia Airlines – can also earn points to fly.

Travellers staying the night at Hilton International hotels can bank 500 air miles with American Airlines' AAdvantage scheme, while members of Marriott Miles receive a similar number for the carrier of their choice. Marriott claims its programme could award as many as 650 million miles within a year – enough for more than 35,000 free air tickets.

Some schemes are free to join, while others cost money. The Hilton Club's 20,000 members pay $150 a year, with the option to pay more for extras such as airport transfers. ITT Sheraton Club International charges $25, offering members coupons for discounts and upgrades, plus the opportunity to earn double or triple club points and convert them to air miles. Inter-Continental's Six Continents Club charges a $100 joining fee, but is free to those staying more than 30 nights a year.

Earning dream holidays

Other schemes are free to all-comers. Members pay nothing to join Westin's Premier scheme – though they will need to stash up a mind-boggling 150,000 points to earn a seven-night dream vacation at one of the chain's top holiday resorts. Hyatt's Gold Passport scheme is similarly free, and provides points for every dollar spent on food and accommodation, plus the chance to stack up air miles. Meridien charges nothing for membership of its L'Invitation club, while Ramada's scheme is free to those who spend ten nights with the chain every year.

TELEPHONE BILL RIP-OFFS

Hotels often slap on scandalously high mark-ups every time you use the telephone. Service charges can be as much as eight times the actual cost of a call – no mean sum if you are dialling long-distance. Some US hotels even charge for unanswered calls, billing users after just six or seven rings. A few also impose hefty surcharges for calls to toll-free numbers.

Hotels in Singapore are now banned from putting more than a 20 per cent mark-up on guest calls, and obliged to set flat rates for local calls. Others may soon see their lucrative telephone revenue nosedive as more and more guests carry personal cordless phones and telephone calling cards.

Hotel phone cards

Plastic cards designed to help travellers avoid rip-off hotel telephone rates – some of them available free of charge – are now flooding the marketplace. Users simply make their call via an operator on a toll-free number, and charges are debited automatically to their telephone number at home, or their credit card account.

As well as avoiding excessive hotel mark-ups, the cards enable users to by-pass local telephone exchanges, and the linguistic difficulties and delays these can entail. They provide a clear breakdown of all calls made – something many hotels still fail to do – and avoid the need to incur costly reversed-charge rates or carry pocketfuls of change.

All good news for business people – particularly since a survey carried out by *Executive Travel* magazine and US telephone giant AT&T revealed that 20 per cent of corporate travellers spend more than £1,000 a year on phone bills, making a significant 68 per cent of their calls from hotels.

Access fees and blocks

The problem is that many hotels anxious to safeguard their telephone revenue now prevent call cards being used. One survey found that card-assisted calls were being blocked in a staggering 50 per cent of French hotels and 75 per cent of those in Switzerland. Some chains, among them Sheraton and Marriott, are now getting round the problem by charging users an access fee – usually around $1 – instead.

While it's not yet posssible to use the cards everywhere, users of AT&T's Calling Card can make calls between more than 50 countries at the time of writing. The AT&T card and fellow American cards MCI and

Sprint are generally the cheapest when making calls from the US, though surveys show British Telecom's Chargecard to be a better bet when calling between Europe and the UK. Clearly, it pays to assess where you'll be using the card most before deciding which to get.

Executive Telecard comes out the cheapest in many call-cost surveys, and moreover claims users can by-pass hotel blocking systems by simply dialling a local number supplied. All cards can, of course, be used at payphones to avoid restrictive hotel blocks – normally indicated by an engaged tone – or unwelcome access charges.

HOTEL TAXES

If it's easy to be stung by hotel phone bills, it's even easier to be caught out by the maze of taxes and service charges that can appear on your bill as you check out.

State and local taxes can bump up your account by 25 per cent or more in some places. Occupancy taxes, luxury taxes at the top end of the market, service and sales taxes – sometimes charged on incidentals as well as on the room rate – are dismal evidence that business travellers are often regarded as cash cows who will cough up come what may.

Australia is one of the few countries to impose no tax on hotel guests. The same cannot be said of the US, where hoteliers in New York have more than once taken to the streets in a bid to get high taxes repealed.

While Sweden recently lowered VAT on hotel bills from 21 to 12 per cent, Czech hoteliers now impose a hefty tax of 23 per cent. India takes the biscuit, however, with extra taxes on hotels charging more than Rs1,600 a night adding a mammoth 45 per cent to the bill. The moral is, clearly, to check out the damage before you check in.

LATE CHARGES

Express check-out systems which allow guests to OK their bill on the TV screen, but let hotels add on any overlooked charges later, can also cause guests aggravation. The same goes for the system of blocking off their credit when a card imprint is taken on check-in. See p168.

OVERBOOKING

Like airlines, hotels often overbook their rooms and rely on the 'no show' factor to run as near to full as possible. First-time guests and those without a guaranteed reservation are usually the first casualties if the house is full.

Unless guaranteed for late arrival with a credit card or through a travel agent, rooms are normally only held till 6pm, after which time they are released for re-sale. Anyone planning to arrive late should ensure their booking is guaranteed, and be prepared to incur the full room charge if they fail to show up.

If the front desk clerk claims there's no room at the inn, you should:

- Ask to see the manager. If you can claim VIP status, have an impressive-looking business card, or can threaten the loss of lucrative future business, he/she will do their utmost to help.
- Expect the hotel to arrange suitable alternative accommodation promptly, and even pay for your first night's stay. They should also pay for a taxi to take you there, and let you use the telephone to advise your office or home. This, of course, assumes you hold a guaranteed reservation.
- Consider whether you are being asked for a bribe. In some parts of the world, rooms can materialize by magic when a crisp note changes hands.
- Check your travel insurance cover. If it comes with a 24-hour worldwide assistance emergency number, now's the time to try it.

Note that if you are cancelling a room instead, this should be done by noon on the date of arrival at the latest to ensure you are not billed for part or all of the cost.

WHICH HOTEL?

Budget restraints aside, corporate travellers have traditionally picked their hotels on the strength of location, location, location. While this remains a key factor, it's by no means the end of the story, however.

Award winners

Choosing a hotel that regularly picks up accolades from other corporate travellers is one of the best ways to pick a winner. Numerous business and travel publications invite their readers to nominate the properties they regard as world beaters, and the results can be seen every year in the columns of *Institutional Investor*, *Executive Travel*, *Business Traveller*, *Expression* and other titles.

Far Eastern hotels – renowned for levels of service their rivals in the West can only aspire to – invariably sweep the awards board. Those such as Hong Kong's Mandarin Oriental and its Bangkok stablemate the Oriental have achieved near-legendary status by regularly topping these and other consumer polls.

Business Traveller readers named the Vier Jahreszeiten (Hamburg), the Georges V (Paris) and the Savoy in London as their top European hotels of 1992, with Sheraton as their favourite overall chain. Readers of *Executive Travel* voted the Shangri-La in Singapore their top hotel of 1993, with London's Copthorne Tara named best in the UK. *Euromoney* readers voted Hilton their favourite chain, picking Hong Kong's Mandarin Oriental as their top hotel of '93.

Inter-Continental claims to have chalked up more awards than any other chain over the last 40 years. Three of its properties feature in *Institutional Investor*'s latest (at time of writing) 50 Best Hotels survey, while two – the Willard in Washington and the Mark Hopkins in San Francisco – made it to the top 15 of the 1992 edition of *Great American Hotels*. The Four Seasons/Regent group is another regular poll-topper.

High-tech havens

Technology has transformed today's hottest properties from unashamed lairs of luxury into havens of high-tech. Fax and computer points have replaced Swiss chocolates and hand-milled soaps as the in-room extras of the '90s, as hoteliers compete to put more byte into bedrooms.

Versatile TV sets can call up the bill, relay fax messages, order breakfast, supply up-to-the-minute flight information and enable guests to check out without leaving the room. Some offer armchair shopping for those too tired to make it to the stores, while at Chicago's Inter-Continental the TV remote control even summons the porter. Videophones should be widespread by the end of the decade.

Voicemail systems that act as personal answering machines are now common at Westin, Sheraton and Ramada hotels, and will soon be installed network-wide by Hyatt. At Heathrow's Edwardian International, where they are also a standard feature, in-room TVs can relay live conference proceedings from downstairs to jetlagged delegates too tired to get out of bed.

Arriving guests will soon no longer even have to wait at the front desk. Hyatt guests can already check into their hotel by calling a freephone number and supplying the details required in advance. On arrival, they present a credit card, sign their already completed registration card and simply pick up their keys. Marriott hopes to extend a similar facility network-wide before long.

Far Eastern hotels are predictably in the driving seat of the high-tech bandwagon. Hong Kong's Kowloon hotel has a computerized directory that prints out address slips in both English and Chinese, ready to hand to the cab driver. Down the road, the Peninsula provides a fax, copier and a Telecentre terminal in every room – the latter able to flash business and flight information, as well as doubling as a word processor.

Hire-out hardware

Business centres are crammed with even more wall-to-wall technology. The best offer hire-out laptops, laser printers, software libraries with hardware to match, and meeting rooms equipped for teleconferencing. Tokyo's New Otani hotel offers work stations, personal computers, video players and a library, while others have machines designed to let guests print their own business cards in minutes.

Not all high-tech features have proved a runaway success. Working out how all the buttons, switches and controls work now threatens to need a degree in computer literacy – especially since most people are fumbling for tips when the porter goes through the ropes. And all the gadgets in the book have yet to replace the trusty Gideon bedside bible.

Spa wars

High-tech health is on the menu at many leading hotels, with computerized equipment designed to test guests' digital skills as much as their muscle-power. Although experience shows that for every nine out of ten people attracted by an impressive-sounding health spa, only one in ten actually uses it, more and more chains are sinking megabucks into building bigger and better facilities.

Top choices for fitness fiends include London's Meridien and Hyatt Carlton Tower hotels, and Chewton Glen in Hampshire, whose luxurious health centre cost a mind-boggling £5 million to install. Some establishments will even provide personal trampolines, Stairmasters and bikes for those who prefer fighting the flab in private.

Designer shrines

Nineties gadgetry is not the only feature keeping today's top properties ahead of the pack. Hotel design has also turned a corner, with the giant atrium properties of the '70s giving way to smaller hotels where the emphasis is less on sweeping public stages than bigger, plusher bedrooms. The latest in contemporary chic can be seen in New York's Royalton and London's Halkin hotels.

Gone – or going – is the bland, businesslike look identical everywhere from Tokyo to Tallahassee. Entertainment centres with games rooms and libraries are ousting the dated bar-and-disco formula, while themed restaurants have replaced the classic *haute cuisine* dining room. Forte Crest, now repositioned as the Forte group's business class brand, is moving away from formal dining towards contemporary brasseries.

Club and executive floors

Hushed executive floors where higher-paying guests can stay well well away from the madding crowds and enjoy peace, privacy and special privileges have mushroomed in recent years. The hotel world's equivalent of business class service in the air, they aim to combine exclusivity with added comfort and style.

Ideal for senior managers not averse to a little discreet one-upmanship – particularly since their names will often be logged on the hotel's VIP guest list – the floors are also well suited to those who value extra security, such as women (see also p192). Run almost as a hotel in miniature, they charge a typical rate premium of around 20 per cent.

Also known as club or concierge levels, the best are accessible only by special lift pass, and offer private check-in desks. Lounges ideal for informal business meetings serve complimentary drinks, canapés and breakfast, and sometimes come complete with mini-libraries, backgammon tables and sets of Trivial Pursuit. Rooms are generally better equipped for working, and feature additional touches such as bathrobes and slippers. Newspapers and other perks often come free.

Joining the club

Most major chains have jumped on the club floor bandwagon since Hyatt launched the concept in Atlanta back in 1967. While some simply offer a few token extras that should arguably be offered to four- and five-star guests anyway, those in many hotels set impressive standards.

More than 70 Hilton International hotels offer executive floors with a separate check-in, extra in-room amenities and private lounges. Rooms at the Brussels Hilton have a stereo, video cassette player and CD sound system, while those in Osaka boast cordless telephones, individual safes and fax lines. There are floor butlers in Kuala Lumpur, separate morning and evening lounges in Perth, and fireside billiards in Toronto.

Holiday Inn is test-marketing Executive Edition guestrooms in the US, featuring recliners or ottomans, an oversized desk, additional toiletries and a shaving/make-up mirror. Marriott offers well-patronized concierge levels, while Ramada Renaissance Club floors offer an honour bar and upgraded room amenities. Ritz-Carlton's Club floors are accessed by a special lift key, and offer a dedicated concierge.

Guest profiles

Computerized guest profiles now keep track of the likes, dislikes and special quirks of club floor guests and other premium-paying travellers.

If you hate a hard bed, can only sleep on goose-down pillows, like to have a room full of carnations or have to see at least three daily newspapers, no problem. Once your preferences are stored on electronic file, your wishes should be fulfilled wherever you go.

Now being systematically developed by hotels at the top end of the market, guest profiles allow hotels to single out VIP guests for special treatment, and to calculate which services are in most demand. Ritz-Carlton, for instance, has a well developed IBM programme to help it keep tabs on the tastes of 350,000 guests.

All-suite hotels

Extended business trips can prove both costly and restrictive in a traditional hotel. All-suite properties are designed to fill the gap, allowing long-stay guests more space and freedom to unwind at often moderate expense. Especially popular with female guests, who dislike having to do business in a hotel bedroom, they are also well liked by hoteliers, since less space is wasted on low-revenue earning restaurants and public areas.

While all-suites have been slow to take off in Europe – where they cater for those after the genuine luxury suite life – they are now common in the US mid-price sector. Chains active in the field include Hilton, Sheraton, Choice, Marriott (with its popular Residence Inns) and Best Western. There are also well over 100 Embassy Suite hotels.

The suite life

Often in suburban locations, all-suite hotels usually provide a fully-fledged kitchen or bar, room service, in-house movies, shops and meeting rooms. Some have a business centre, while many provide breakfast and drinks. Rooms can vary from basic studios to luxury apartments.

Europe's all-suite hotels tend to be plush, spacious and priced to suit the guest who cannot make do with just one well-appointed room.

Among the best known is the Conrad Chelsea Harbour, peacefully situated on the Thames and easily reached by limo, helicopter and river bus. Ample two-room suites are sumptuously fitted out, and guests can make use of the excellent health club downstairs.

Other luxury properties offering a high suite-to-room ratio include the Ritz in Taipei, which has 100 of each, and the Cipriani in Venice, which has 36 suites to 39 rooms. La Mamounia in Marrakesh, a former palace once graced by Sir Winston Churchill, has 57 suites to 171 rooms, while New York's all-suite Rihga Royal is also built for the top end of the market.

Business apartments

Serviced business apartments are another option for executives planning a longer than usual trip away. Those in London claim to have enjoyed far higher occupancy levels than top hotels during the recession, and promise comfort and space without fuss and five-star prices.

Bookable on short and long lets, most are well-appointed and in smart locations. The best have video entryphones, a 24-hour concierge, daily cleaning and even private tennis courts. Staff can usually arrange shopping, welcome grocery packs, secretarial services, dry cleaning and even full-scale business catering.

Some firms find it commercially viable to take on a permanent serviced apartment for managers spending 100 or more room nights a year in a particular city. Short lets are not necessarily cost-effective since, while weekly rates can work out significantly cheaper than those of comparable hotels, flats often have a minimum stay requirement of three months.

Major apartment chains in Europe include French-based FBM-Orion, with nearly 3,000 properties, and Citadines Residences Hotelières, with nearly 2,000. Another market leader is the London-based Apartment Service, which forecasts major growth in the sector over the next three years. The company offers serviced units in both the UK and Europe, many of them graded by Egon Ronay inspectors.

Greener gables

If your preference is for an address run on eco-friendly lines, you're in luck. With growing pressure on the hotel industry to do its bit for the environment, some now cater for the green business traveller in a big way.

Many guests feel a pang of guilt over the lavishly wrapped toiletries, piles of fluffy towels and throwaway literature now littering five-star hotel bedrooms – not to mention enough lamps to light up the World Trade Center. Breakfast trays come bedecked with miniature glass marmalade pots worth more than their contents, while bathrooms are crammed with designer-packaged knick-knacks.

With research revealing that the typical hotel room can generate nearly 400lb of rubbish a year, the battle is now on to cut energy bills, step up recycling schemes and switch to re-usable product lines. Notices often hang in even the snootiest establishments these days asking guests to turn off lights, save water or do without fresh bedlinen for an extra night. Room key cards often double as power activators.

Hyatt and Inter-Continental both issue green purchasing directives to their properties, while Forte's London hotels use only environmentally friendly toiletries. Hilton has taken part in a number of worldwide eco-initiatives, recycling 30,000 bottles a year at its London hotels. Marriott is also formulating a network-wide environmental programme.

Green travellers can now find politically acceptable havens at both ends of the market. At the top, Washington's Willard Inter-Continental has won accolades for its sensitive restoration and energy management schemes. At the budget end, energy-saving technology now runs many a no-frills hotel. You'll find showers, not baths at a Sleep Inn, and self-cleaning showers and loos at a French Formule 1.

NOTHING BUT THE BEST?

Well-heeled travellers tired of high-rise living are deserting modern hotels in droves and flocking behind the historic facades of some of the world's sumptuously restored *grandes dames*. Dozens of Europe's faded palaces are being restored to their former splendour for those who would sooner pay for nostalgia than '90s high-tech.

Hotels high on old-time grandeur include Edinburgh's turreted and towered Balmoral, with its welcoming fires and superb restaurant. London has the Regent, one of the finest examples of Victorian architecture in the city, while Amsterdam has the Amstel Inter-Continental, another 19th century gem recently remodelled at a cost of $40 million.

Canadian Pacific has turned many icons of Canadiana – rambling heritage hotels built for the railway age – into properties equipped for the B747 traveller. Bangkok's Oriental retains its 19th century Author's wing, while Singapore's much-lauded Raffles – re-styled with a little too much fervour for some purists – is another frontrunner in the classic hotel stakes. London's historic Langham is now a Hilton flagship.

Eastern Europe has also seen some of its decaying monuments re-emerge in swish new finery. At Moscow's Metropol, diners now enjoy Sunday brunch in the Art Nouveau restaurant used as a film set in *Dr Zhivago*. Yet more luxury awaits guests at St Petersburg's Grand Hotel Europe, whose interiors compete with some of the city's tsarist palaces. In Warsaw, Forte has transformed the historic Bristol hotel with a £23 million cash injection and period-style Polish furniture.

Castles and châteaux

Many of the world's best hotels are not to be found in any of the directories published by the big chains. Elegant French chateaux, Spanish stately homes, Scottish castles and other privately-owned deluxe properties trade on their exclusivity and have no wish to tap the mass market.

Often littered with antiques, sprawled in landscaped grounds and boasting an ancestry spanning two or three centuries, they offer discerning travellers style, service and character that is often far preferable to the efficient anonymity prized by their bigger counterparts.

Many of these elite properties increase their marketing firepower by joining small, select hotel consortia such as Leading Hotels of the World, Relais & Chateaux and Small Luxury Hotels. Some have a foot in more than one camp. You'll find the Lowell hotel in New York featured by both Relais & Chateaux and Small Luxury Hotels, for instance. New York's splendid Mark hotel is promoted as a member of the Rafael group, Leading Hotels and Small Luxury Hotels.

Exclusive clans

Becoming a member of these small exclusive clans is not easy. Small Luxury Hotels has fewer than 100 properties in its portfolio, and bigger Leading Hotels says it is unlikely to ever exceed 300.

Joining the Relais & Chateaux group, marketed as the world's most exclusive group, is probably toughest of all. Some 400 individually owned properties worldwide display the group's coveted brass plaque.

Other small exclusive hotel groups such as Orient Express, the Savoy group, Mandarin Oriental, Shangri-La and Ciga (whose stable includes the Danielli and Gritti Palace in Venice) also offer a portfolio of luxury properties for those with the cash to splash out on the best.

Townhouse hotels

Small townhouse hotels – sometimes nicknamed baby grands and boutique hotels – have enjoyed great success in recent years, confounding those who predict that the successful hotels of the next century will be the mega-chains.

These tiny bastions of excellence often reflect the eccentricities and tastes of their owners. Small exclusive addresses in London include Fortyseven Park Street, owned by one of the Roux brothers, and 22 Jermyn Street, which can arrange picnic hampers and even breadcrumbs with which to feed the ducks in London's parks. The Pelham provides a hot water bottle in each bed, while the Portobello even features a fully-working Victorian bathing machine.

SEEING STARS

Wherever you're tempted to stay, don't make the mistake of judging a hotel by its stars. Not only are star ratings given for different reasons in different countries, but many guides use an assortment of other symbols to distinguish the best from the rest. Try working out what all the stars, crowns, diamonds, rosettes, ribbons and four-leaf clovers have in common, and you'll end up more mystified than when you began.

Stars relate to facilities – so an uninspiring high-rise hotel with a swimming pool and second restaurant will merit a higher rating than a charming olde-worlde property with neither. To add to the confusion, hoteliers in countries where higher levels of VAT are levied on luxury properties (among them Spain, Italy and France) often decline five-star status, and opt for a lower grading instead.

Guidebooks are moreover subjective, so properties winning plaudits galore in one may earn barely a mention in another. Inclusion does not mean a hotel has been hand-picked, either. Hotels frequently pay for a mention, while others write their own copy – so literature supposedly designed to help consumers is often simply a marketing tool. Some publications are also more choosy than others. While Egon Ronay inspectors select only the best, tourist boards may reject only one hotel in a hundred.

Star systems are run in the UK by the AA and RAC motoring organizations. A large hotel with two restaurants, uniformed staff and 24-hour room service usually gets four- or five-star status, though the AA awards them percentage ratings as well. Properties such as the Savoy, Claridges and Gleneagles get an extra star, thus effectively ranking as six-star establishments.

Egon Ronay guides assess hotels on 21 different counts, arriving at an overall percentage rating which is 80 per cent or above for deluxe categories. Restaurants making the grade earn stars for cooking, crowns for ambience and arrows to show if they are at the top of their league. Michelin stars remain the most sought-after accolade for culinary excellence.

Brussels bureaucrats are, not surprisingly, keen to introduce a pan-European grading system to help standardize star ratings within the EC. The idea has not won universal approval, since comparing a country club in Scotland with a beach hotel in Greece could prove well nigh impossible. Work is nonetheless now underway to develop a new symbols system.

TAILPIECES

- What are hotel guests most likely to leave behind? Westin says its finds have included a 4-foot snake and a collection of live chickens. Hyatt's list includes everything from false teeth and contact lenses to marital aids and naughty videos. Strangest of all were the Christmas trees forgotten in Dubai and the rabbit left under a bed in Belgrade.

- Sleepwalkers need look no farther than the Holiday Inn Crowne Plaza Midland Hotel in Manchester, where an average of two guests a month are apparently found locked out of their rooms in various states of undress. Likely candidates can have a spare key to tie round their ankle, or a walkie-talkie to clip to their nightwear. Pots of flowers handy for guarding modesty now adorn the corridors.

- Britain's National Bed Federation has been inviting nominations for the Best Bed Awards. Guests filling out nomination forms are asked whether, when moving in bed, they hear creaking or crunching sounds. There's just no answer to that...

8
☐ Staying Safe

Safety looms large in the league of factors influencing the way corporate travellers plan their trips. So large, in fact, that surveys conducted in the wake of hijacks, air crashes and other life-threatening dramas show it to eclipse the more practical questions of cost, convenience and comfort.

Street crime, political unrest and terrorist activity are facts of life in many parts of the world, while the seemingly unstoppable growth in air travel threatens to make the skies dangerously crowded.

Knowing how to minimize risks and deal with the unexpected – whether a mugging, a room theft, or a mid-air drama – will make your travels not simply safer, but much more enjoyable.

FLYING – YOUR SAFEST BET

Your chances of not walking off the plane at the end of your flight are less than one in a million. The fact is, flying is the safest form of travel.

According to Lloyd's of London underwriters, you are 25 times safer in a plane than a car. Figures from Britain's Department of Transport are equally reassuring, confirming that you are safer in the air than on a bike, in a car, on your feet or on the water. The average number of aeroplane deaths per billion passenger kilometres is just 0.2, compared to 72 for pedestrians.

UK aviation expert David Learmount has even calculated that, based on air crash fatalities in 1990, the average traveller would have to make more than four million flights before boarding a doomed aircraft. The odds on engine failure on take-off are around 350,000 to one, and more than half the passengers involved in major crashes survive.

Having said that, not every carrier, aircraft type or airport has the same safety record. Some are reckoned to have a higher risk factor than others. You can narrow the already slender odds of not surviving your flight by learning a little more.

Assessing plane risks

Travelling in the latest high-tech, fly-by-wire Airbus is unquestionably a safer bet than taking off in a rattling Russian workhorse with 12 million miles on the clock. But while the jet engines of the 1990s are up to ten times more reliable than their forerunners, no aircraft is risk-proof.

Statistically, you are far safer aboard a large wide-body jet than a small commuter plane. Fatal accident rates per million hours are eight times lower for large jets than for small business jets and turboprops, and 17 times lower than those for light twinjet aircraft operating in the US. Bigger, sturdier wide-bodies are not only more likely to survive an accident, but harder for hijackers to commandeer. Two engines are better than one, and four are an even better bet.

Ageing aircraft

Most people feel safer aboard a brand new jet than an old one. The subject of aircraft age became a hot chestnut during the late '80s after a string of incidents involving ageing aircraft – the most dramatic of which involved a 19-year-old Aloha Airlines B737 making a near-miraculous landing in Hawaii after its roof tore off 5 miles over the Pacific.

Studies conducted shortly afterwards showed that half the jets being flown by major US airlines were over 16 years old. Even now, one B747 in ten has flown more hours than it was designed for, though maintenance procedures ensure that by the time a plane reaches its late teens, very little of its original bodywork remains.

Air carriers deny that older planes are less safe, rejecting the idea of a compulsory retirement age and claiming that with proper care, planes can fly almost indefinitely. It's also true that even younger aircraft put in some awesome flying time these days, with many chalking up double-figure flying hours every day of the week.

Some carriers pride themselves on operating younger fleets, however. In 1993, average fleet ages varied from 4 years for Qantas, to 5 for Singapore Airlines, 6 for Lufthansa, 8.5 for SAS, 10 for British Airways and 12 for Air Canada.

Metal fatigue

Aircraft operating on shorthaul sectors are most at risk from corrosion and metal fatigue – the two big enemies – since it is the constant round of take-offs and landings that stresses the plane. Since maintenance requirements vary from country to country, those stationed in some parts of the world can also be more at risk than others. Travel trade insiders still joke that if you want to bump off a friend, you simply book them on a ramshackle Ilyushin 62 trundling around Russia.

No youthful fuselage, high-tech cockpit or rigorous maintenance policy comes with a gold-plated guarantee against the unexpected, of course. Most air crashes are simply caused by human error.

Which airline?

Experts disagree on ways to compare the safety records of major airlines. Should they tot up a carrier's number of crash-free flights, accident-free air miles, passengers carried safely or years without a fatal incident? Comparing like for like can be a daunting task.

Third World and certain Latin and East European carriers have less impressive safety records than those from more affluent parts of the world. Having flown in planes with neither seatbelts nor safety cards in China, seen spare passengers squatting in the aisle in Russia, had goats herded on board in Afghanistan and landed on an airstrip amid grazing sheep in Nepal, I can't say I'm surprised.

Accident rates in South America – Colombia in particular – are higher than in many other regions. India also enjoys a none-too-rosy reputation, with Indian Airlines having suffered a series of disasters over the last 20 years, including four hijackings and two accidents (one killing over 70 people) in the first half of 1993 alone. By contrast, El Al's reputation for bullet-proof security probably makes flights to and from Israel some of the safest in the world.

Soviet carrier Aeroflot came bottom in an airline safety league table compiled in 1990 by the US magazine *Conde Nast Traveler*, which reviewed accidents occurring over a 20-year period. The airline had had at least 40 known fatal crashes during the period 1969–88 – a far cry from Dallas-based Southwest Airlines, which had made more scheduled flights without a fatal accident than any other carrier.

And which seat?

Having picked the right airline, there is the question of choosing the right seat. Unfortunately – since it's impossible to predict exactly how or where an airliner may crash – there isn't one. Since three out of four air accidents occur within sighting distance of the airport, however, seats offering greater mobility may be the best bet. Your survival chances are greater, according to some experts, by sitting near the exit doors, on the aisle and – to lessen the chances of being turned to charcoal – away from the engines.

Your prospects will also be greater if you pay attention to the in-flight safety demo instead of burying your head in a newspaper. Studies show that people with a better knowledge of exit locations and emergency procedures can not only help themselves, but others too, in the event of a crash.

Making flying safer

There is now a broad consensus that features such as smokehoods, cabin sprinkler systems, rear-facing seats and more space alongside over-wing exits could significantly improve air crash survival rates. Unfortunately, safety costs money.

Some airlines also claim that smokehoods could hinder, rather than help, the evacuation of an aircraft in an emergency. They argue that rear-facing aircraft seats would be expensive to fit and significantly increase an airliner's load – and that, anyway, most passengers don't want to fly backwards. In the meantime, smokehoods are on sale for £50 in stores such as the Spycatcher store in London's Knightsbridge.

Individual carriers are meanwhile taking other initiatives on the safety front. British Airways is developing a safety information system known as BASIS, which uses computer electronics to spot any worrying blips or trends in an aircraft's flying pattern.

BA is also trialling tiny cameras mounted on the aircraft fuselage which let the flight crew check out any problems with engines or wing flaps visually, and global positioning systems able to pinpoint the location of an aircraft anywhere in the world. Other carriers are developing equipment to detect and pinpoint dangerous clear air turbulence – invisible to both humans and radar.

Cockpit mechanics

All the whines, whirrs, vibrations and thumps you may hear in-flight do not actually denote impending doom. Wing flaps are tested before take-off, engines are cut back as the plane climbs, and the aircraft may bank steeply as the pilot sets its course. On landing, the deafening roar of reverse thrust engine power is a normal occurrence.

In-flight turbulence is seen as more of a nuisance than a danger by flight crew (who reckon parking the plane is a lot harder than actually flying it), and is sometimes simply a jet stream, or narrow band of fast-flowing air that can speed up your journey. Hard landings are preferable to those that simply dust the runway, since they minimize wear on tyre tread, avoid aquaplaning and make it easier to slow down.

Cockpit radar picks up thunderstorms (and your captain will be sure not to fly straight into one of those), while ground proximity warning systems emit a shrill warning should you get a shade too close to planet earth. Cabin doors have such powerful in-flight pressurization that even an army of body-builders couldn't shift them.

Crowded skies

If the prospect of planes falling apart in the sky is a worry, so too is the fact that there may be too many up there in the first place. Mid-air congestion is not only crowding out the airlanes on busy routes, but costing carriers a fortune in holding time and fuel.

Mid-air shaves are now regular headline-grabbers in the media both in Europe and the US, though statistics show that the skies over Britain, at any rate, are safer now than they were some years ago. Civil Aviation Authority statistics show that while the number of commercial aircraft involved in UK air misses reached a peak of 95 in 1988, the figure for 1992 was less than half.

Terrorist threats

Terrorist attacks on airports and airliners peaked in 1985, when US Federal Aviation Authority data revealed a chilling catalogue of 36 hijacks, 32 explosions and a spate of other violent incidents that left 473 people dead and nearly twice that number injured. Aviation insurance claims for the year totalled $1.2 billion.

Since then, violence in the skies has dropped sharply as a barrage of counter-measures has come into force. Should you get caught up in a one-in-a-million terrorist drama for any reason, however, here's what the experts suggest:

- Stay calm, alert and observant.
- Remain inconspicuous. Don't catch the assailant's eye.
- Follow instructions, and don't argue.
- Don't be a hero. Foolhardy action might spell disaster for everyone.
- Don't advertise your nationality. American passport holders have occasionally learned this to their cost.

AIRPORT SECURITY

Airport security has been dramatically stepped up in recent years, both in terms of employee vetting and luggage searches. Even checked-in luggage is now routinely screened at many airports, where check-in times have been lengthened as a result.

Safety versus convenience

But while surveys show that most passengers would not object to paying a small surcharge to finance watertight security, measures have been tempered with what is considered acceptable in terms of time and inconvenience.

Luggage checks remain patchy even at major airport hubs. While metal detectors for picking up knives and firearms are now standard, the same cannot be said of electronic sniffer machines capable of detecting explosives and plastic guns, or giant X-ray machines designed to screen 40ft freight containers. Metal detectors often stay obstinately silent, or squeal at the mere presence of some loose coins, while the Latin guards manning them at some airports are more interested in eyeing up attractive females in the queue than watching the males behind.

Efforts are well underway to equip major airports with a new generation of security devices. Standard X-ray and metal detector units will ultimately give way to sophisticated scanners responding to temperature, matter and density.

Individual airlines have varying standards of security. El Al's strict measures, which prevented a bomb being planted on board a flight at Heathrow in one well-publicized incident, are reckoned to be the best in the business. Passengers travelling to the States from Britain with US carriers are now quizzed in detail about their luggage, while those flying to and from Northern Ireland are subject to tight security.

Complacency remains the biggest danger. Ways are now being sought to beat the boredom factor for security staff checking thousands of bags every week at airports around the world. At Heathrow, machines have been trialled capable of superimposing random images of a gun, knife or other dangerous object over that which the operator is viewing. Those spotting the highest number of trick pictures are rewarded for staying on the ball.

TOUTS AND TAXIS

Feeling safe at an airport does not always hinge on overt security measures. Some travellers can end up fleeced or simply flustered by having to run the gauntlet of crooked officials, taxi touts and assorted hangers-on.

International travel agency Wagonlit has launched a meet-and-greet service at Lagos airport, reckoned to be one of the most dangerous in the world, after clients complained of being relieved of their cash, cigarettes and goodwill before even reaching the arrivals hall. Bogus escorts had occasionally even managed to find out travellers' names, accost them at the arrivals gate, then drive them off and rob them. Customers are now given confidential security numbers to identify themselves.

Other airports known to be less than safe include Bucharest, where some business travellers have been driven off by unscrupulous cab drivers and robbed. Indian and African airports can be awash with pirate cabs and pestering porters. Others are notorious for pilferage, while a few – among them Jakarta – are said to have baggage staff involved in the drugs trade.

George Albert Brown, author of *The Airline Passenger's Guerilla Handbook*, tells a salutory tale about getting into a pirate airport cab at Bogota, in Columbia. Two burly locals climbed in on either side of him as the car pulled away. Realizing the situation spelt trouble, Brown asked the driver where he might get a woman, adding that he would first need to call at his hotel for some money. Once there, he invented an urgent appointment and sent the driver packing with a healthy tip.

Airport carparks can not only be costly, but less than safe. Carpark operators are rarely liable for damage or theft, and owners of smart sports cars occasionally return to find their wheels gone. Off-airport carparks can be a better bet, since cars are often ferry-parked in blocks, making them virtually impossible to steal.

Hassle-free arrivals

You can improve your prospects of a hassle-free passage through the airport if you:

- Make sure your case has a stout lock. Leave the matching monogrammed Gucci at home.
- Ensure you are met if arriving somewhere deemed to be in the passenger peril league. Most bigger travel agents can arrange for a meet-and-greet service to speed you safely to your hotel, day or night.
- Stick to official airport cabs – preferably those taking pre-paid vouchers issued in the arrivals hall.
- Share a taxi with a (trusted) fellow traveller or see if a share-a-cab system operates.
- Avoid being dropped at lonely long-term carparks in the dead of night.
- Consider staying at the airport till dawn, if you arrive after midnight.

- Carry a 24-hour emergency telephone number. A good travel agent or travel insurance company will provide one.

Getting cabs around town

Keep an eye on even official cabbies in cities such as Lagos and Cairo. In Rio, where drivers are often reluctant to wait at lights after dark, lest a rolled-up newspaper wrapped around a gun barrel is thrust through the quarterlight, some hotels even have their own car fleets. While these may cost twice the price of the yellow city cabs, they are often the safest bet.

- Avoid taking pirate cabs, whatever the money-saving temptations.
- Agree a price first, if the cab is unmetered.
- If there is a dispute, make sure it's not in the middle of nowhere. You may be left with a long walk.
- Object loudly if the driver tries to pick up other passengers.
- Beware of the over-inquisitive cabbie or the one who hangs around, pesters or tries to 'adopt' you.

For further hints on taking taxis, see Chapter 6.

DRIVING A CAR

Hiring wheels can also invite trouble in some parts of the world. In Miami, where visitors have been tailed from the airport and robbed in their hire car within minutes of driving off, authorities have put a ban on tell-tale Y and Z rented car number plates, and urged hire firms to remove giveaway advertising bumper stickers.

With 130 visitors mugged there every month – and 35,000 a year becoming victims of crime in Florida as a whole – Miami's Chamber of Commerce now issues visitors with explicit safety notices, warning them to keep car doors locked and not to pull over except for police. STAR patrols (Safeguarding Tourists Against Robberies) escort drivers who have strayed into unsavoury areas back to the main highways. The Streetwise Map Company now issues warts-and-all maps of the city showing no-go zones, and plans to cover other US cities.

Car theft is rampant in countries like Italy, where hire car insurance often carries a hefty premium. Vehicles left in the wrong part of town in other countries can be stripped to the bones by the time you return, and leaving luggage and valuables on show is asking for trouble.

Road safety is another nightmare. Figures compiled by the International Road Traffic and Accident Database for 1990 show some stark differences in road fatality rates around the world. Deaths per 10,000 motor vehicles ranged from a low of 1.7 in Sweden to a high of 12 in former Yugoslavia. The rate was 1.9 in Japan, 3.2 in New Zealand, 7.2 in Greece and 10 in Hungary.

Drink is a common culprit, though fatigue can be a bigger killer. The US Department of Transportation estimates 200,000 accidents each year are caused by people feeling tired or falling asleep at the wheel – the danger time being between 3am and 7am. Mini-computers capable of alerting drivers will soon be on the market.

Safer driving

- Service your own car thoroughly before setting off.
- Don't try and be flashy. Slow down if you're not a local.
- Don't drink and drive.
- Invest in additional car safety features. Miniature road scanning mirrors can now be fitted above the wheel arch to show the road ahead when you're stuck behind a truck.
- Avoid clearly designated hire cars. Local number plates are preferable.
- Keep doors locked and valuables out of sight. Never leave cash and credit cards in the glove compartment while the car is unattended.
- Report thefts to the police, if only to obtain the forms necessary for an insurance claim.
- Don't pick up hitch-hikers. Stay in the car if you break down on the motorway.
- Consider hiring a car and driver in some countries. Find the right one, and you'll have someone who will make your safety a priority.

BEING STREETWISE

Street crime is on the rise in almost every major city. The huge rise in tourism to poorer nations, where visitors casually spend more on lunch than some locals earn in a year, has exacerbated the problem even in regions once considered crime-free. Violence has long reached epidemic proportions in South America, and is now climbing fast in parts of Asia. Lawlessness is legion in cities such as Bogota and Lima, where you enter some streets at your peril.

Muggings, murder and car theft have soared in Russia and the former Soviet satellite states since large-scale social change got underway. Westerners, with their gleaming cars and consumer trappings, are not surprisingly plum targets. It's much the same in Havana, where an influx of foreigners has paralleled Cuba's steady move towards a market economy, and brought a tide of black marketeers in its wake.

Big-city crime

A survey published in London's *Evening Standard* in early 1993 showed big-city murder rates to be highest in Rio de Janiero. The chances of becoming a victim of violence were said to be 1 in 64 in Rome, 1 in 120 in Toronto, 1 in 166 in New York, 1 in 178 in London, and 1 in 191 in Sydney. The safest city of all? – Tokyo – where the chances of becoming a victim of violent crime are apparently just 1 in 2,332.

Crime rates in the US are higher in Boston, Dallas and Washington than in New York, often portrayed as the country's most crime-ridden metropolis. Numbers of police employed in the Big Apple have risen by 300 per cent since 1990, according to the city's Convention and Visitors Bureau, with crime – down by nearly 7 per cent in the first half of 1992 – dropping steadily as a result. Things are not so hot elsewhere, though. Parts of downtown Miami, Dallas and Houston are no-go areas even by day, and visitors are advised to carry 'mugger's money'.

Thieves are sometimes tiny tots. The scruffy gypsy children pleading for sweets and gum in St Petersburg are notorious thieves and pickpockets. Elsewhere, culprits can even be police. Clued-up travellers going through land border points in Latin America stay in twos and threes, to guard against crooked officials planting drugs in their bags and then claiming a handsome bribe for not making trouble when they are 'discovered'. In Lagos, organized road gangs dressed as police have accosted unwary drivers.

Survival tips

Having a bag snatched containing credit cards, cash and Filofax – the latter often containing all manner of personal details – can not only ruin a trip and wreck your social life, but badly knock your confidence. Make sure you carry a toll-free emergency number for reporting loss or theft of plastic cards, and:

- Stay clear of notorious no-go areas. If in doubt, ask the concierge.
- Stick to well-lit or busy thoroughfares after dusk.
- Avoid standing on street corners poring over a map. You might as well hang a sign round your neck saying 'Mug me – I'm a tourist'.
- Avoid flaunting wealth and expensive jewellery. Some thieves will grab a necklace from around your neck.

STAYING SAFE ■ 143

- Wear shoulder bags under your coat – straps can be slit in seconds with a razor. Zipped handbags are harder to open than those with a simple catch.
- Invest in a thief-proof wallet. You can even buy one that holds pressurized dye capsules which break open and permanently discolour the contents if the wallet is forced open.
- Try the rubber band trick. Wrap two large ones around your wallet, and the friction makes it almost impossible for the wallet to be slid from your pocket unnoticed. You can learn to live with the inconvenience.
- Remember back trouser pockets are notoriously vulnerable. Money belts make cash harder to snatch.
- Remember, pickpockets often work in pairs – one to distract and one to steal. The tomato ketchup trick (one squirts you and offers to clean it off, while the other lifts your wallet) is a favourite.
- Tuck some notes into a sock when sightseeing. Alternatively, try a Tubigrip – an elasticated bandage sold at chemist shops which you wear round your calf. John Hatt, author of the *Tropical Traveller*, recommends them for keeping money safe.
- Think about taking some self-defence classes. If nothing else, they will increase your confidence.
- Resist carrying any kind of weapon – it could be wrenched out of your hands and used against you. A piercing whistle may be more useful.
- Keep a note of the emergency services number in the country you're visiting, eg 911 in the US, 999 in Britain.

Getting mugged

It's usually best to hand over your cash than to put up any heroics. Although every situation is different, the golden rules are:

- Don't fight back unless you know you can win. You may end up arguing with the wrong end of a shotgun. Besides, your assailant may be, drunk, angry, or a lot bigger than you.
- Try not to panic. That way, both you and your assailant may lose control. Remember your credit cards are worth less than your life.

Ways to deal with sexual assault are discussed in Chapter 12.

Money can sometimes resolve a trivial matter if the police themselves are the problem. Otherwise, take the names of any obstructive individuals and insist on seeing the most senior officer available. Don't be afraid to name-drop and mention the names of prominent contacts.

TERRORISM ON THE GROUND

Watching your wallet may be the least of your worries in some countries. Kidnapping, terrorism, civil unrest, guerilla warfare and political coups are rife in the world's danger spots. Leading London kidnap underwriters, Cassidy Davis, say the worldwide kidnap and ransom insurance business is now worth $80 million a year.

Countries currently high on the danger list include Afghanistan, Bosnia and Serbia, Iraq, Lebanon and Somalia. Other less than safe havens include Angola, El Salvador and Northern Ireland. Westerners have also been deliberately targeted by bombers in Turkey and Egypt, and caught up in riots in India.

Seeking advice on security is essential before setting off for known trouble spots. Control Risks, which operates offices in London, Washington and Melbourne, provides up-to-date briefings on more than 70 countries for travelling executives and claims to run the world's most sophisticated risk assessment network. Briefings include advice on local transport – even down to which taxis to take into town – and all other relevant matters. Risks, both current and future, are spelt out, with information stored on database and updated daily.

Should you have serious cause for concern, heed the following:

- Make sure a large group of company seniors does not travel together on the same flight.
- Avoid carrying political literature. It may be confiscated or attract unwanted attention.
- If staying in a high-risk destination for any length of time, avoid routine and keep a low profile. Take advice from local expatriate colleagues.
- Avoid arriving on public holidays – they are favourite terrorist attack dates.
- If you're being followed, head for other people fast – whether at a shop, café or bus stop.
- Hire a cop. Off-duty policemen are often keen to bump up their income with freelance work. A good tip can often secure protection for the evening.

Gadget junkies who are deadly serious about safety can snap up a range of protection devices from specialist security shops. Visit the Counter

Spy Shop in London or Beverly Hills, and you can pick up anything from bugging devices to bullet-proof raincoats. Top-selling lines include blinding lights to immobilize attackers, fake cans for spare cash, electronic watchdogs to listen through walls and anti-kidnap devices that transmit your whereabouts on a fake Rolex.

Other items include night vision binoculars (better than carrots), phone scrambling devices, wristwatch cameras and voice gender-benders guaranteed to turn the weediest voice into a good imitation of Rambo. You can even order an 007-style supercar fitted with hidden gun portholes, secret transmitters, emergency oxygen units and oil slick emitters.

AT THE HOTEL

Fire risks

Being woken up at four in the morning by the piercing shriek of a fire alarm can make your hair stand on end. In my case, at the Edinburgh Sheraton, it was fortunately a small kitchen fire that was almost out by the time bleary-eyed guests stumbled into the carpark.

That needn't have been the case, however. The fire could have spread. We could have been staying 30 floors up. The exit doors could have been blocked, or locked. And nine out of ten of us would have failed, as usual, to bother reading the fire safety instructions on the back of the door.

Lack of care
No corporate traveller expects to check into a death trap for the night – but survey after survey reveals that hotel fire precautions are often woefully inadequate. Locked escape doors, blocked exits, unprotected stairwells and unmarked escape routes are commonplace. So too are badly sited exit signs and escape plans hung upside down.

Guests are not necessarily safe even with the big chains. Fires at the Heliopolis Sheraton in Cairo in 1990 and at the Dupont Plaza in Puerto Rico in 1985 claimed 17 and 96 lives respectively. Fire regulations around the world differ widely, and many chains settle for the minimum with which they can get away. Experts have rightly demanded that fire safety standards be included in the star rating system for hotels, so that five-star comfort means five-star safety, too.

Sprinkler systems are now fitted to most new hotels in the US and Europe. A number of chains, among them Marriott, Hilton and Sheraton, are also retro-fitting them to existing properties. A few hotels even boast new high-tech electronic watchdog systems which monitor smoke detectors and can instantly pinpoint the location of any fire, summoning the fire brigade if need be.

Playing it safe

- Find, and read, the fire escape information in your room on arrival. If you don't see it, complain.
- Check out escape routes. A few minutes spent casing the joint may make all the difference in an emergency.
- Ask to stay on a lower floor, if standards look questionable.
- Remember, smoke is the real killer. It can spread faster than you can run. Stay low if you have to combat smoky corridors, and use walls for orientation.
- Don't smoke in bed.
- In an emergency, don't use the lifts unless instructed to by firefighters. Once outside, report to the right evacuation point. Someone may be searching for you.
- If trapped in your room, shut the door and use wet towels to block the gaps. Run the shower to soak the carpet.

In-room security

Don't imagine you've paid for privacy when you pick up the keys to your hotel room. Room and minibar attendants, floor supervisors, electricians and even salespeople showing clients around can all obtain a duplicate set and simply walk in. Some are not even deterred by clearly posted 'Do not Disturb' signs.

As a result, your room is not exactly Fort Knox in security terms. While few employees would risk their job simply to swipe a bottle of duty-free gin, it's clearly courting trouble to leave valuables lying around.

Lost and stolen goods
Hotels won't generally take responsibility for anything that goes walkabout from your room – unless it's lost, stolen or damaged due to their own negligence – though they are clearly liable for items lodged in a safety deposit box. UK hotels are required under the Hotel Proprietors Act to give guests free use of their safe. If not, their liability for losses from the room is limited to two items up to a value of just £50 each.

The answer is clearly to put valuables into a hotel safe, secure them in a locked suitcase or keep them on you. In-room safes that can be digitally locked with a self-selected code are now increasingly common, though some incur a daily usage fee. While some hotels also charge for their front desk safes, a few have at least introduced shatterproof screens, booths and other safeguards. Instances of credit cards being fraudulently used while in hotel safekeeping are mercifully rare.

Numberless electronic key cards reprogrammed for each guest are improving guestroom security, since they cannot be copied and don't have giant tags emblazoned with numbers for all to see. Spyholes and chains – some engaging automatically at the press of a button – are now fairly standard.

Most good hotels are also increasingly discreet with room numbers. Keys may be deliberately marked with wrong numbers (albeit confusing for the guest who has had a Scotch too many), or handed over in a small card folder. The porter who picks up a female guest's case with an ear-splitting 'Room 202 was it, love?' is fortunately a dying breed.

Hotels such as Heathrow's Edwardian International are now kitted out with state-of-the-art security systems which log each entry to each room, showing not only the time, but precisely which key was used. Video watchdogs can not only freeze-frame shots of any suspicious looking character in the corridors, but provide an instant colour print-out.

Devices are also on sale to prevent anyone else from opening your room door. You can purchase a Doorkeeper electronic wedge with an inbuilt alarm for around £45 from good security stores, or a Touch Me Not alarm which hangs on the door handle. It's worth remembering that crime rates are worst in budget hotels – where, incidentally, you are more likely to be burgled by your fellow guests.

Guarding valuables

A few basic precautions can guard against problems:

- Keep your room locked, and check who's there before opening.
- Don't hang the Make Up My Room sign on the doorknob when you leave. It advertises the fact that no one's there.
- Make sure you shut your room door properly. You'd be surprised how many people don't.
- Don't leave your numbered room key on the bar or restaurant table in full view.
- Give creepy corridors and carparks a wide berth. Ask for a room near the lift and tip the doorman to park your car.
- Remember, flash designer luggage may impress the porter, but it will tell thieves you're loaded.
- Use the hotel safe rather than hiding cash in the room or carrying it all

with you. There's nothing to stop you renting a safety deposit box on arrival, even if your room's not ready.
- Remember, thieves will often take the last cheque and stub from a carelessly discarded cheque book. That way, you won't discover the damage till later.
- Make sure staff are discreet with your room number. If they're not, complain.

According to police, you are most at risk in the lobby of your hotel than anywhere else on the property. Theatre ticket touts, petty thieves and other undesirables often loiter there, and a favourite trick is to drop a newspaper on top of keys tossed on the counter by guests leaving for the day. Make sure yours go in the key return box provided.

Pickpocket gangs who invade busy hotel lobbies in the summer are another hazard. Working in teams, they rely on the power of distraction to relieve unwary guests of their money. One might bump into you, dropping an armful of papers, or wiping ice cream down your clothes. As he apologizes profusely, his accomplice empties your pockets from behind. Before you've realized what has happened, the pair are outside the door.

Considering the numbers of people who stay in them, London's hotels have a surprisingly low crime rate. Just seven armed robberies were committed in the capital's top hotels during 1992 – all against staff in the early hours of the morning. Hotel crime in Hong Kong during the year included 220 cases of assorted theft and 33 reports of serious assault or wounding.

MEANWHILE AT HOME ...

So much for security while you're away. What about your empty pad back home? With break-ins on the rise, it's vital to make your home as burglar-proof as possible. The growth in mini-sized electronic gadgetry has made it easier for thieves to make off with rich pickings, since many goods can now be lifted with one hand.

All manner of slick home security systems are now on the market, including alarm systems that will ring through to friends or monitoring services. If you hate the idea of leaving the place empty, house-sitting agencies can provide anything from basic caretaking to live-in sitters who will feed the cat and even paint the bathroom while you're gone. Identifying your possessions with a marking kit and keeping a note of serial numbers will help police return any stolen goods recovered.

You can deter an opportunist thief, if not a determined villain, by taking some basic precautions:

- Don't leave valuables on view. Fit blinds or net curtains.
- Lock away ladders and tools. They make splendid burglar aids.
- Make sure your answering machine doesn't tell the world you're away for the week.
- Cancel the milk by phone, not by leaving a note on the doorstep.
- Get neighbours to pick up your mail, and fit light timer switches.
- Don't leave papers with your address on the dashboard of your car in the airport carpark.

TAILPIECES

- It's not simply political zealots who cause havoc in the air. Fellow passengers who are drunk, drugged or just plain batty can also cause mayhem. British Airways carries plastic handcuffs on board to deal with troublemakers, and says over-indulgence in the demon drink is the usual reason they are used. It hastens to add that 'very few' passengers leave the aircraft manacled.

- Londoners suffer 500 burglaries a day – or one every three minutes. UK break-ins reached a value of £750 million in 1992 – double the haul recorded in 1990.

- It's not simply travellers who are at risk from theft at hotels. Light-fingered guests cost many properties a fortune every year in towels, ashtrays and glasses – but if you know anyone who stole some from the Ritz in London before 1945, they could be welcomed back with open arms. The reason? The Ritz is building up a memorabilia museum.

9
☐ After-hours Fun

It's the end of the day. The last meeting is finished, the last handshake proffered and the last coffee cup drained. You can snap your briefcase shut till the morning and head back to base for a welcome drink and a shower.

On the other hand, the night is yet young. You're in an exciting city 5,000 miles from home that boasts some of the world's most talked-about nightlife. Neon-splashed frontages are flashing into life. Clubland is coming alive. Bars are suddenly buzzing. Why turn in early?

Deciding how to kill time after dark can pose a dilemma for those on foreign shores. Not everyone has a tailor-made network of contacts certain to extend after-hours invitations to dinner, shows or sports fixtures. At the same time, the prospect of dining out alone, or staying in with a tray supper every night is distinctly unappealing.

For the reckless few, casual sex is on the agenda regardless of the risks. Many a hotel concierge receives calls from male guests enquiring where paid-for female company is to be had, as well as supplies of the magic balloons that help ensure any horizontal encounters are safe.

THE RED-LIGHT TRADE

Business visitors are a lucrative source of revenue for the purveyors of sex in its many forms, and the huge growth in corporate travel over the last decade has been paralleled by the worldwide growth of the sex industry.

Punters, voyeurs and tourists alike flock the streets of Amsterdam, Hamburg, Bangkok and a score of other cities to see, if not to sample, the supermarket-style array of peepshows, porn shops, hostess bars and ladies of the night in action-packed red-light districts.

Whether it's under wraps or openly flaunted, prostitution thrives in the world's big business capitals. The breakdown of the Soviet empire has even brought it into the open in cities once famed for their after-dark sobriety – Moscow and Prague being prominent examples.

A global industry

Other places boast a long-established sex-for-sale tradition. Porn cinemas and all-night bars abound in Berlin, for years an outpost of West German decadence in the East. Amsterdam has windows full of scantily clad girls, as well as a tawdry Sex Museum and an aptly named Condomerie. Hamburg has its notorious Reeperbahn, whose striptease bars and live shows cater for scores of visiting ship crews.

Sleaze has entered the '90s in the sidestreets surrounding New York's Times Square, where many girls now carry pagers and bleepers, promoting their services through escort agencies featured in Yellow Pages rather than on the streets. Elsewhere in the Americas, Rio's Copacabana area has a glut of anything-goes streetwalkers catering to both tourist and business trade.

Singapore's Bugis Street, once home to hordes of transvestites, has been cleaned up in recent years. But the red-light trade continues to flourish in the Itaewon area of Seoul, where the authorities have tried to curb the night-time activities of the notorious barber shop girls by imposing a midnight curfew. Male visitors to Lagos and Havana may find local hookers knocking at their door unless requests are left to the contrary at the front desk.

Vice crackdowns

Tough action from the authorities is now closing down scores of establishments (many of them employing the city's notorious blind masseuses) in Manila's Ermita district, long popular with male tourists. But while the city's mayor reportedly wants to see antique shops and ice cream parlours replacing the live shows and sex salons, the crackdown is merely driving the trade out to Angeles City, two hours drive from the capital.

The flesh trade continues to prosper in Bangkok, whose sex merchants comb the streets of Patpong to round up customers for bars offering a range of anything-goes entertainment. Sex tourism is on the wane, however, following a tide of publicity over child prostitution and rapidly rising HIV rates.

Tough laws have been proposed to combat a new vice boom in London's Soho, where dozens of unlicensed peep shows and hostess bars have replaced small businesses bankrupted by recession in recent years. New ways of outlawing the sex traders and streetwalking 'toms', as hookers are known by London's police, are being sought by Scotland Yard and Westminster council's legal eagles.

AIDS AND OTHER NASTIES

Whether it is regulated, legal and licensed, or conducted in a twilight world of pimps and porn shops, prostitution is a major factor in the relentless spread of AIDS and other sexually transmitted diseases. Studies by the World Health Organization (WHO) confirm that the disease is now well entrenched, despite the vigorous efforts of safe-sex campaigns in many countries.

Male expatriate workers have a higher risk of picking up sexually transmitted diseases (STDs) than most other groups, according to WHO studies. Airline crews (occasionally said to run a lucrative sideline in providing sexual favours for customers), and business travellers are also vulnerable.

Careless risks

Travelling executives can take risks abroad that would be unthinkable at home. Caution is often cast to the wind thousands of miles away, where there is little fear of a casual encounter turning into something more serious. Host companies may lay on sexual entertainment for visiting clients, prostitutes may openly tout for business in hotel lobbies, and bars may be peopled by hostesses paid to use every trick to pull customers.

As a result, unwary travellers can return home carrying more than they bargained for. It's an irony that those who go abroad without any particular intention of having sex are often the ones to end up at the STD clinic, since they are the ones who fail to carry protection. Celibacy is not surprisingly the best safeguard.

WHO figures show that 2.5 million people were infected with AIDS at the end of 1992, putting the figure of HIV positive people worldwide (including children) at 13.5 million. More than half were in Africa, with 2 million in the Americas, 1.5 million in Asia and half a millon in western Europe. The figures were lowest in Australasia, where estimated HIV cases reached the 25,000 mark. Most new infections are occuring in sub-Saharan Africa and Asia.

HIV blackspots

HIV is known to have its blackspots. Kenya, Uganda and Tanzania have some of the highest rates in Africa, with one survey showing nine out of ten Kenyan prostitutes to be test-positive. Brazil and Bombay are other danger spots where many hookers routinely offer unsafe sex for a higher fee.

In Thailand, one in three Patpong girls and nearly half of all heroin users are said to carry the virus, leaving health authorities struggling to contain a growing HIV epidemic. In New York, where many girls work the streets to feed a drug habit, up to one-third are reckoned to be positive. Transvestite and male prostitutes can be an even greater risk.

Other sexually transmitted diseases are admittedly easier to treat than AIDS. The days of dying of syphilis (a fate allegedly suffered by Cleopatra, Mussolini and van Gogh), are now rare. Herpes, which can turn into a friend for life, has become widespread instead, while hepatitis B is commonly contracted through having sex with a carrier.

STDs aside, there are several other good reasons for refraining from casual sex abroad. One is the cost. The sex industry has more than its share of sharks, touts and rip-off merchants notorious for taking their clients to the cleaners – knowing most will be too sheepish to complain to police afterwards.

Sex-for-sale sharks

Scores of men lured into the hostess bars and sex salons of Soho emerge an hour later having been soundly fleeced with absurdly priced drinks – some costing over £100 – and other questionable charges. Those without enough funds to pay are escorted to the nearest cash dispenser by burly bouncers.

Careless clients of prostitutes operating on the fringe of the law also risk being robbed, compromised and blackmailed. Some are even rounded up during police raids and arrested. Being caught in such circumstances is not something most business people want on their CV.

Illicit sex also carries the danger of being found out by more than the law. I once worked for a blue-chip British company which had unexpectedly lost one of its chairmen to a heart attack in the throes of a lustful encounter in Hawaii. The problem was that he was meant to be in Australia on a business trip – and the secret soon leaked out.

MEETING PEOPLE

Being stuck on your own after hours in a strange city can be one of the most dispiriting – and distinctly unglamorous – aspects of business travel. There is nonetheless no need to forfeit company and become a recluse in your room. Fortunately, there are plenty of ways to meet people and socialize without patronizing a house of ill repute, ringing an escort agency or sitting alone in the hotel bar. You could:

- Use the hotel pool, health bar or fitness centre. Friendly overtures won't be misconstrued, and it will do you good at the same time.
- Find out what's on. Listings magazines detail talks, sports events and workshops, as well as cinema and theatre. Get a copy of *Village Voice* or *New York Magazine* in the Big Apple, *City Life* in Amsterdam, and *Checkpoint* in Berlin.
- Call the tour desk for details of after-dark sightseeing. Boat rides, dinner-and-show evenings and organized trips to concerts, jazz venues and casinos can be a good way to meet other travellers. While you're there, book up a safari or snorkelling trip to fill an empty weekend.
- Catch up on culture. You can buy half-price theatre tickets on the day from booths in both London and New York. Cinema is even cheaper – though you'll pay 12 times more to visit a picture palace in Tokyo than in Prague.
- Try a supper club. Those offering food, dancing and cabaret are currently enjoying a rebirth in New York City. Catering for a mixed audience, they attract a number of single diners.
- Make friends with the hotel bar staff. They may be glad to chat between serving customers, and will keep unwanted company at bay if you don't wish to be bothered. Note that bars in Moscow are often credit card only; a device used to deter local prostitutes.
- See if your hotel offers a travellers table for solo guests wishing to eat together. While these are rare, they can make dining alone more pleasurable.
- Sample a singles bar. They're not all out-and-out meat markets. New York has dozens, catering for both straight and gay clientele.
- Join a meet-and-eat club if you visit the same city often. Many arrange regular evenings for professionals to dine together at restaurants – and not everyone is after a hot date.
- Try a lonely hearts page. Many ads are placed by business people looking for no-strings friendship or fun during their visits to a particular city.
- Do the inviting yourself. Schedule less formal meetings over breakfast or lunch, or invite contacts to join you for dinner, drinks or a concert at night.

DATING CHEZ VOUS

If your hormones are tap-dancing on the ceiling, and dating or more is on the agenda, you might as well go about it the right way. There's no need to make tracks for the seedy side of town when you can entertain in style on your doorstep.

Hoteliers are often all too familiar with the sexual proclivities of their guests. Doormen turn a blind eye to the single guest who rolls up at two in the morning with a companion, while room service staff asked to provide champagne on ice ten minutes later are well aware that the recipient is unlikely to be Sir's real spouse.

Japanese style

Properties catering in a big way for close encounters of the transient kind include airport hotels – which often rent rooms by the half-day or day – and Japan's so-called love hotels, popular with young couples prevented from doing what they do there, at home. The so-called *Rabu Hoteru* cater for those after their weekly passion ration (*sekkusu* in Japanese), but with limited time to spare.

So discreet are Japan's thousands of love-inns that you often don't even need to show your face. Money is taken through a hatch in the wall, while doors are remote-controlled. Rooms are thoughtfully furnished with mirrors, large beds and adult videos, while more practical necessities are to be found in the mini-bar. Sophisticated addresses provide (so I'm told) waterbeds, videos to film your antics, and an assortment of props and costumes. Racy comments can be left in the visitor's book.

Passion breaks

Business hotels are traditionally keen to persuade their executive guests to stay on over the weekend, when occupancy rates take a dip. Some even market weekend passion breaks aimed at executives whose high-stress lifestyle gets in the way of amorous activity during the week. Ask, and you'll probably find the penthouse suite complete with four-poster, jacuzzi and candelit dining table can be yours for a remarkably modest outlay.

Before booking into a love hotel or ordering the Dom Perignon on ice, you may of course wish to arm yourself with other essentials. Apart from those familiar little silver-foil packets, these may include items such as:

Aphrodisiacs

Shops selling powdered rhino horn, dried bats and other so-called aphrodisiacs do a roaring trade in some parts of the world. I once called at a tiny shop in the Cairo bazaar, where buyers were signing credit card bills that would have bought a week at the Savoy for thimble-sized pots of whale lard promising users instant Herculean stamina. In Taipei's aptly-named Snake Street market, the locals were queuing up to quaff freshly tapped reptilian blood for much the same reason.

Magazines certainly come cheaper – though don't forget they will be confiscated if you arrive with an armful in places like Saudi Arabia.

Linguistic guides

Phrase books designed to help the traveller seeking to chat up prospective dates and entertain them till breakfast in a variety of languages are now on sale. Well-thumbed volumes of *Wicked French* and *Wicked Italian* can be spotted at airport bookstalls amid the tour guides and expandable clothes lines.

Latest of the slender volumes to appear is *Love Talk in Five Languages*, which leads the amorous but linguistically fumbling traveller through the minefield of trans-national intimate encounters. It tells you the French for inviting your date back *chez vous* (*Aimerais-tu venir à mon hotel?*), the Spanish for asking him or her to stay over (*?Te quedas esta noche?*), the Italian for 'don't stop' (*Non fermarti!*) and the German for 'how was it for you?' (*Wie war es für Dich?*). Handy put-downs for pests are also included.

Adult movies

Should you retire to your room alone, it needn't spell a night with nothing for company but your files and the BBC World Service. Soft-porn entertainment is now available at the flick of a switch in many hotels.

Blue movies are, by all accounts, handsome revenue earners. Marriott hotels say they are very popular with both sexes, and that few guests, if any, complain at being offered a choice of bedtime porn. While Holiday Inn says it does not permit X-rated films to be screened, other chains leave the decisions up to individual managers, who must clearly take local norms and customs into account. You are thus more likely to be offered no-holds-barred viewing in Denmark than Dubai.

Granada Business Communications, which supplies films to 30,000 hotel bedrooms in the UK, says all adult programming is certified by the British Board of Film Censors and only played after 9pm. Guests with minors in tow can bar access to the relevant pay channel to prevent junior from accidentally flicking straight from Tom and Jerry to a three-in-a-bed orgy.

Movie titles should not be detailed on your bill – so if you've spent the night watching *Danish Dentist on the Job* or *Vice Vixens in Soho*, you will be spared any blushes when your boss gets to sign it.

THE MILE HIGH CLUB

Anyone who cannot wait to get to their hotel room to try out position 999 can always try joining the élite ranks of the Mile High Club and have a go in a plane. Although much has been written about the fun and jinks airline crews and their charges supposedly get up to in-flight, any veteran of longhaul flying will confirm that you'll need some Olympian skills to succeed.

Unless you and your partner happen to have the upstairs first class cabin of the plane to yourselves, can discreetly commandeer the entire centre row of seats or don't mind emerging from the loo at the same time, mile-high sex is probably best left to airport best-sellers. Rumours that airline amenity kits are soon to include condoms along with the toothpaste and combs have so far proved false.

Hanky-panky upfront

British Airways denies there has been an outbreak of mile-high hanky-panky since launching its first class Sleeper service and inviting passengers to strip off, change into romper suits and jump under the duvet. 'Certainly not. The atmosphere in our first class cabin is very clubby – rather like Blades or Boodles', says a spokesman sniffily. Should any couple have other ideas, BA's policy is to ask them to refrain, or to shield the spectacle from fellow passengers.

If the Mile High fraternity is not élite enough for your tastes, you could always go one better and join the Ten Mile High club, by achieving your goal on Concorde. Would-be members will have to be both quick and agile, however, since the plane is the narrowest in the fleet and flies the Atlantic in half the time of the average B747. Those in the know say greater success has been had in BA's Club World loos instead. These have wider than usual doors, and a full-length mirror.

Crew layovers

If passengers rarely get the chance to get at it in-flight, air crews complain they scarcely get time on the ground these days. Long layovers (as it were) have become a thing of the past, while flight attendants – some of them now even grandparents – are more likely to be rushing home for PTA meetings than looking for extra-curricular fun. All of which puts them in much the same boat as their executive charges – who crash out with a cocoa most nights, to dream about Around the World in 80 Lays.

TAILPIECES

- An entertaining tale is told in the book *Both Feet in the Air* – written by a former airline pilot – concerning one of the old Stratocruisers, which were fitted with bunks for weary passengers to rest in. One couple climbed in, drew the curtains and decided to do a little more. Unfortunately for both, the man had his elbow pressed against the crew call button. A steward duly arrived and swept the curtains aside to enquire what was needed. 'Honey, you're ringing the bell!' cried the woman, realizing what had happened. Continuing with gusto, her beau merely retorted 'Babe, you ain't seen nothin' yet!'

- Room staff often barge in unwittingly on guests engaged in sexual frolics between the sheets. Sometimes the shoe can be on the other foot, however. One flustered Sydney guest recently arrived at the front desk to complain that he had stumbled on the maid and the butler busy making his bed – from the inside.

10
☐ Money

Money can cause huge headaches for the frequent traveller. Exchanging it into other currencies without being taken to the cleaners, safeguarding it against theft or loss, and replacing it quickly if the worst comes to the worst is often easier said than done thousands of miles from home. Handling money well also means knowing how to balance cash funds with plastic, when to tip, how to oil the wheels of business and where to cash in on the bargains.

BUDGETING FOR TRIPS

Spending two days in Blackpool will cost the firm a good deal less than two days in Buenos Aires. To find out how much money you'll need for your travels, seek advice on local living costs. In Britain, organizations like the Economist Intelligence Unit and Employment Conditions Abroad issue regular cost-monitoring reports on major cities.

Running some checks is vital. It would be foolish to set off without realizing that living costs have more than trebled in Madrid and Berlin since 1986, that Buenos Aires and Caracas are now two of the costliest capitals in the world, that Budapest is Eastern Europe's priciest destination and that Tokyo remains the world's most expensive city. While $150 a day will cover your needs in Lima or Bogota, you'll need more than $500 to get by in the Japanese capital.

Currency shake-ups, devaluations and runaway inflation mean budgets may need to be radically revised for trips just months apart. At the time of writing, hyperinflation in former Yugoslavia has halved the value of the dinar every fortnight, forcing visitors to Belgrade to carry around stacks of notes fatter than a phone directory just to pay for lunch. Inflation of up to 2 per cent a day in Moscow plays similar havoc with budgets, while monetary mayhem rules in Argentina, where locals have endured five currency changes in the last 20 years.

Taking the right funds

Don't rely on a single form of money for your trip. Once stolen, cash is gone for good. Travellers' cheques can be cumbersome, while personal cheques may not be accepted outside your home country. While it's tempting to rely purely on plastic – after all, your hotel is unlikely to let you past the front desk till you provide a credit card imprint – cards are not welcome in some parts of the world. The answer is to spread your assets and take a balanced portfolio of money.

While some local currency is useful for incidentals, it can be largely redundant in countries where dollars now rule the day. In the way that English has become the business world's lingua franca, greenbacks are now king when it comes to financial transactions. The proverbial fistful of dollars will get you farther in Eastern Europe and much of the Third World than a suitcase full of local shekels. Keep a supply of small-denomination bills handy for tips and thankyous.

CHANGING MONEY

So widespread are the rip-offs at the world's currency exchange counters that it's all too often a case of heads you lose, tails they win.

Banks and bureaux de change make their money not only from the differential in buying and selling rates, but by slapping hefty commission charges on top. Surveys comparing the value-for-money at assorted banks and exchange counters confirm that failing to shop around can leave you short-changed by 10 per cent or more.

Punitive exchange rates are one factor in favour of the proposed ECU (European Currency Unit), since it would save travellers having to hand over money at every EC border post. Former president of the European Commission Lord Jenkins once calculated that if a traveller left Britain with £100 in banknotes, visited all 12 EC capitals and changed money 11 times, he or she would be left with just £28.50 by the time it was converted back into sterling.

Executive Travel magazine came up with similarly dismal findings when reporters were sent to a range of money-changing outlets to change £100 into US dollars, then back into sterling. This seemingly straightforward transaction left them with as little as £83.60.

Interestingly, it can sometimes pay to change currency at a local branch of an appropriate foreign bank. In a test carried out by *The Daily Telegraph*, no commission was deducted when changing £500 into

Italian lira at a London branch of the Banca Nazionale del Lavoro, or into Spanish pesetas at the nearby Banco Bilbao Vizcaya.

Bear in mind that many soft-currency countries – among them India, Morocco and Tunisia – prohibit visitors from taking currency in or out of the country, while others limit the amount to small sums. Excess funds may be confiscated or re-converted at punitive rates at the airport as you leave. Currency declarations must be completed in countries like Algeria and Ethiopia, to guard against visitors trading their D-Marks or dollars for a sea of local money on the black market. Those leaving the country will be asked to produce bank exchange slips and explain any discrepancies.

Getting the best rate

- Airport bureaux de change rely on captive custom. Don't expect the best rate in town.
- Use a bank, rather than a hotel, for the best rate. Shop around to see which one offers the best deal.
- Exchange rates can differ from country to country. You'll sometimes get a better deal at home than at your destination.
- A wide gap between buying and selling rates usually means fat profit margins.
- Exchange desks taking fixed commission may be better than those taking a percentage. Do some quick arithmetic to see which works in your favour.
- Look out for hidden charges. They are often posted in a way that makes them easy to overlook.

BLACK MARKET TRADING

Entrepreneurial travellers often succumb to the temptations of the black market in countries whose punitive official exchange rates make living costs absurdly high, or where yards of red tape turn money-changing into a four-hour marathon. This carries well-publicized risks, however, since apart from the danger of being stitched up by crooks it can leave you in trouble with the law.

It's not unknown for plain-clothes police officers to tempt travellers into a deal, then march them off for questioning. Customers can also be tricked by sheer sleight of hand and end up with worthless, out-of-date banknotes. Scores of visitors to Bucharest and Sofia have encountered the backstreet money changers who manage to make off with their sought-after hard currency for what turns out to be a wad of newsprint wrapped in a few real notes.

If you must do deals on the side, hotel porters will be a safer bet than someone on the street, since they won't want to lose their job. Bear in mind that, if you have filled in a currency declaration form, you should ensure you also change enough money through official channels to avoid suspicion. Airport officials know full well you cannot get by on fresh air.

Only change what you need, to avoid carrying around large amounts of cash. Many insurance policies limit the amount of cash they will refund in the event of theft, and you could end up paying out yet more commission if surplus cash has to be re-converted at the end of your stay. Only show a black market trader the amount you wish to change – and make sure the cash is counted out in front of you.

TRAVELLERS' CHEQUES

Despite the plastic revolution, travellers' cheques (TCs) remain best sellers with the travelling public. Stores, gas stations and taxi drivers are known to accept them in the US, where some $25 billion worth are issued each year. Market leader American Express says its sales of TCs grew by 500 per cent between 1971 and 1991 – disproving the view that they have been usurped by plastic cards.

TCs are without doubt the safest form of money. Refunds can often be authorized in a matter of minutes in the case of loss, with replacements sometimes hand-delivered within hours. These have even been rushed to passengers changing planes at Heathrow airport, who discovered over the Atlantic that their original batch was missing.

Nevertheless, travellers' cheques do have their downside. They must be ordered in advance, signed by the purchaser in front of the issuing cashier, then countersigned at the point of sale. What's more, they must be paid for upfront, which can tie up large sums of money.

Commission penalties

TCs also carry a weighty commission penalty, since charges may be levied by the issuing bank, the encashment point, and the bank where unused cheques are converted back into local currency. While charges are normally 1–2 per cent, hotels routinely slap on twice that amount. Cheques can also be impossible to use on the black market. Smaller issuers may not have the resources to refund stolen cheques anywhere, anytime, and may limit the amount that can be refunded.

Reduce business travel costs

Recover VAT on European business expenditure

- travel and accommodation
- business entertaining
- exhibition and conference expenses
- consultancy & lawyers' fees

Call on Cash Back, the world's leading VAT recovery people - WE DO THE REST. Representation in over 20 countries.
(Recovery varies country by country)

CASH BACK

Cash Back Consultancy (UK) Ltd. 20 St Dunstan's Hill, London EC3R 8HL. Tel: 071 626 3262. Fax: 071 626 0384.

It's easy to claim your VAT back.

Cash Back recovers VAT paid on business expenditure incurred throughout Europe

- travel and accommodation
- business entertaining
- exhibition and conference expenses
- consultancy & lawyers' fees

Call on us, the world's leading VAT recovery people – WE DO THE REST. Representation in over 20 countries.

CASH BACK

Cash Back Consultancy (UK) Ltd, 20 St. Dunstans Hill, London EC3R 8HL
Tel: 071 626 3262   Fax: 071 626 0384

Banks recommend carrying cheques in the currency of the country you plan to visit, to avoid commission for cashing them, as well as worries about exchange rate fluctuations. If this is not an option (since even the large issuers deal only in a dozen or so currencies), dollars are the best bet.

Holders of American Express travellers' cheques benefit from a 24-hour Express Helpline, which provides pre-travel information and emergency medical and legal referrals while abroad. The company's Brighton refund centre, which handles 50,000 claims a year, says 75 per cent of all refunds are approved immediately.

Cheque safety

When taking travellers' cheques abroad, remember to:

- Keep the receipt listing serial numbers separate from the cheques themselves – preferably with a duplicate copy left at home. Cross the numbers off as you use them.
- Keep your refund assistance number handy in case of problems.
- Keep unused cheques somewhere safe – preferably in a safety deposit box. Most are stolen from hotel rooms and cars, which should tell you where not to leave them.
- Report any losses to local police. Keep a copy of their report for insurance claims.
- Keep a mental note of the number of cheques left in your wallet. Thieves often tear out the last one, so you don't discover the loss straight away.

EUROCHEQUES

While personal cheques are of little use abroad, Eurocheques are a handy alternative. Issued by European High Street banks, they come with a guarantee card supporting cheques in the appropriate local currency up to the equivalent of £100, and enable holders to draw on their own bank account for funds. There is a fixed bank conversion charge – often 5 per cent or more – for each cheque.

Despite their name, Eurocheques can be used in countries on the fringe of Europe like Albania, Israel, Lebanon, Tunisia and Morocco. Unlike travellers' cheques, they don't tie money up in advance, and can be made out for the precise sum of money you choose. On the downside, they are often unknown in remoter parts of the world.

CREDIT AND CHARGE CARDS

Today's world of international corporate travel runs largely on plastic. Leaving home without a pocketful of credit and charge cards is as unthinkable to most business travellers as failing to pack a toothbrush and spare shirt.

Checking into a hotel, renting a car and securing any number of other travel services is now well nigh impossible without providing a credit, debit or charge card imprint as security. Without your magic piece of plastic, you are likely to be treated like a leper by counter staff and face the indignity of pre-paying your bills in cash.

Global plastic power

There are good reasons for the rapid growth in plastic power. Visa cards are welcomed in more than 10.5 million outlets worldwide and can be used to withdraw cash from nearly 430,000 banks and automated teller machines (ATMs). American Express cardholders – a global army of 36 million – can use their cards in 3 million establishments and 55,000 cash machines. The world's 7 million Diners Club members can patronize 2.3 million merchants and 18,500 cash dispensers.

Cards outlets are now mushrooming in Latvia, Estonia, Lithuania and Albania, not to mention the rest of more-travelled Eastern Europe. The rest of the world is now largely a plastic realm, though restricted zones include the Lebanon, Haiti, Vietnam, North Korea, deepest Africa and parts of former Yugoslavia. By the year 2000, it's predicted there will be over four billion plastic card transactions a year – ten times more than in 1985.

Corporate cards

Three out of four UK companies now issue at least some of their employees with corporate credit or charge cards, and the figure is even higher in the States. Research indicates that firms in Sweden and Britain are Europe's most enthusiastic users – billing more than half of all travel and entertainment costs against them – with Portuguese companies coming bottom of the league.

Corporate card schemes provide useful insurance and travel inconvenience packages, as well as the usual cardholder benefits. Individual firms can decide on spending limits, as well as whether the cards may be used to draw emergency funds from ATMs around the world. Gold cardholders enjoy greater privileges and access to cash.

Airlines have also jumped aboard the plastic card bandwagon. British Airways joined forces with Diners Club in 1991 to launch a joint corporate card, while Visa has since teamed up with Lufthansa, Iberia and Aer Lingus. In addition to the usual benefits and access to cash, the cards provide extras such as priority waitlisting, extra baggage allowance, worldwide travel assistance and duty-free discounts. BA/Diners cardholders enjoy use of Diners Club airport lounges.

Smart cards now being trialled will effectively soon become versatile plastic purses for buying incidentals like newspapers, tube tickets and cups of tea as well as major items. Users will simply insert them into machines that load them with a chosen sum of money – invisibly marked on the card's magnetic strip. By the turn of the century, other cards will let users book airline tickets from roadside ATMs using a simple swipe and handprint scan.

Problems with plastic

Despite their seemingly unstoppable spread, plastic cards have not won universal applause. Some retailers have taken exception to the commission imposed on them by card companies – notably Amex – and unpeeled their window stickers in protest. Paying for petrol by card on the Continent can be a problem, while cards are generally not accepted in war zones or in many places off the beaten track.

Merchants in parts of South America – notably Brazil and Argentina – are known to slap on handsome surcharges for payment by cards, while cash withdrawals worldwide attract service fees of 1–3 per cent. Pay with plastic in the former Soviet Union, and you could be stung with stiff conversion rates that turn your bargain buy in roubles into a major outlay in dollars or pounds.

Credit card bills cost more the longer you delay paying up. Those adept at stretching free credit to the limit can hold off payment for up to 56 days with a Visa Barclaycard, though billing schedules vary among Britain's other 20 Visa issuers.

Credit card fraud

Fraud costs the card-issuing giants millions of pounds every year. Of the 80 million cards in circulation in the UK, more than 5,000 go missing every day, with losses amounting to £5 a second. Card fraud soared fourfold between 1988 and 1991, and cost the UK banking industry £165 million in 1992, with Barclays alone suffering losses of more than £50 million. Issuers spent £7 million during the year simply rewarding vigilant shop staff handing over 'hot' cards.

Electronic swipe machines are helping to cut fraud, though it's still advisable to hang on to slips till your statement arrives – if only to ensure that a dishonest trader has not added an extra nought and turned your $80 dinner into an $800 debt at the stroke of a pen. Since cards are occasionally fraudulently used while lodged in a hotel safety deposit box, you can also double-check there has been no mischief afoot.

While work continues to develop biometric cards, which will use fingerprint or retina identity systems, card companies are becoming increasingly quick off the mark when it comes to checking out suspected card abuse. No-nonsense 24-hour fraud units now swing into action if purchases fall well outside a cardholder's usual spending pattern.

Losing your cards

Since you are unlikely to receive replacements for 24 to 48 hours you can minimize the inevitable hassle by taking the following steps:

- Never leave cards in cars or hotel rooms, where they are most at risk. Use your in-room safe.
- Don't be tempted to use your phone number as a code on the latter. If it's written on your registration card, it will be the first combination a crooked hotel employee tries.
- Treat your PIN (personal identification number) as top-secret. That means not writing it in your address book under the entry 'Mrs Pin'.
- Report card loss at once. Use a toll-free number or reverse the charges. Make sure replacements will be issued and delivered pronto.
- Cover your cards with a card protection plan. The cost is peanuts, and it takes just one toll-free call to invalidate all cards in the event of theft or loss.

While you are waiting for new cards, you may well be on your uppers in terms of ready finance. If so, your best bets are to:

- Contact your company to arrange for funds to be transmitted without delay. While wiring money abroad used to be akin to sending it by mule train, electronic banking means it can now be done within minutes.
- Try a bureau de change. Some offer an instant international money transfer facility, for which the sender normally picks up the tab. American Express has a useful MoneyGram service, enabling funds to be transmitted to some 12,000 worldwide locations.

- Go to your nearest consulate, if local contacts or colleagues cannot help. Although they won't advance emergency cash unless it's life-and-death, they can contact family or friends and provide other practical help.

Hidden card charges

Having your cards stolen and used on fraudulent spending sprees is not the only hazard you may face on your travels. There is also the business of late charges, which allows hotels to debit your account with charges even after you have checked out.

This so-called final audit facility is common where guests use the hotel's express check-out facility, which enables them to OK their bill on the in-room TV, then simply drop their keys off at reception when leaving. Since they will have provided a signed credit card imprint on arrival, the trader simply adds any charges overlooked at the time of departure – a final breakfast or mini-bar drinks, for instance – and completes the voucher later.

Not surprisingly, mistakes can occur – and disputes are clearly more difficult to resolve once you are back home on the other side of the world. It's vital to compare your monthly statement against the original bill, and check for discrepancies. Any late charges should be clearly itemized and entered as such on the voucher. If you suspect they are bogus, contact the card company without delay. The trader will then be asked to justify his or her position.

Card companies recognize that many travellers have misgivings about final audit facilities, and have in some cases revised their billing procedures. Visa operates a tracking system which checks complaints received, and says any hotel whose name recurs is automatically investigated.

Hotel credit blocks

Yet another moot point among credit cardholders is the hotel practice of blocking off their credit, to ensure there will be sufficient funds in the account to cover their likely bill. By calling the card company for authorization of the sum they anticipate will be spent, the hotel effectively cuts the cardholder's spending power at a stroke, leaving them at risk of having their card refused in restaurants and stores when charges overstep their remaining credit.

In some instances, a cardholder's credit may even be blocked off twice – once on arrival, and once on departure – if the earlier authorization is not cancelled when the final bill is totted up. Since smaller traders without electronic swipe machines may still rely on the post to submit vouchers, this can take days to put right. What's more, some travellers claim hoteliers try to block off credit for sums vastly higher than their likely bill. To minimize any inconvenience, you should:

- Ensure your card account is in credit before setting off. If you plan to use the card extensively, settle all outstanding charges and if possible pay in extra funds on top.
- Travel with a ceiling-free charge card, corporate or Gold card to maximize your spending power.
- Ensure that if after supplying a credit card imprint, you pay the bill by other means, the signed voucher is destroyed when you check out.
- Try asking the hotel how much they are estimating you will spend.

TIPPING

Knowing when and how to tip can be a headache even for seasoned travellers. Finding the right change, pressing it into the right hand, and being certain that you have neither grossly insulted the recipient nor handed over the equivalent of a month's wages is not always easy. Guidebooks offering advice are moreover usually out of date.

Failing to tip the right person can be as bad as mistakenly tipping the wrong one, as I discovered when trying to thank a nice young man who had carried my bags upstairs at a swish New York hotel. He turned out to be the assistant general manager.

Tipping customs vary greatly from country to country. Americans do it all the time – and handsomely. Japanese and Icelanders hardly bother. Australians and Britons do it in moderation, while cruisers at sea do enough of it to buy a weekend at Claridge's. Americans often tip the *maitre d'* as well as the waiter, while diners in Moscow tip the doorman just to be sure of a table.

Social minefield

Confusion reigns in restaurants, since some include a compulsory service charge, while others leave it to the guest's discretion. Yet more levy a charge, but leave a gap on your credit card bill in the hope that you will leave still more. Hotels can also be a tipping minefield, since there are room service waiters, parking attendants and porters to worry about – not to mention the concierge who manages to get tickets for a big match, or the butler who painstakingly presses your best suit.

Fortunately, those expecting a tip usually make it clear. The coach driver will invariably have a bold notice pinned above his head. The waiter will hover at the door, while the doorman who has hauled your bag out of the cab and carried it all of five yards will deposit it on the lobby floor and tell you that's as far as he goes. If you have just arrived and have nothing in your pocket but the equivalent of a $50 note, tell him you'll see him later. Avoid any awkwardness by:

- Checking out tipping guidelines in an up-to-date guidebook.
- Asking for some small-denomination notes when collecting currency from banks and bureaux de change.
- Keeping a wad of dollar notes handy. Packs of Marlboros are also welcomed in some countries.
- Not worrying. You won't get it right every time.

BRIBERY

Dash, baksheesh, chai – call it what you like – is a universal currency in parts of the world where bad management, bureaucracy and black economies flourish. Crossing the odd palm with silver to oil the wheels of business may be a necessity somewhere along the line.

Bribery comes in many forms. Every veteran Third World expatriate will swear by his local Mr Fixit – the chap who not only knows anyone worth knowing, but who can also get just about anything done. He's guaranteed to avert a police summons, arrange an audience with a minister, get hold of luxury items in short supply and have visas renewed within hours. Making sure he gets his reward will be worth every penny.

Other forms of bribery are less palatable. Every picture has its price in some parts of the world, where locals have learned how to milk snap-happy tourists with demands for money every time a shutter clicks. Elsewhere, officials may ask for payment (or a 'birthday present') before carrying out what is technically their job.

Tell-tale signals

Travellers unused to the tell-tale signals often fail to realize a bribe is being sought, and get bogged down in tiresome arguments as a result. Others hear the alarm bells ringing but refuse to accede on principle. Yet more cause red faces on both sides by offering money when it is the last thing on the other party's mind.

While bribery is an unsavoury business – and there's no doubt that every time you offer a bribe, you make it harder for the next person to avoid doing so – there are times when it is counter-productive not to. Difficult officials become downright intransigent, and seemingly trivial problems threaten to turn into major international incidents.

If an 'error' is discovered in your papers at the airport that threatens to debar you from entering the country, you can often resolve the situation by getting out your wallet and asking whether an on-the-spot fine is appropriate. The chances are that it will be. Passports are not infrequently handed over with a note or pack of cigarettes at some Indian and African airports, to avoid such problems.

Begging

To give or not to give – that's the dilemma. Despite the all too real poverty of the Third World, handing money to street beggars is not necessarily a good idea. You can end up under siege. You can also end up unwittingly contributing to a growing industry of takers – from children to sophisticated confidence tricksters. Try rewarding individuals for a genuine service rendered – even if it's just a few coins for the boy who watches your car while you pop inside for a meeting.

BARGAINING

Sooner or later you'll want to take home souvenirs from your travels. Whether we are talking about costly Persian rugs or cheap fake watches, you'll need to get to grips with the art of bargaining.

Haggling is *de rigueur* in many parts of the world. Even department stores are not averse to a little negotiating in the capitals of Asia, where traders in markets and bazaars rarely sell goods any other way. Since some shopkeepers will shamelessly treble the price as soon as they sniff a foreigner in the doorway, it makes sense to ensure you're not going to be taken for a ride the moment you reach for your wallet.

Knowing where to start is often the biggest problem. Before diving in with a ludicrously low offer, try and find out roughly what you should be paying in the first place. Compare prices in neighbouring shops or ask your contacts. Once you have countered the vendor's opening gambit with an offer of, say, half, both of you haggle it out till you agree on a fair price.

Striking a deal

A few well-tested techniques can improve your success rate:

- **Be an early bird.** It's a tradition in the East that the first customer of the day brings luck. Naturally, he or she also gets a good price.
- **Say you'd like a discount for cash.** And have it ready.
- **Ask for a trade discount.** Your credentials may not be questioned.
- **Play down your wealth.** Letting the shopkeeper know you are staying at the best place in town is inviting prices to match.
- **Beware of hospitality.** Once you are drinking tea with the trader's three cousins, it will be harder to say no.
- **Don't be over-aggressive.** Staying firm but good humoured gets better results.
- **Walk away.** The farther you go, the lower the price tends to fall. If not, the vendor's last offer was probably a good one – and you can always pop back later.
- **Take a local contact.** They will have a much better chance of getting the best price.
- **Don't get carried away.** Prices may be cheap, but are friends really going to thank you for Ali Baba slippers, Moroccan water pipes and colourful fez hats at Christmas?
- **Keep things in perspective.** Paying 50 pesos too much for a straw donkey is not the end of the world.

SHOPPING SPREES

Every big business capital has its meccas for shopaholics. You'll find them in droves snapping up antiques in London's Portobello Road, ponchos in Mexico City's Zona Rosa, cheap watches in Kuala Lumpur's Chinatown, bric-à-brac in the celebrated Paris flea markets, and fake Reeboks and Raybans in Bangkok's Silom Road.

Markets are the cheapest bets for presents, though don't expect anything to come with a five-star warranty. If the colour runs, the paint cracks or the fake Lacoste label drops off when you get home, tough. Stick to recognized dealers and get a receipt if you're after electronic goods.

Bogus antiques abound in the backstreets of Delhi, Taipei and Cairo, where it will be hard to tell the old from the newly minted. Tempting buys can also include antiques, weapons or endangered species you are not allowed to take out of the country or bring back home. Banned items regularly seized at UK airports include python skins, ivory necklaces, live parakeets, stun guns, CS gas canisters and ceremonial daggers.

Stick to recognized dealers if you plan to have your goods shipped home. Horror stories abound of those who part with their money in good faith and never see their bargains again. Others can receive unexpected bills from local shipping agents that add up to more than the cost of the goods.

The real thing?

Buy fakes strictly for fun, and don't be surprised to find a Made in China label on the back of your authentic-looking Buddha when you get home. Pick up the vouchers from tax-free stores for reclaiming VAT at the airport, and remember that tax-free goods – among them perfumes, jewellery, make-up, electronic goods and cameras – won't be such good bargains as duty-free liquor and tobacco, which come free of tax, Customs and excise duties.

CLAIMING EXPENSES

While some companies wouldn't dream of asking travellers to account for every last rouble, zloty or yen, others go strictly by the book. Some provide take-it-or-leave-it daily allowances, while others refund strictly against receipts – regardless of whether your Mexican cab driver had ever heard of them.

Whether to protect their guests from the temptations of free-rein expense claims or to save themselves from nit-picking queries, hotels now break down their bills into tedious detail, revealing not simply what you ate every night but the time, and frequency, with which you extracted bags of peanuts from your mini-bar. Supper for two on room service with a bottle of house champers will be unsparingly shown for all to see – though most hotels resist the temptation to note that you spent the evening watching re-runs of *Nymphets Whipped into Shape*.

Bear in mind that crooked expenses can spell trouble at home, as well as at the office. The TV show 'Whicker Down Under' once mentioned an Australian brothel which billed clients as the Mammasan Bistro on credit card slips in order to spare their blushes.

Inevitably, the item was watched with great interest by a lady who instantly recognized the name from her husband's credit card bills. Boldly challenged, he managed to convince her that joke-playing colleagues had made off with his cards and gone there instead.

TAILPIECES

- Travellers rightly get annoyed with cash dispensers that eat up their cards without coughing up a nickel. One London policeman was even more chagrined recently to realize that he would not simply be left without cash for the night, but that he had just fed in his brand new warrant card.

- Cartier spends more than $5 million a year in its battle to fight counterfeiters. The company employs over 40 full-time lawyers and currently has over 3,000 litigations pending worldwide.

- Travellers' cheques were invented in 1891 – the year thermos flasks were invented, beer mats were patented, toothpaste went on sale in a tube and Tchaikovsky wrote the *Nutcracker Suite*. American Express takes the credit.

11
☐ In the Pink

International travel may broaden the mind, but it can play havoc with your insides. Falling prey to a bout of the Rangoon runs or Tokyo trots is no laughing matter when you're 5,000 miles from home and due to address your firm's number one foreign client in an hour's time.

Sickness abroad is bad news for both you and your company. It can not only run up a daunting bill, but ruin a well-planned trip. Yet research suggests that frequent flyers used to boarding planes at the drop of a hat can be astonishingly blasé about health risks and are often less well prepared than your average holidaymaker.

What's more, travelling executives often work harder away than at home. Under pressure to complete a deal or pack in dawn-to-dusk appointments, they can eat, drink and smoke far more than usual as meetings and mealtimes overlap.

Staying on top demands five-star fitness – not always easy, given a cocktail of stress and five-star living – but you can improve your chances of staying in the pink by observing some golden rules. Complacency is the biggest killer in the book.

IMMUNIZATIONS

While World Health Organization figures show that traffic accidents are the leading cause of death among travellers, plenty more have succumbed over the years to diseases that would have been preventable but for a jab in the arm.

Failing to ensure you are properly immunized against common fatal diseases is foolishness of the first order. Call a travel immunization centre or consult your travel agent to see which shots are needed for your next trip. Family doctors can be out-of-date when it comes to giving advice, while national tourist offices often play down the risks.

Remember, some inoculations do not take immediate effect – a yellow fever jab is not valid for up to ten days – while others, such as rabies, may require more than one trip to the surgery. Keep a record of all injections, since they can have a cumulative effect.

Diseases for which vaccinations may be required include:

Yellow fever
Endemic in parts of Africa and central America, this originates in monkeys and is transmitted by mosquito bites. Immunization is highly effective, and lasts ten years.

Cholera
Acquired from contaminated food or water, cholera is rare but can cause death within hours in extreme cases. Vaccines offer only partial protection, and last for only three to six months.

Tetanus
Cuts and wounds from animals or thorns can lead to tetanus, for which many children are now routinely vaccinated at home. The booster lasts ten years.

Hepatitis A
Now a common travellers' hazard, this viral disease of the liver causes lethargy and jaundice. A shot of gammaglobulin before departure gives short-term protection. However, it is vital this is HIV screened. Better vaccines are now being developed.

Hepatitis B
Transmitted through body fluids, hepatitis B is 100 times easier to catch than AIDS. While early symptoms resemble flu, victims can end up off work for months. A course of three injections provides at least three years' immunity.

Typhoid
Sometimes fatal if untreated, typhoid starts with flu-like symptoms. The vaccine can lead to a sore arm and fever, though pills are now coming on the market.

Polio
Contracted from infected water, polio can cause paralysis. The vaccine is highly effective, and usually taken in a sugar lump.

Rabies
An animal viral infection that causes delirium and convulsions, rabies is untreatable once symptoms have developed. While an effective vaccine exists, it is normally reserved for those working with animals.

Bilharzia
This is transmitted by larvae living in stagnant water, which burrow through the skin and reproduce in the internal organs, causing kidney and other infections. A vaccine may soon be on the market, though the disease can be treated with drugs.

Japanese encephalitis
Inoculations are available to combat this serious viral infection caught from mosquito bites, as well as meningococcal meningitis, a rare but potentially fatal infection of the brain and spinal cord.

Other diseases
No injections are necessary for smallpox, now officially eradicated worldwide, or for TB. Travellers can also strike diphtheria off the danger list, since most people receive adequate immunization during childhood.

Malaria

Far from being stamped out, malaria is on the rise worldwide. It is now thought to account for up to a million deaths a year, and was contracted by 2,300 people returning to the UK during 1991 alone. Some unfortunates have become victims during even the briefest stopovers abroad.

Transmitted by mosquito bites (also a cause of dengue fever, which is occasionally fatal), malaria is endemic in tropical Africa and parts of South America. It comes in two strains, both of which exhibit initial flu-like symptoms – later turning to fever, shivering and violent diarrhoea – which may not start for weeks or even months after the traveller's return home. For this reason it is often wrongly diagnosed by doctors, and can kill with vicious speed in extreme cases.

Anyone travelling to a country where the disease is prevalent should take daily or weekly antimalarial pills. Newer brands like Lariam are now gaining favour over older ones like Nivaquine and Avloclor as it becomes clear that mosquitoes are fast developing resistance to chloroquine – traditionally prescribed to combat malaria.

Guard against being bitten in the first place by using insect repellents and keeping legs and arms covered in the evening. If you're staying at a less than pristine address, invest in a plug-in vaporizing mat, mosquito coils or a mosquito net impregnated with DEET.

ANIMAL NASTIES

The thought of encountering snakes, scorpions and eight-legged foes can cause some travellers more angst than the prospect of coming down with TB or dengue fever. However, bites are rarely fatal, and the dangers are in general greatly exaggerated. If you are keen to get off the beaten track and camp out in the bush, take advice from the locals. They'll be a far better judge of animal hazards than you.

GETTING ADVICE

British Airways runs more than 30 franchised travel clinics around the UK offering health advice, immunizations and supplies of useful items. Thomas Cook also runs an excellent immunization centre at its main London outlet.

MASTA, the London-based Medical Advisory Service for Travellers Abroad, also advises on jabs and other health precautions, keeping clients' immunization records on computer and sending reminders when necessary. It keeps a computerized databank, updated daily, on health hazards in more than 230 countries, to which on-line company subscribers have 24-hour access. Personal health briefs can be ordered using the Travellers' Health Line.

Detailed information on inoculations and other health matters can also be had from books such as Dr Richard Dawood's *Travellers' Health*, or John Hatt's *The Tropical Traveller*. Some airlines supply medical factsheets on request, while travel agencies within the EC are now required to supply clients with information on health hazards, if asked.

STOMACH UPSETS

The chances are that you will be struck down with a bout of the traveller's trots – also known as Delhi belly, Cairo curse and the Aztec two-step – at some stage. Stomach upsets are on the cards for almost anyone without cast-iron innards, and can play havoc with a busy meetings schedule.

Four out of ten international travellers are hit by stomach bugs abroad, with a third of those confined to bed and many more obliged to alter their plans. Flying first class and staying at the best place in town is no copper-bottomed guarantee against gastric upsets, which can strike at short notice and turn a productive trip into a nightmare.

While four out of five cases of diarrhoea clear up in a few days, others can lead to dysentery and other debilitating conditions. Salmonella victims can easily end up on the danger list, and any prolonged stomach troubles should be checked out with a doctor.

Commonsense rules

If your stomach has a tendency to play up, you should:

- **Avoid tap water** – both for drinking and teeth-cleaning. Stick to fizzy, rather than still bottled brands, since the latter can easily be refilled from the tap. Skip the ice in your G and T.
- Follow the dictum **cook it, peel it or leave it**. Unless you can vouch for the chef, that means no salads and strawberries.
- **Steer clear of shellfish and underdone meat** – including your rare T-bone.
- **Avoid food kept warm for long periods** on a buffet. Make sure yours is freshly cooked.
- **Veer towards veggies**. Meat can harbour some of the worst bacterial nasties. I turned vegetarian in China, where the meat resembled boiled chow, and stayed fighting fit.
- **Skip the dollops of ice cream, mayonnaise and coleslaw**. They are a frequent source of salmonella.
- **Resist the temptation to nibble at roadside stalls**. Singapore's rigorously checked hawker food stalls are an exception.

In theory, diarrhoea is best treated by letting your system clear itself out for a few days with plenty of fluids. In practice, waiting for nature to take its course can be a trial. If you're on a short, pressurized trip, keep a supply of stop-you-up pills such as Imodium, Arret or Diareze handy. While many doctors don't recommend the stronger remedies (those containing clioquinol, like Enterovioform, have now lost favour), they will at least see you through an important meeting.

Stick to plain, non-greasy foods for a few days, avoid milk and take plenty of soft drinks. Rehydration remedies such as Dioralyte can also be useful; otherwise try adding a teaspoon of salt and eight heaped teaspoons of sugar to a litre of water.

SUN HAZARDS

Even the sun can be the traveller's number one enemy at times. Fail to heed the warnings about mad dogs and the midday sun, and you could end up in bed with sunburn, heatstroke or – at some time in the future – skin cancer. Don't underestimate the sun's power – buy some sunscreen, wear a hat and tan s-l-o-w-l-y.

Numerous off-the-shelf remedies (aloe vera gel being one of the best) can be bought to soothe sunburn. Heatstroke – symptomized by a temperature and nausea after being out in the sun – is another matter. Take an aspirin to lower your temperature, drink plenty of fluids and use ice packs or a cold bath to cool down.

Skin cancer is another good reason to give the midday sun a wide berth. More than half a million Americans are treated for it every year (President Reagan being one well-publicized victim), and there is growing evidence that holes in the ozone layer may soon make it even more common. Moles that are itchy or inflamed can signify malignant cancers and spread to other parts of the body if untreated.

BUYING DRUGS

Take care if buying pills and potions overseas – fakes abound in some parts of the world. Many of the big pharmaceutical groups have been through lengthy court battles to stop cheap counterfeit drugs flooding Third World shops and markets, but have yet to stamp out the pirates.

Skilfully packaged fakes have included eye drops capable of causing blindness in Nigeria, sub-standard polio vaccines in Lebanon, medicated shampoos containing petrol and water, and products found to contain chalk instead of penicillin. Churned out in unhygienic factories and sold at huge profit, they can fool consumers and pharmacists alike. Make sure you buy any medical supplies from a reputable dealer.

AIDS AND HIV

The dangers of casual sex are now so well publicized that few travellers can be unaware of the risks involved. AIDS has advanced ominously in recent years, and travellers abroad are 100 times more likely to contract the disease than the stay-at-homes they leave behind.

While sufferers in the West are predominantly male homosexuals and drug users, AIDS is now well entrenched in the heterosexual communities of many parts of Africa. More than 13 million people worldwide are now thought to carry the virus.

If celibacy is out of the question, it's clearly vital to minimize the risks attached to having sex with someone whose bedroom track record you know next to nothing about. Failing to use a condom is madness. If you've missed the shops, try having a discreet word with the concierge.

Medical risks

Sex is not the only way to come home HIV positive, of course. The dangers of receiving medical or dental treatment involving unscreened blood and contaminated syringes cannot be underestimated. Recent studies indicate that in many parts of the world, less than half of all donated blood is guaranteed HIV free. Receiving some can also be a shortcut to contracting hepatitis B.

If you're unlucky enough to end up on a Third World operating table, there may be little you can do but say your prayers, of course. If not, make sure you are treated only with thoroughly sterilized or disposable hypodermic needles, syringes and razors. If an emergency blood transfusion is on the cards, colleagues or friends should at least try and ensure you are being treated in a reputable hospital. It's useful to keep a note of your blood group.

AIDS travel kits

Packs containing syringes, needles, dressings and other sterile medical items – commonly called AIDS kits – are now widely on sale for travellers visiting high-risk parts of the world. UK residents can buy one from MASTA (see above), which also sells other useful items, and from firms such as Homeway and Nomad.

Britain's Department of Health now distributes *Travel Safe* leaflets aimed at helping travellers minimize the risks of contracting HIV overseas, and giving a list of golden rules. These include only buying good quality condoms, and avoiding all unnecessary medical and dental treatment.

HEALTH INSURANCE

Don't just rely on pills – make sure you have adequate company medical cover. Some experts recommend having up to £2 million of health insurance if you are visiting the US, where your first treatment may well be a wallet biopsy. Some clinics will refuse to admit you unless you can settle your bills on the spot, and many travellers have been bankrupted by having to pay up single-handedly for costly treatment or emergency repatriation.

While travel insurance is often sold on a per-trip basis, it makes sense to opt for a renewable year-round policy. *Executive Travel* magazine's Executive Club International offers cost-effective worldwide health cover, while IAPA's worldwide personal accident programme offers up to $2 million protection. See Chapter 3 for more details.

EC nationals are entitled to free or reduced-cost emergency medical care when visiting other EC states and certain countries where reciprocal agreements exist. Details are given in the free UK government booklet *Health Advice for Travellers*, which can be ordered via the freephone Health Literature line.

JETLAG

Globetrotting would be a cinch if we could re-set our body clocks as simply as our wristwatches the minute we set foot on foreign soil. Annoyingly, it's anything but the case. New technology may have shrunk the planet into a global village, but you still can't get from one side to the other without feeling out of kilter for days at a time. Hardly the best prelude for a series of high-powered business meetings.

Jetlag can make you irritable, fatigued and disorientated for days at a time. You're liable to lose concentration, cat-nap during meetings, feel ravenous at three in the afternoon, and then spend half the night doing *The Times* crossword. Eight out of ten people experience it in some form or another.

Time zone traumas

The traumas of time travel are triggered by disruption to the body's circadian rhythms – our patterns of waking, feeding and sleeping. These are in turn related to our senses of balance, co-ordination, reaction time and memory. Throw these rhythms out of step and our internal clock is thrown into turmoil.

Jetlag is linked to geographic time zones rather than distance. While flying from Johannesburg to London – only two hours apart in time terms – should leave you feeling no worse for wear, travelling from Tokyo to New York – a time difference of 14 hours – will leave you out of sorts for days. Jetlag is generally worse going east, when clocks are put forward, though your body theoretically needs 24 hours to recover for every time zone crossed.

Beating your body clock

Pre-flight diets are the answer, according to some experts. American doctors Ehret and Scanlon, authors of *Overcoming Jet Lag*, have devised a feast-and-fast diet to be stuck to for three days prior to departure. However, there is little conclusive proof that it actually works.

Using gadgets ...

Electronic gadgets are also claimed to beat jetlag. You can buy a pocket-sized Bioclok for around £80, designed to analyse flight plan timings and tell you which hours to stay in darkness or light after you land. Alternatively, you can invest in Acu-Health, a hand-held device using acupuncture techniques that passes a tiny electrical current into key points on the skin through a slender metal probe.

Research is underway into the use of the neuro-hormone melatonin, regarded as something of a seasonal synchronizer in the animal world. Triggering breeding and other cycles, it is thought to act as the main control on our biological clocks. While tests involving melatonin on animals have shown that dramatic adjustments to the body's natural clock can be made, what's good for hamsters is not necessarily good for humans. Jet travellers may have to wait a few more years before fully tested melatonin-based jetlag tablets go on sale.

... or essential oils

Aromatherapy, which uses the aromatic essential oils of plants, may help slow down or speed up your system as you are being catapulted through time zones. Try a few drops of lavender on your pillow or in a hot bath before you retire, with rosemary or basil on your wrists and temples to get you going in the morning.

Air New Zealand and Virgin are among the airlines now promoting aromatherapy. Virgin's in-flight masseurs use aromatherapy-based products, while ANZ's premium-fare passengers receive a free after-flight regulator kit containing 'Awake' and 'Asleep' essences. Designed to last three days, they are used in the bath or shower, according to the time zone you've arrived in. Also promoted by Brazilian carrier Varig, they can now be bought at the world's first jetlag shop – Daniele Ryman Ltd – at London's Park Lane hotel.

JAL passengers can down a glass of vitamin-packed 'Sky Time' brew, containing kiwi fruit extract and energy-giving royal jelly, or try out a humidity-promoting honeycomb mask. Guests staying at the Ritz in Paris can step into its Ozotherm machine, which claims to help jetlagged guests meet the demands of fast-track living with a mixture of hydrotherapy and aromatherapy. However, at least one user has compared the experience to going through the fast-rinse cycle of a washing machine.

Introducing jetlag hotels

Research is underway into the ways that light and dark – the most powerful social cues in moving the hands on our body clock – can be used to accelerate zonal adjustment. It seems that controlled post-flight exposure to bright lights and dark could do the trick, helping to iron out the peaks and troughs in our daily circadian rhythm. So convincing is the theory, that some forward-looking hotels now offer their guests the sleep–wake treatments promoted by US-based company Circadian Travel Technologies (CTT).

At the Tudor in New York and the Rembrandt in London, for instance, special rooms fitted with blackout curtains to banish daylight and bright lights to simulate artificial sunshine can create midnight, dawn or high noon as needed. Would-be inmates can purchase a CTT trip guide before setting off, giving an hour-by-hour plan for light exposure for the duration of their trip.

Light–dark DIY therapy

If the kitty won't stretch to customized jetlag-beating accommodation, you can at least try some DIY light–dark therapy. Experts advocate travelling eastbound early in the day, then dining and turning in when the locals do. Westbound journeys should start later (preferably after a morning lie-in), to minimize tiredness during what will be an elongated evening.

However, let's say you've just stepped off the body-sapping red-eye from New York to London. It's 8am local time, and your body clock reads 3 in the morning. Don your Raybans and avoid bright light before midmorning if possible, then have a couple of hours of fresh air before lunch.

Going back to New York, take a mid-afternoon flight that arrives early evening – already midnight on your body clock. Resist the temptation to turn in, and try to get a few hours' daylight exposure before heading to bed after nine. If you wake (as you surely will) before 5am, keep the room dark and rest with your eyes shut till it's time to get up.

Anti-jetlag drill

Following the basic commonsense measures below will also help:

- **Stay on home time** for very short trips, sticking to your usual sleeping and eating routines.
- **On longer trips**, set your watch to destination time when you board the plane and start adjusting your resting and eating patterns to suit. A short-acting mild sleeping tablet will help you get some rest at the right time. On arrival, try to eat and sleep when the locals do, rather than when your body feels like it.
- **Don't get dehydrated** in-flight. Resist the temptations of endless alcoholic drinks and coffees, since both are major dehydrators. Stick to mineral water or orange juice – ideally a glass every hour.
- **Take some exercise**. Stretch your legs every hour or so in the plane, and take some exercise on arrival – whether a jog, a workout or a brisk stroll. Physical activity oxygenates the blood, shakes off lethargy and helps speed up the time zone adjustment process.
- **Travel first or business class** if budgets permit. Ten hours stretched out in a roomy sleeperette-style seat will leave you in far finer fettle than the same time squeezed in the back of the plane.
- **Don't expect peak performance** if you have just flown halfway around the globe. That one-degree-under feeling is certain to last for a bit. Keep important meetings for the next day.

IN-FLIGHT FITNESS

Long-range B747 and Airbus jets have made stopovers redundant on many routes, paving the way for even longer hours of sedentary tedium for trans-continental travellers. Rather than pace up and down the aisle like a caged lion, you can try practising some of the in-flight mini exercise programmes now being promoted by a number of carriers.

Lufthansa, Northwest and British Airways have devised a series of airline flyrobics – illustrated on videos and literature – designed to combat the effects of immobility and flex the muscles, boost circulation and release tension. Most are a matter of commonsense stretching and flexing – doing a bit of imaginary jogging and rowing on the spot, arching your back, rotating your ankles and circling your shoulders. The problem is that most people feel a bit of a Charlie actually doing them.

Choosing a smoke-free flight may also help, since tobacco fumes, coupled with poor in-flight ventilation and dry cabin air, are often to blame for headaches, sore eyes and lethargy – not to mention flu next day from other people's recycled germs. Air Canada and Virgin both offer smoke-free travel across the Pond, while most domestic US flights now ban the dreaded weed.

Wear glasses instead of your contact lenses and use a moisturizer on your face and hands to prevent your skin drying out. You could even invest in a Humidiflyer – a strap-on mask made in Australia that filters out dust and smoke – if you don't mind raising a few eyebrows.

Dressing for comfort

Remember, too, that although glossy airline advertisements imply that everyone flying upfront is power-dressed for the occasion, you'll be much more comfortable in loose clothing. While they are not very glamorous, your feet will be happier in those little woolly airline sockettes than in tight shoes. Use the blinkers and Do Not Disturb stickers in your comfort kit if you want to sleep.

Various patches, potions and pills are now available for anyone prone to feeling queasy during turbulence, though your faithfully supplied airsickness bag in the seat pocket will be on hand in emergency. Aromatherapy fans say sniffing peppermint or lavender oil on a tissue can also help beat the problem.

More prevalent is discomfort and pain in the ears when descending – often acute if you have a cold or sinus problems. Chewing sweets or gum, yawning or swallowing will normally prevent pressure building up in your ears. If that doesn't do the trick, use a decongestant or squirt a few drops of Otrivine in your nose before and during take-off and descent. Users say it works a treat.

Fear of flying

Some of us are doomed to be permanent members of the white-knuckle brigade. One in two travellers experience fear of flying, whether it's simply mild anxiety or sheer unquenchable panic. Lurid media coverage of plane crashes does little to quell the secret fear, lurking inside even the most blasé traveller, of being the one-in-a-million victim of an engine failure, fire or mid-air collision.

Airphobia is reckoned to be the third most common fear, after spiders and social situations. Even a mild case can lead to tension and sweaty palms as the aircraft is buffeted by bad weather or a sudden change in air speed. Serious sufferers are known to start sobbing, lock themselves in the loo or even try to hurl themselves off the plane. One or two have started hammering their way through the windows at 35,000 feet to do just that.

How do you put the fright to flight? Maurice Yaffe's book *Taking the*

Fear out of Flying should prove a useful bedtime read for starters. If paranoia still rises at the thought of taking off, try a one-day Fearful Flyers course, when an experienced pilot will give you a reassuring talk, show you some relaxation exercises and take you on a short flight with others far more scared than you.

Relax Air and Aviatours run courses in the UK, though most national carriers should be able to refer you to an operator. Hypnosis can also be very successful in helping fearful flyers. If a course of that fails, you'd better face the fact that your best bet is a clinical psychologist's couch.

If it's more a case of mild butterflies than major panic, playing a relaxation tape before boarding will help. Many sufferers feel happier in an aisle seat close to the exit, and say that having a drink or two before take-off helps. Visiting the cockpit and learning more about the way the flight crew work can also be helpful. And remember, pilots are subject to more health and performance checks than even world-class athletes.

TAILPIECES

- Travellers flying overnight from the States to Europe can now buy a $380 anti-jetlag Combat Kit, complete with dark specs to banish daylight and a visor with tiny lights underneath to simulate it. Let's hope it meets with more success than the welder's goggles worn to ward off morning sunlight by a Harvard medical student arriving at Heathrow. He was promptly marched off by airport security guards.

- Fearful flyers will no doubt identify instantly with George S Kaufman's verdict on air travel: 'I like terra firma – the more firma, the less terra!'

- Sign spotted in a Kampala hotel bedroom: 'Condoms are available in the staff clinic. Please call if the need arises.' And at a Bangkok drycleaner's: 'Drop your trousers here for best results' (*Executive Travel*).

12
☐ The Female Factor

Being woken by the telephone at 3 in the morning is not exactly fun – especially when it's the night porter calling up to see whether you fancy a bit of nocturnal company. But as a businesswoman travelling alone, it's one of the hazards you may well face sooner or later. Never mind coping with jetlag, missed flight connections and a hectic meetings schedule – as a solo female traveller, you'll have a whole lot more to contend with as well.

Whether it's the Lothario in pinstripes propping up the hotel bar, the toffee-nosed *maitre d'* who reckons any unchaperoned female is on the game, the barman who thinks it's OK to make a pass over the salted nuts, or the bellboy who lets the entire lobby know your room number, headaches galore can lie in store for today's unwary woman traveller. Learning some sensible survival tactics is a must.

WOMEN – A GROWING MARKET

Twenty years ago, female business travellers were treated rather like aliens from Mars. Now, the hand that rocks the cradle is increasingly the one that picks up the room key. The number of women travelling on business has rocketed in the last two decades. *The New York Times* forecast back in 1988 that by the year 2000 half the world's corporate travellers would be women. In the States, they've almost reached that point already.

Women now make up nearly 20 per cent of the UK business travel market. They account for one in four Holiday Inn guests – a figure projected to double by the turn of the century – and nearly half the guests at Marriott hotels. Some 14 per cent of British Airways Club World customers were women in 1992.

Hotels and airlines now acknowledge that they ignore the needs of the female market at their peril. Today's woman executive wields not only a string of credit cards, but formidable corporate buying power besides.

La dolce vita?

Despite the female market's rapid growth, life on the road for today's single woman executive is often anything but *la dolce vita*. Businesswomen may be mushrooming in the boardroom, but they'll be treated like the Invisible Man by the bar staff at a smart hotel. Many, not surprisingly, feel they get a raw deal on their travels.

When a business women's travel club was launched in Britain in the late 1980s, nearly two-thirds of new members claimed to have suffered some form of unpleasant experience on their travels. Hotels were slated for slapdash security and insensitivity. Airlines took the rap for offhand cabin service, ticketing all passengers as Mr, doling out amenity kits packed with razors and shaving foam, and making women less than welcome in airport lounges.

Members cited being ignored or asked for dates by hotel staff, treated like off-duty stewardesses by cabin crew, followed down solitary corridors and having to use unguarded, badly-lit carparks. One traveller, terrified when a man burst into her bedroom at night, discovered her room number had been passed on by the doorman.

Gender on the agenda

While efforts to put gender on the agenda have undoubtedly paid off, the slate has not been entirely wiped clean. In a pan-European survey carried out in late 1992 on behalf of Official Airline Guides, 86 per cent of UK respondents said that most business hotel rooms were not geared to the needs of women, while 59 per cent felt airport lounges were designed with only men in mind.

Some blame the gender stereotypes used in glossy travel advertising for failing to further the cause of independent women travellers. The suave-looking businessman picking up the keys to his hired Porsche from a dishy blonde, or being fussed over in the air by seductive Singapore Girl, is a familiar figure. The same can't be said of the dashing Mr Universe ushering an equally suave female exec to the door of her hired limo – though Virgin, it has to be said, has come refreshingly close.

PROBLEMS AND PITFALLS

Women's problems fall into roughly three areas. They can be practical – needing an ironing board or a make-up mirror, for instance. They can concern security – having to negotiate gloomy corridors, carparks or subways. They can also be intangible, such as having to put up with hassle, inconvenience or second-rate service.

Practical problems remain widespread. It's a fact that while trouser presses and razor sockets are standard fare in the hotel world, skirt hangers, hairdryers and irons – typically wanted by women – are more elusive. To add to the problem, electrical sockets are invariably 10 feet away from the nearest mirror.

Lack of discretion

Safety remains another common headache. Few women feel secure in a room that lacks a chain, deadlock or spyhole on the door. The fact that most hotel locks – including many electronic types – can be slipped in seconds by a determined thief, does little to induce a sense of wellbeing.

Lack of discretion over room numbers has yet to be erased. Too many hotels still have the porter who calls them out for all to hear, the waiters who demand them instead of simply asking for a signature, the switchboard operator who hands them out freely to callers, or the front desk clerk who slaps down room keys, number face up.

Intangible problems are often the hardest to define, and the trickiest to deal with. Many hotels still have restaurant staff capable of driving the most confident woman upstairs with a tray supper. Poor tables (those next to the kitchen are favourites), noisy male diners and slow service ('Weren't you waiting for someone?') remain commonplace.

Matters can be even worse when a woman decides to entertain. Despite booking the table, choosing the wine and requesting the bill, her male guest ends up tasting the Sancerre and being presented with the bill. Both parties have fortunately developed a wry sense of humour about it all.

Ladies or tramps?

Female executives also risk being mistaken for women seeking to do business of a very different kind. Ordering a drink in a hotel known to be a favoured haunt of local ladies of the night can often lead to unwanted propositions from other guests, being pointedly ignored by staff, or even asked to leave.

London's Metropolitan Police says that, while there are incidents of bona fide hotel guests being asked to leave top West End hotels (the wife of a well-known UK travel company boss was recently ushered out of the Ritz), most staff suspicious of a woman's motives in waiting alone will simply keep an eye on her. They are more likely to enquire if she's waiting for someone, says the Met, than to be in any way insulting.

FINDING A FEMALE-FRIENDLY HOTEL

With research showing that women are more likely than men to regard their hotel as a genuine home-from-home – staying in at night and making greater use of room service, fitness centres and other amenities – both big chains and independents are now keen to convince customers they are female-friendly.

Most are well aware that women travellers are not, of course, identical in their needs and behaviour. They can range from the assertive, dominant type – nicknamed Boardroom Barbara in a Ramada hotels survey some years ago – to the mouse-like junior making her first trip away from home. But whatever their style, the fact is that many women used to calling the shots at home can feel singularly ill at ease on their travels.

Most hotels have abandoned the rose-on-the-pillow approach of the '80s. Women-only floors and guestrooms decked out in pinks, pastels and florals are largely history. The trend now is to ensure that guestrooms cater well for every traveller. Feminine frills and gimmicks have given way to practical extras like multi-use hangers, hairdryers and well located extra sockets. Many hotel rooms now have dual shaving/make-up mirrors and a wider range of soaps and skincare products, in addition to spyholes and chains on the door.

Hotel designers have taken on board the fact that not even men wish to sleep in a bedroom that feels like the MD's office. Yesterday's officious-looking steel lamps and tobacco-brown swivel chairs have given way to pastel rag-washed walls, country-house fabrics and squashy sofas.

Bar areas are becoming less of a gentleman's club than a comfortable lounge with magazines, coffee tables and easy chairs. Fitness facilities have been enhanced, while restaurants offer lighter dining alternatives to once-standard meat-and-potatoes fare. More chains are also providing irons for anyone needing to steam the creases out of a jacket without paying through the nose or waiting all night.

Discreet security

Despite this overtly even-handed approach to the sexes, hotels often take discreet steps to ensure their female guests enjoy added security. Many have a policy of allocating women rooms close to the lift area, offering to escort them upstairs on check-in or to vet incoming calls. Some see to it that if a male waiter delivers room service to a female guest, he props the door open till he leaves.

Larger chains have also tackled the thorny issue of staff attitudes – not easy in cultures where the male/female status quo is very different from that in the West – with training videos and workshops highlighting the needs and concerns of female travellers. Staff are taught to spot, and deal with, unwanted male pests, and to help women feel at home.

Helplines and hairdryers

Holiday Inn promise female travellers prompt attention in reception, bar and restaurant areas, a choice of room location, and the option to have external telephone calls screened. A 24-hour Helpline is available for emergencies, while extras such as an iron, bathrobe or spare tights are supplied on request. Reading material is made available in restaurants and bars.

Hyatt rooms now feature skirt presses, hairdryers, full-length mirrors, retractable clothes lines, hair sprays and facial creams. Ramada also tries hard, describing its policy as 'addressing women's needs without making them feel wrapped in cotton wool'. Female restaurant guests are seated against a wall or mirror, rather than surrounded by fresh air. Those using the bar are consulted, should a man wish to buy them a drink.

Britain's Forte Crest chain, 17 per cent of whose guests are women, has confidently bucked the trend away from conspicuously branded products with its Lady Crest rooms. These feature brighter, lighter decor, a bigger bed (why, no one's saying), fresh fruit, women's magazines and a dedicated range of toiletries. There is an adjustable make-up mirror, an iron and ironing board, plus an L-shaped desk with flip-up lid that doubles as a dressing table.

Take-up rates for Lady Crest rooms are high, says the chain – and not just by women. It seems that men, who frequently request one of the rooms, are just as keen to snuggle down with their free copy of *Cosmopolitan* and get their hands on an ironing board.

Executive floors

Hotel executive floors, with their hotel-within-a-hotel concept, have proved a godsend to the female traveller. Comfortable and secure, they also come with private lounges – usually serving complimentary breakfast – where conversations can be struck up in a relaxed way, and drinks can be enjoyed without having to do battle in the main bar.

Hilton has executive floors at more than 70 properties worldwide, charging a typical premium of $50 a night. Some provide free local phone calls, personal computers and small meeting rooms, while most offer extra in-room amenities such as bathrobes and slippers. Ramada's Renaissance brand has club floors offering lounges with free refreshments, reading material and an honour bar.

At the top end of the scale, Ritz-Carlton's Club floors are accessed by a special lift key and offer a private drawing room, dedicated concierge and all-day drinks and refreshments. Hyatt's Regency Club floors, which are particularly popular with women guests, are accessible only by a special pass key and offer boardrooms and lounges.

In Asia, Shangri-La has 15 executive Horizon floors, where guests pay a 15–30 per cent room rate premium, while the giant Imperial Queen's Park hotel in Bangkok has two women-only floors. Three floors of mini-offices have also been built for those wishing to avoid conducting business from their rooms. See also p126.

Dining comfort

Chains such as Hyatt and Marriott now have small tables complete with reading lamp, notepaper and magazines, to help single diners of either sex feel more at home. Others ask single female diners if they would like to share their table with another to avoid eating alone.

One potentially good idea which has been tried with mixed success is that of a captain's table, at which single travellers can dine together. London's Langham Hilton tried the concept and abandoned it after a few months, claiming that most guests either met colleagues in the evening, were happy to eat alone or preferred a room service supper anyway.

Most hotels confirm that female guests are now happier to dine alone and are more confident travellers in every way than even a few years ago. As Marriott hotels put it: 'The difference between business travellers now is not their sex, but their experience. The more experienced they become, the fewer problems they encounter. So the more women travel, the better it becomes.'

Women at the helm

Does a woman general manager make a hotel more female-friendly? Indirectly, yes. Female GMs are often more approachable, better listeners and more likely to influence staff attitudes than their male counterparts. Since many also have a better eye for detail, they may be more likely to ensure that guests don't need to be left-handed acrobats to use hairdryers or sockets.

London hotels managed by women at the time of writing include the Sheraton Belgravia, Conrad Chelsea Harbour and Mayfair Inter-

Continental. They also include the 28-room Beaufort Hotel, whose owner Diana Wallis gives guests their own front door key, puts Walkmans and hairdryers in the rooms and has compiled her own tried-and-tested restaurant guide where female diners should feel at ease. Drinks are free, and resident cat Harry is on hand to provide no-strings male company.

TRIALS IN THE AIR

If hotels often earn black marks from their female clientele, airlines fare little better. Straw polls show that women are more likely to be challenged walking into a business class lounge, more likely to be seated next to bawling babies on board and less likely to be fussed over by cabin crew.

While Asian stewardesses – well known for cosseting male passengers while ignoring the women next to them – can be some of the worst culprits, western flight attendants are far from blameless. Flying upfront once with the late Pan Am, I was studiously ignored by cabin staff for the first hour of the flight. After finding my own seat, putting my own coat away, finding my own newspapers and fetching my own drink, I gave up and decided to get on with some work. As the briefcase came out, the service switched on as if by magic as it dawned on the crew that I might be a bona fide passenger instead of an off-duty stewardess. Needless to say, by that time I had written them off as a disaster.

British Airways says crew are told never to assume that if a man and woman are seated together, he's automatically in charge. 'Our staff are taught that whether they are colleagues or a couple, she may well be the boss,' says a spokesman. 'The problem is that this policy could cause offence with passengers from countries with an unequivocal men-first culture – so we temper our approach accordingly.'

Ticketing troubles

Tighter airline security is causing problems for married female executives whose business travel arrangements are usually booked in their professional name while their married name appears on their passport. A colleague of mine on a recent two-day business trip to Paris was refused permission to board until she had cancelled her ticket and re-booked it in her married name. The airline's argument was that she could not prove she was the person on her ticket – despite her business card, company documents and the colleague travelling with her!

Airline comfort kits packed with mainly male necessities are now on the way out. Air France – which publishes a dedicated women's in-flight magazine, *Air France Madame* – provides separate his-and-hers kits. BA does the same, including Body Shop handcream and cleanser in the women's pack. Virgin provides female flyers with a range of excellent Molton Brown preparations.

Travelling with children

One in six parents, according to one study in the States, now packs the kids along with the cabin bags when going on a business trip. Needless to say, the parent is generally Mum. Travelling with children can be a feat of organization. While most airlines provide funpacks for kids, fellow business class passengers may not thank you both for flying upfront. If junior threatens to cause mayhem amid snoozing executives, a mild sedative is probably the answer. On arrival, it pays to stay somewhere with a pool, plus good laundry and babysitting services.

SURVIVING ABROAD

Women's status and role in business varies greatly from country to country. As a result, so too do the courtesies, problems and threats you can expect to encounter.

North America, Australasia and much of South East Asia pose few menaces, though the same cannot be said of Latin America, Islamic states and parts of the Mediterranean, where you could be forgiven for thinking that the brains of most of the male population are lodged in their trousers.

Having said that, your travels may spring some surprises. Women who rate Britain as a bastion of misogyny often claim doing business in the Arabian Gulf is a breeze, since the roles of the sexes are so clearly defined. Others report that far from being excluded from the whirl of male after-work socializing in Tokyo, they have been deluged with dinner invitations.

Nonetheless, whether on the road, in the seeming sanctuary of your hotel or in social situations that threaten to get out of hand, it's vital to be prepared. One of my least pleasant travel experiences probably illustrates the point.

I'd been staying in Lagos – one of the world's most threatening cities. After spending a day in the north of the country, I was due to fly on to the Ivory Coast. This entailed backtracking to Lagos to change planes.

Suffice it to say that I missed the connection, and found myself marooned in one of the world's least hospitable airports at nearly midnight with no company, no accommodation and – through my own folly – no ready cash. To make matters worse, the phone lines were down.

Too nervous to set off alone in a ramshackle cab through miles of unlit highways, I ended up spending the night in a nearby dormitory used by Nigerian flight crews. It was not an experience I'd recommend.

Getting around

As a female, you'll need to be more safety conscious than male colleagues when getting from A to B. Most women have tales to tell of near escapes from the clutches of rogue cab drivers or philandering fellow travellers. Ignoring the rules and trusting things to luck is simply not enough. When getting around town, you should:

- **Take taxis after dark**. Companies such as Lady Cabs, in London, offer a women-only service.
- **Avoid pirate cabs**. The backstreets of many big cities are no place to end up with a driver you can't trust. Don't jeopardize safety for the sake of a few bucks.
- **Avoid being dropped off last**, when sharing a cab with male colleagues. You could find the driver has other ideas.
- **Beware of being too chatty**. Once a cabbie knows your name, your address and the fact that you're alone – or simply misinterprets your friendly smile – your brisk goodbye may not be the end of the story.
- **Avoid carrying too much cash**. Even drivers are held up in some cities.

Choosing a safe haven

Bear in mind that the safest hotels are not necessarily in the middle of town. Business districts are often deserted after six, while downtown areas are strictly no-go zones in some US cities. Since city-centre hotels can also be a favourite haunt of prostitutes, those catering for the family market are sometimes a better bet. Take advice before you travel.

Residential style hotels like Marriott's long-stay Residence Inns are popular with many women. University and other clubs can also be convivial places to stay. For ultimate peace of mind, some cities even have women-only hotels. Reeves in London, run by women for women, has never yet housed a male guest, and prides itself on top-notch security. Whatever your choice, remember to:

- Avoid staying anywhere that means negotiating dark subways, dimly lit sidestreets or deserted carparks.
- Treat your room number like a state secret. Don't inadvertently reveal it by walking ahead of someone you don't like the look of from the lift.
- Ask for your calls to be screened. Don't be caught off guard and reveal your room number or name to someone either making arbitrary calls or trying to track you down.
- Keep the chain on your door to ensure no one can simply walk in. Alternatively, invest in a keyless security lock or electronic door wedge. They're cheap and easy to use.
- Use valet parking to avoid using dark unattended carparks. If unavailable, tip the doorman to park or fetch your car.
- Avoid being a night-time prisoner. Use the pool, sauna or health centre – bigger ones often have aerobics or gym classes.

Eating out

- Try a pre-emptive strike. Don't wait for the waiter to leave you marooned in the middle of the restaurant, or stuck behind the potted plants. Say where you'd like to sit.
- Choose restaurants with care. Romantic candle-lit bistros are not the best place to dine alone.
- Schedule meetings for lunch or dinner, if budgets will allow, to minimize solitary mealtimes.
- Drink in the bar, but make friends with the barman. A good one will make sure you're not bothered by pests or prowlers. Otherwise, stick to the hotel's executive floor lounge.
- Don't be intimidated. Remember you're the customer. If you're getting shoddy service, make sure the manager knows.
- Regard eating in your room as a treat. You can have your feet up, your hair in a towel, eat with your fingers and have the telly on.

Dressing the part

Appearances do matter. If you want to be treated like a manager rather than a Girl Friday, dress like one. Wild hairdos, sloppy outfits and wrists a-rattle with cheap jewellery are not going to win you any points.

While informal garb is often acceptable in western business circles, it will do little to enhance your credibility in countries where women play a subservient role. Keep your appearance conservative and adopt a scrupulously professional approach. You'll be judged by the way you look as much as by the way you behave.

If you've got it, don't necessarily flaunt it off duty. Flout the rules of social decorum in Muslim or orthodox Jewish areas, and you run the risk of being ogled, groped, or – in extreme cases – even spat at. Keep a wrap handy for visiting mosques or sacred places, where sporting bare arms, legs and shoulders can be tantamount to going topless.

On the streets

While women are often much more attuned to the dangers around them than men, female intuition is not infallible. Consult the concierge about no-go or unsavoury areas before strolling out alone. You may be in danger of wandering into a neighbourhood where muggers regularly make mincemeat of bag-toting visitors. Take care, and, if possible, a companion.

- **Don't advertise the fact that you're a stranger.** Dithering on streetcorners with your nose buried in a map is an instant giveaway.
- **Use a money belt or secure inner pocket** to store cash when sightseeing. Jeans with hidden velcro pockets are handy for credit cards.
- **Walk purposefully.** Remember those most at risk from being mugged or assaulted tend to behave like victims to start with.

Health matters

Some brief reminders:

- Contraceptive pills may lose their effectiveness if you have a bad tummy upset.
- Feminine toiletries may be hard to come by in Beijing, Bucharest and other cities. Forewarned is forearmed.

DEALING WITH HARASSMENT

Even simple eye contact can be misconstrued as a come-on in certain Latin or Islamic countries. Men unused to independent females often have a simplistic view of Western women, drawing their stereotypes from American movies where sexual favours appear to be freely given. These are no places to lounge around in bars on your own, or behave in the matey fashion you might otherwise do with male pals. While being one of the boys can make travelling as a woman plain sailing at home, it can simply invite trouble elsewhere. The same goes for studious eyelash-fluttering designed to open doors that would otherwise stay barred.

Heavy make-up and red lipstick could class you as a prostitute in India, while revealing clothes can not only incite the bad guys, but embarrass the good ones. Flirt at your peril – there is great kudos attached to bedding a western woman, and every trick may be used to achieve it.

Defence tactics

You can minimize the prospect of harassment if you:

- **Don't admit to being alone.** Wear a wedding ring, call yourself Mrs or make copious references to children. One friend even swears by calling herself Doctor.
- **Find a male escort.** Locals who view you as a scarlet woman alone will at least assume you're an honest one.
- **Team up with another female.** Two women tend to suffer less hassle than one.
- **Wear sunglasses.** The reflective kind are ideal for avoiding eye contact in the streets.
- **Beware of confined spaces.** Lifts are classic places for being groped.
- **Don't accept rides with someone you've just met.**
- **Keep a defensive device in your handbag** – whether a metal nail file or a rape alarm.

If you are being pestered, you should:

- **Keep your cool.** Losing it can sometimes simply make things worse. A touch of humour is often better than letting your anger or frustration show.
- **Invent some influential local contacts** – or a burly brother-in-law working for the police.
- **Expand your vocabulary.** Learn how to say an emphatic and colourful no – with some meaningful variations – in six languages. Know the word for police.

If through folly or sheer bad luck you end up in a seriously unpleasant situation, with assault or worse on the cards, intuition may be your best ally. In a nutshell, the options are:

- **Screaming loudly** to attract attention and running away.

- **Talking your way out** with appeals or reason.
- **Confronting your assailant.** If loudly challenged, some will beat a hasty retreat.
- **Getting physical** – scratching or kicking your attacker where it hurts most.
- **Putting them off.** Telling the other party you are a carrier of herpes or HIV will be a major turn-off.
- **Buying time.** The 'let's go to my hotel' tack often works.

TAILPIECES

- Passengers on a BA flight to Leipzig were startled to hear the captain's voice asking whether, since he was extremely thirsty, someone would please locate a stewardess and send her up to the cockpit with some coffee. This was followed ten minutes later by an announcement from one of the female flight attendants to say that as passengers were now extremely thirsty, the captain would be coming down the aisle to serve duty-frees. Which he did.

- In a survey published by UK singles tour operator The Club, two-thirds of the men admitted going abroad with hopes of finding holiday sex. Ominously for them, only 7 per cent of the women quizzed said it was on their agenda.

- If you've ever fancied taking your pooch along for the ride, try checking into a Consort hotel in the UK. One-bone establishments supply feeding bowls and chocs; two-bone hostelries provide doggie food, bones and complimentary baskets; while a three-bone rating includes walkies by staff, and a deluxe dog's dinner.

13
☐ Doing it Right

Pitfalls and perils abound for those who fail to do some cultural homework on their destination. Jet travel may have shrunk the planet to a global village, but spiritual chasms remain between many of its townsfolk.

Knowing how to build bridges socially, as well as commercially, with your foreign partners is a vital part of doing business. Clinching the deal will hinge as much on winning their trust and respect as having the right product and price. Failing to learn the unspoken rules of business etiquette around the world and exercising the social skills demanded can mean the difference between coming home with a contract and simply clocking up a series of social blunders.

BASIC POINTERS

Word of mouth

The spoken word is clearly your biggest tool in the communications game – providing you get it right. One hapless Dutch businessman visiting Spain promptly said goodbye to his contract when his clients took him to see a bullfight. His was the only voice to emit a robust 'Olé!' when the bull gored the bullfighter in the pants.

While English has become the lingua franca of the business community in much of the world, learning a few basic social niceties in your hosts's native tongue will win full marks for effort. Since language courses now come on tape, compact disc and video, as well as on the telephone, there's little excuse for not trying.

Getting it right matters. A friend of mine once spent two days in Lisbon bidding everyone *'Buenos dias'*, before realizing he had been memorizing his Spanish, and not his Portuguese, phrase book.

Oriental tongues depend heavily on intonation. Deliver a badly-learned few words of Chinese – notorious for its delicately nuanced inflections – and instead of asking for your jacket to be dry-cleaned, you may well have made a bawdy suggestion to your host's wife.

Then there are the mysteries of double-speak, business-speak and slang. There is little point an English person describing their boss as 'loaded', 'gobsmacked' or 'over the moon' to a Japanese listener stretched to grasp linguistic basics. An American telling a German about time windows, golden parachutes and corporate shark watchers will have the same problem. Keep the jokes and witty one-liners for when you're back home.

Forms of address

While clarity of word is the keynote when communicating by fax and phone, crossing the cultural and linguistic divide in meetings demands the right manner, as well. Some nationalities are forthright in their approach, while others are anything but. The straight-talking New Yorker is a million miles apart in stylistic terms from his oh-so-subtle Tokyo counterpart.

English speakers fumble clumsily with the formal and more familiar forms of address in other tongues. Start calling your French and German hosts 'tu' or 'Du' prematurely, and you commit a fatal social gaffe.

Jumping in with an American-style 'Hey Jacques, it's good to meet you', will go down like a lead balloon in the formal business circles of many European cities. Err on the side of caution and let your counterparts set the tone and pace of your relationship.

Germans often stick to surnames in the office, and set great store – as do the Italians – by professional titles. Familiar forms of address are more commonplace in Scandinavia ('du' is widely used in Norway), and while the Nordics can be formal on first acquaintance, their reserve can melt in a tidal wave over a bottle of Scotch.

Body talk

Body language is as vital as the one you speak. There's little point memorizing neat phrases designed to impress your foreign hosts in their native tongue if the way you say it does the opposite. Throwaway gestures can unwittingly spell social suicide in the wrong place. Mannerisms that may win you friends for life at home can earn you a left hook somewhere else.

This minefield of social subtleties extends to kissing codes (should it be one, two or three?), queuing etiquette (do you or don't you?) and letting rip when it comes to complaining. Losing your cool to register anger or displeasure is one of the most un-cool things you can do in some parts of the world, where the locals will simply see it as loss of face.

Even the seemingly universal introductory handshake may not be the right answer. A polite mutual bow still comes more naturally to the Japanese, while Middle Eastern men may not only dislike a western male extending a hand to their wives, but refrain from doing likewise with their visitor's spouse. The back-slapping jollity that comes easily in the Mediterranean can be anathema elsewhere.

Make a circle with your thumb and forefinger in the US, and you are signalling that everything's OK. Do it in parts of Latin America, and you are saying 'get lost' in the rudest possible way. Beckoning someone over with an index finger in Indonesia is akin to calling the dog, while shying away from hearty man-to-man embraces in Latin or Arab countries could leave you labelled a cold fish.

Shake hands or eat with your left hand in the Islamic world at your peril. Only the right one should be used – the other is used for personal ablutions. Patting people on the head or pointing the soles of your feet at your hosts in Buddhist or Arab countries is likewise to commit social hara-kiri. Smiles are fortunately pretty universal.

Doing business

Full-frontal assaults with lawyers in tow may be fine in the States, but can be counter-productive in countries where rolling up your sleeves to get down to business in no-nonsense fashion is unheard of. Building a platform on which to negotiate can be a gradual process that is wrecked by gung-ho haste. It can mean building in a few rounds of golf in Japan, drinking endless tea in the Arab world or hosting a lively dinner in Latin countries.

Timekeeping

Punctuality is another area where a *faux pas* is easily made. 'Mañana' attitudes still prevail in Latin countries, where apparent disorganization should not be taken at face value. Teutonic timekeeping is similarly not a feature of Arab lands, where hosts may turn up late and spend half the meeting chatting between themselves.

Trying to squeeze too many meetings into the day in the Third World, where constant interruptions can frustrate all endeavours to get things moving, can be a mistake. Impromptu calls can sometimes yield better results than trying to secure appointments by phone.

Card games

Exchanging business cards is a vital part of the meetings ritual – and that doesn't simply mean dishing them out by the score. The way your card is given and received can be as important as the title it bestows upon you in some countries. Cards are proffered with both hands rather like a gift in the Far East, where they may be carefully read and consulted during the meeting.

Woman-wise

Life for the female business traveller is yet more complex. Western women accustomed to being the boss on home ground may be treated with bemusement, suspicion, or even derision elsewhere. They risk not being taken seriously as well as taken for something other than a bona fide business executive.

As well as learning to tread carefully with their hosts, they must deal skilfully with unwanted sexual overtures, and risk being excluded from the swirl of after-hours male socializing. They may need to emphasize their qualifications, abandoning informality in favour of a studied executive style, down to the briefcase and tailored suit. Honour in social matters may be deemed as important as the title shown on their business card.

Sexual stereotyping remains strong in Japan and Korea, where older men in particular may find it difficult to deal with a young female westerner. It is also a fact of life in much of the Arab world.

Hospitality

Entertaining can be another cultural minefield. Muslim or Jewish guests won't thank you for being offered pork fricassée, while Hindus – for whom cows are sacred – may spurn beef or veal. Likewise, you should not be upset if your Arab guest bolts for the door while still chewing his last mouthful of food. To stay longer would imply he has not had enough to eat.

Try and be sporting when urged to taste local specialities. Speaking as someone who was once offered deep-fried moose testicles (fortunately they were off that night), I can confirm this is easier said than done. Just remember, your oriental hosts may not go a bundle on haggis, Irish stew or jam roly-poly when the ball is in the other court.

Avoidance tactics can sometimes pay off. The classic tale that comes to mind is that of an eminent British diplomat who is invited to dine with an Arab sheikh. A servant arrives at his side, bearing the dish specially prepared in his honour which, in keeping with local tradition, he must now sample. It is the dreaded plate of sheep's eyeballs. Displaying the best of British sang-froid, the diplomat thinks on his feet. 'We too have an important tradition which I would not wish to break,' he tells his host, passing the platter firmly on to his wife: 'Ladies first'.

Hitting the bottle

Toasts also have their dangers. Every country boasts its own brand of fiery hooch guaranteed to raze your taste buds. Writing in *Signature* magazine, Perrott Phillips sums up the perils of downing a Green Tiger – pink gin laced with chillies – in one fatal gulp as 'a nuclear explosion in your mouth ... followed by a flaming torchlight procession down your gullet ... and ending with Last Night of the Proms inside your stomach.' Be warned.

Bars are an extension of work for Japanese businessmen, who are renowned for getting home at midnight and seeing nothing of their families. Visitors will be taken to *baa* and *pabbu* (pubs) serving Scotch and frothy beer before being whisked off to the nearest Karaoke bar. There, singing for their supper with gusto – certain to be greeted with hearty applause, no matter how awful – is *de rigueur*.

Le power breakfast

Power breakfasting – the latest executive trend to roll out of the States – has usurped expense-account lunching in some quarters. Corporate breakfasters can talk shop over the bacon and brioches and still be at their desk by 10 in the morning. What's more, they won't have had one brandy too many or decimated the firm's dining-out budget.

If you can't get your guests to recce for brekkie (and le power breakfast has even taken off in Paris), lunch is the obvious option. Let your Gallic guests choose the wine in France, and ideally the venue – they are not known as connoisseurs of fine food for nothing. Hospitality is often just a beer and a sandwich in The Netherlands, while Germanic guests will bring hearty appetites to the table and show little regard for low-fat, low-cholesterol ideas. Long lunches are unusual in Scandinavia, where work starts and finishes early.

Try to learn something about the cuisine you will encounter. I once sat next to an Englishman on a flight to Tokyo who proceeded to drink the contents of his fingerbowl, before dipping his mitts in the clear soup to rinse them off.

Giving gifts

Exchanging gifts is another side of the business etiquette game – and it's not just the thought that counts. What you give will say as much about you and your company as it will about the relationship you hope to cement.

Well-known branded goods in the tax and duty-free line will be the safest bets – whether a top-label malt whisky, discreetly logoed fountain pen, designer leather wallet or Wedgwood china plate. Never give tack, nor refuse a gift, unless it's clearly a bribe.

Don't bother packing the dozen copies of your company's latest calendar, complete with views of the Dagenham depot. Remember not to offer alcohol in the teetotal world of Islam, and check that even your gift-wrapping doesn't offend local sensitivities. Choose white paper in the Far East – where the colour denotes mourning – and your gesture may end up looking like a condolence offering.

Taboos

Knowing which subjects can kill a conversation stone dead and spell social calamity is also vital. Launching into an impassioned debate over the Salman Rushdie affair with a party of Muslims could put the kiss of death on the next day's talks, for instance. Criticism, brusqueness and tactless candour can also do untold damage.

Each country has its superstitions, too. Filipinos won't wish to visit offices on the 13th floor, while their neighbours in Hong Kong will be careful to observe the ancient laws of *fung-shui*, which dictate the siting of new businesses. They and their Singaporean cousins – for whom spitting is a taboo – will be avid fans of oriental dragon dances.

Silver handshakes

Endless supplies of baksheesh will help oil the wheels in countries whose inefficiency, draconian bureaucracy or flourishing black economy make it vital to know the short cuts. Anyone who has tried to speed up a deal in Moscow, cope with top-heavy officialdom in India or get things done in Nigeria – where enlisting a middle man is the best answer – will be familiar with the routine. Bribes are discussed more fully in Chapter 10.

Stereotypes

Xenophobic stereotyped images of other nationalities will do little to help your cause abroad. Americans don't all exude superficial *bonhomie* any more than Germans all operate with teutonic precision and the British declare 'I say!' every minute. The Japanese do, however, mutter 'hai, hai, hai'. That simply means they're listening.

Most nationals have nicknames – derogatory or otherwise – for folk from elsewhere. As a Westerner, you will rank as a Gweilo in Hong Kong, a Gaijin in Japan, and in all probability a Gringo in Mexico. *C'est la vie*.

GETTING BY IN ... NORTH AMERICA

George Bernard Shaw's apt observation that England and America are two countries separated by the same language is as true today as it was when he said it. Even the dogs go to shrinks in the world's biggest meritocracy, where Disney World takes on the importance of Mecca, homeowners keep handguns, fast food has been turned into an art form and 'Have a nice day', trips off every tongue.

Americans are known for their straight-talking, hard-assed approach to business. Time is rarely wasted socializing if it can usefully be spent at the negotiating table, and executives will readily get straight down to business with people they've never met. More women operate at senior management level in the US than anywhere else.

Subjects likely to go down like a lead balloon with your US hosts include jokey references to how the Japanese are devouring corporate America. Over the border in Canada, where one in four nationals speak French, your biggest gaffe will be to call everyone American.

JAPAN

More is written about business etiquette in Japan than any other country. Dealing with the hardworking corporate warriors that have turned the country into an economic superpower takes tact, patience and an insight into the complex cultural traditions that govern the Japanese way of life.

Timekeeping is precise, and the pecking order strictly observed. The exchange of business cards (printed in both Japanese and English) is taken seriously. Talks are rarely conclusive first time around (a certain amount of beating around the bush is inevitable), and decisions are usually made committee-style.

Drinking starts once work is over, and the visitor is certain to be swept into a round of after-hours socializing. Clients will be expected to join in the singing at the inevitable Karaoke bar, though being invited to play golf is the ultimate honour. Western women may be graciously entertained, even if their local counterparts are nowhere to be seen. Scotch and sake will be much in evidence.

While the Japanese are tolerant of western ways, social taboos still exist. Among them are public shows of affection, pointing with an index finger and blowing one's nose close to others.

THE LATIN WORLD

Flamboyant, friendly and outgoing, Latins on both sides of the Atlantic are known for their love of sartorial chic and a lingering fondness for siestas. They are also notorious for poor timekeeping (though they like their visitors to be on time), a reluctance to put things down on paper and a tendency to get physical. Back-slapping embraces and hugs are all on the cards.

Latins also have a propensity to entertain at a time when other nationalities are ready for bed. Dinner invitations can be as late as 11 o'clock at night. Socializing is a natural part of business – even if only to check that you are (as an Italian would say) *simpatico*.

When it comes to gifts, money talks. A no-expense-spared approach pays off, and extravagance is preferred to understatement. Designer labels, style and exclusive brand names are relished.

Chauvinism is alive and thriving in the Latin belt – France being one of the few countries where many women hold senior positions. Female execs may be treated with old-fashioned charm and courtesy, but not necessarily as business equals. Few make it right to the top.

All Latin countries should not be tarred with the same brush, however. The laid-back style of the Caribbean is distinct from that of cooler Madrid and Montevideo, while Chileans have more of an American jackets-off approach to business.

Frank comments on South America's all too pressing drugs, crime and national debt problems are not always appreciated. Even a well-intentioned discussion on efforts to combat the drug barons and shore up the region's ramshackle economies may be taken amiss.

EASTERN EUROPE

Things have changed dramatically in the former Soviet empire since the first flutterings of *glasnost* swept through the Kremlin. The collapse of iron-fisted state bureaucracy has instead spawned a new set of problems for those doing business in the region.

Don't be surprised to find yourself dealing with a new breed of middle men – Russia's thriving black economy has created a business Mafia bigger, some claim, than in Italy. Many organizations now lack a clear chain of command, and getting paid at the end of a contract can be as time-consuming as getting it rolling in the first place. Women play a prominent role in business.

'Blat' – whether a $5 bill, pack of Marlboros or bottle of Scotch – undeniably gets things done, whether to secure a restaurant table or set up a vital meeting. The good news is that, while open political discussion was stifled in the past, it's no longer taboo.

ARAB STATES

An irreverent cartoon gracing many an expatriate bookshelf in the Middle East depicts a portly Arab seated at his desk and poised to turn his attention to a wobbling pile of papers. In each hand he holds an all-important rubber stamp – one marked Maybe, the other, Maybe Not.

This tongue-in-cheek comment on the Arab style of doing business sums up some of the frustrations felt by visitors in a world where delicacy is all, where nepotism is widespread, and where haggling plays an essential role. The Arab states are not one-stop, hard-sell markets offering instant returns.

While Saudi Arabia is the strictest of the Islamic lands, the traditions of the Koran govern all aspects of Arab life. Meetings will invariably start late, and may be briefly interrupted for prayer. Others may be present, or come and go. Declining the obligatory coffee or failing to allow for a little social chit-chat will be deemed rude and churlish.

While western women will be well treated – if with some bemusement – their Arab counterparts will probably stay well hidden. Modesty is a must, and the sexes may be segregated at mealtimes.

Taboos include alcohol (unless proposed by your host), pointing the soles of your feet at someone and eating with your left hand. Instigating a discussion on the Arab–Israeli conflict will not win many points, either. Don't expect to get much business done during the holy month of Ramadan.

AFRICA

Africa is a melting pot of ethnic groups, tribal cultures, religious loyalties and the vestiges of colonialism. The Francophile states of the West are very distinct from those which once regarded Britain as their ruler.

Westerners are well advised to make the mental switch from operating on home time to local time. Things happen when they happen. Getting hot under the collar over delays will achieve nothing but raised blood pressure.

Women play a more prominent role in business than in the Islamic world. Entertaining is often done at sports or country clubs, where it may not be politic to order South African wines or launch into discussions on that country's much-publicized race problems.

THE ORIENT

The complex customs and social graces of the oriental world – whether social, sartorial or superstitious – can make business etiquette in Asia and the Far East something of a Chinese puzzle. Like trying to chase a peanut with ivory chopsticks, business deals can be elusive to those who fail to try and get beneath the skin of the oriental psyche.

Deals are struck in the bar rather than the boardroom, even if the venue chosen differs wildly from Bangkok to Beijing. While back-slapping informality is out, business venturers hoping to hit it off with their would-be partners will need a strong head, as well as the ability to rattle off the odd flowery speech of thanks.

Hong Kong's hard-nosed business community has little time for the traditional hospitality and formality still found in Taiwan and mainland China. There is also less of the avid after-work socializing found in Japan.

Avoidance of conflict and loss of face are vital sides of the oriental business mix. Women play a prominent role in commerce in some countries – notably Thailand and Hong Kong – while golf is increasingly popular as a sport and ice-breaker between business contacts.

Avoid contentious issues (Tianamen Square, for instance) and curb western candour. Remember to refer to China as the People's Republic – the Taiwanese call their own country the Republic of China.

Don't puzzle too much over what you're eating – sought-after oriental delicacies include monkey brains, snake soup and shredded pig's ear. And in a region known for its thriving counterfeit industry, make sure your gifts are the real thing.

EURO-PALS

Dealing with the 12 different cultures now welded together in the so-called Single Market can make even the most well-intentioned executive feel rather like a corporate chameleon. Business is still done in a palpably different way almost everywhere from north to south of the continent.

While the British are somewhat indignant at Brussels' failure to ordain English as the Community's official Eurospeak, language schools countrywide are packed with executives trying to get to grips with other nations' linguistic nuances. For the moment, a meeting in Brussels may be conducted in English, French or German.

Even closer political affinity looks unlikely to iron out the differences in national characteristics. The Germans will still wait for the little green man before crossing the road, the French will still be enveloped in a fog of Gaulois and the English will still be muttering about the lack of entente cordiale across the Channel. Everyone, however, will be sporting their standard-issue Euro passport.

LONG-TERM SURVIVAL

Eliciting pointers of etiquette from a guidebook will be of limited use if you plan to live and work in another country for any length of time. Preparing for the rigours of expatriate life demands a little more commitment.

Residential courses for business people heading abroad *en famille* are held in most countries. Among the best – so well known it even attracts orientals needing to learn about other parts of Asia – is medieval Farnham Castle, in the heart of Surrey commuter country.

Intensive courses prepare executives and their families for assignments in virtually every part of the world, briefing them on all aspects of coping with an alien culture, community and language. Sessions even include simulated socializing and role-play – just the thing to pave the way for the many rounds of breaking bread with your business partners before the real talking is done.

TAILPIECES

- Names are all-important in the international marketing game. Top-selling lines unlikely ever to win the hearts of British supermarket shoppers include Italy's Mukki yoghurt, France's Pschitt lemonade and items like Krapp toilet paper, Bum's biscuits and Plopp toffee bars from Sweden. Cypriot wines like Arsinoe also have a slight image problem.

- Phrasebooks are striving to move with the times. New Berlitz editions now tell you how to get condoms and advice on VD rather than castor oil and weight reducing tablets. Church service times have given way to the lowdown on casino gambling.

- Funny how the Germans always get there first – whether it's around the pool or in the plane. After a BA aircraft at Heathrow was given a 30-minute take-off delay, a German plane also waiting was cleared for immediate departure. The furious British captain immediately buzzed Air Traffic Control to know why. Before the tower could reply, the Lufthansa captain broke in. 'Ve got to ze airport early,' he said, 'and put our towels on ze runway.'

14
☐ Business Holidays

Trading your suit for a surfboard and spicing up a business trip with a dash of holiday can turn a run-of-the-mill visit abroad into an unforgettable one.

Heading for the same city for the umpteenth time can be a less than enthralling prospect when you are simply going to review next year's budgets or audit the books. Mix it with a few days in the Caribbean, a weekend on the ski slopes or a spot of white-water rafting, and it takes on a very different appeal.

Having a bit on the side – whether a weekend on the beach, a conference trip with colleagues or an unashamed corporate jolly with your partner, can be a powerful antidote to nine-to-five stress.

What's more, the cost can be minimal. Sidetrips can often be arranged at little extra expense, while company-paid get-togethers can cost little more than presents to bring back home. Whatever the option, even those for whom travel is an occupational hazard agree that having the chance to mix business with leisure now and then is a chance too good to miss.

SIDETRIPS

One in four travellers tack on some time off when taking a business trip abroad – and for compelling reasons. Cheap weekend rates at luxury hotels and a greater choice of flights to both mainstream and far-flung destinations have made the idea of an almost-free sidetrip once in a while irresistible. Tiny island hideaways once considered inaccessible are now just a short hop away from many busy hub airports.

Since airfares often tumble when a Saturday night stay is involved, even the firm can gain when managers take a weekend break during their trip. As many hotels now charge on a per-room basis, taking a partner along need not bump up the accommodation bill, either.

Organizing a sidetrip demands a clued-up travel agent and the readiness to do some air fares homework. Knowing how to make the most of maximum permitted mileage rules when purchasing a round-the-world or multi-sector ticket will be a big help. Don't get the terminology wrong, though – more than one bemused agent has been asked to book a business trip with some free legovers (rather than stopovers) thrown in.

Keeping abreast of fare offers, seat sales, hotel weekend deals and short break programmes will also pay off. Many carriers offer excellent rates at hotels on their home ground specifically to attract stopover traffic and the revenue it brings. Many firms are moreover prepared to turn a blind eye to a little creative ticketing, and don't object if a traveller chooses to trade in one business class ticket for two in economy.

Top destinations

Having decided that a sidetrip makes sense, where can you go? Most of the Caribbean lies within easy reach of the big east coast US cities, while Nassau in the Bahamas is a mere half-hour hop from the Florida mainland. A trip to the States offers limitless possibilities, with ski slopes and beaches alike lying within easy reach of the major gateways. Miami is a natural stepping-stone to much of Latin America.

The choice is equally impressive in the Far East, where a score of tropical idylls lie within a few hours' flying of the big business capitals. Both Phuket and less developed Koh Samui are easy to reach from Bangkok, while Bali is an obvious choice for anyone doing business in Jakarta or Singapore. Visiting some of the Pacific islands can also be a breeze from Sydney or Auckland.

Malaysia has its highlands and islands, wildlife and old colonial architecture. The Philippines – whose hotel capacity has doubled in recent years – offers both some celebrated nightlife and a string of fine beach resorts. South Korea has its honeymooners' isle of Cheju.

Europe, too, offers endless scope for the traveller prepared to get to grips with a pocket flight guide. With much of previously-cloistered Eastern Europe now on the main tourist beat, numerous cities formerly hard to reach are now easily accessible.

CONFERENCE AND INCENTIVE TRIPS

Designed to satisfy wanderlust and the work ethic at the same time, conference and incentive trips mix work and play in a style that makes them out-and-out winners for most executives.

Some are centred around busy trade fairs and conventions, while others are thinly-disguised junkets for the company's star performers.

They generally combine a quota of meetings and workshops with delights ranging from tailor-made sightseeing tours to lavish themed events with no expense spared. Pure incentive travel is thought to make up 10 per cent of the meetings and conventions industry in the US.

Tax benefits

Despite their cost, the trips do not drastically dent corporate coffers. Nothing motivates like travel, and since salespeople and dealers will pull out the stops and out-perform each other to earn an expenses-paid jaunt to the sun, their rewards are effectively self-financing. Incentive trips can also be tax deductable providing they have a specified meetings content – currently 40 per cent in the US.

Spending on incentive-based trips has admittedly cooled in recent years. No boss wants to be seen living it up in Barbados when half the office have just joined the dole queue, and domestic events have replaced some of the exotic get-togethers of the '80s. Travel has been scaled down rather than abandoned, however. Travel agents estimate that as many as one in four business travellers are on a conference and incentive trip of one kind or another.

Which destinations top the polls? Florida, favoured for its sunshine record and wealth of man-made attractions, has become a top choice for companies on both sides of the Pond. Anywhere between New York and LA is now popular with Europeans, tempted across the Atlantic by free-fall air fares in recent years.

London, Paris and Amsterdam are perennial favourites in Europe, with newer destinations such as Seville, Istanbul, Budapest and Prague dislodging older favourites. Cyprus and Spain's Costa del Sol are popular with the budget market, with Rome and Florence attracting culture fiends. Strong contenders in Asia include Singapore and Hong Kong, plus newer destinations in Thailand, Korea and Malaysia. Elsewhere, more adventurous firms are whisking their high achievers off to places as diverse as Dubai, Mexico and Venezuela.

Theme parties

Incentive trips feature themed events in a big way. Go to Palm Beach, and you could find yourself invited to a '50s night packed with Elvis look-alikes and pony-tailed chicks, jiving to juke box hits and sipping sodas. Try Hong Kong, and you could be swept up in a pirate's raid as invaders swarm aboard your ocean-going junk. Go to Texas, and you'll eat round a camp fire on a dude ranch before stepping out at a cowboy-style barndance. In Rio, you'll be off to the samba school.

Arizona cook-outs, hot-air balloon rides over the Grand Canyon, breakfast at the Pyramids, Bedouin feasts in the Jordanian desert, river rafting in Switzerland, pearl diving and dhow trips in the Arabian Gulf – even lunch in prison – ensure that those lucky enough to take part will be doing things they would never normally do.

Activities are also designed with team-building in mind. They might include four-wheel drive desert safaris, war games in the forest, sailing on the Solent, beach olympics in California or treasure-hunting in the Everglades. Team members may have to build a raft, navigate water taxis, or unearth hidden treasure armed with clues and compass.

Getting an invitation

Your best ploys to get on a good conference or incentive trip are to:

- Get your head down and bust the sales targets.
- Convince your boss that three days spent discussing metal stress at a small-bore rifle symposium in Rio really will benefit the office. Or that your supplier's invitation to enjoy a three-day jolly on the Riviera will be just the place to discuss widget design.
- Join the speaker circuit. Try trading your services for a trip to the sun.
- Be a valued customer. Suppliers like being nice to the people giving them the orders.
- Organize a trip yourself. Write a proposal, present it to the board and offer to take personal charge.

Practical pointers

If the last ploy wins, deciding where to go will be your next headache. This will be governed by:

- **Budgets**. The buck stops at the bottom line.
- **Convenience**. There's no point flying your team halfway round the world for a two-day event.
- **Cachet value**. People want to go somewhere they can tell their friends about, not where they take granny every year.
- **Originality**. If your firm is known for pulling surprises out of the hat, you'll need to top the previous act.
- **Luxury**. Attendees will expect the VIP treatment. They won't be impressed at being stuck with a bill for extras.
- **Practical matters**. The top factors influencing destination choice are hotel availability, ease and cost of transport, and distance.

What counts most at the hotel? Research shows fine food to be the most important factor, followed by the choice and quality of meeting rooms, negotiable rates, accommodation and support services. Flexibility is also important – if you want a smorgasbord and dancing girls at midnight, the hotel should be prepared to provide it.

Many hotel chains promote key properties as incentive destinations in their own right. Inter-Continental offers Ultimate Incentive programmes at most of its North American properties, in addition to those in Tokyo, Sydney, Cannes, Rio and elsewhere. Conrad has an impressive incentive product at its Istanbul and Brussels properties.

On the high seas

Starting the day with a leisurely breakfast on deck, before dropping anchor at some palm-fringed Caribbean island, is the stuff dream incentives are made of, as far as many travel veterans are concerned.

Cruise ships are trawling for a bigger slice of the corporate meetings cake as more and more conference delegates discover the pleasures of being all at sea. With their reputation for good food, luxurious living and island-hopping itineraries, lines are having little problem convincing companies to cast off for a get-together on the ocean waves.

Floating resorts

Today's new-generation superliners are floating resorts complete with shopping arcades, sweeping atriums, panoramic lounges, cinemas, themed bars and sports ranging from shuffleboard to mini-golf. What's more, they sail everywhere from the Baltic to the Black Sea, and Alaska to Mexico. With vast new capacity dumped on the Caribbean in recent years, prices can moreover be temptingly low.

Conference and incentive trips afloat have inbuilt novelty value – always a plus. Delegates are more likely to mix outside working sessions – it's difficult, after all, to slope off anywhere – and the venue is secure from prying eyes. Food is generally so good that most passengers throw their calorie counter out of the porthole and spend the week grazing at banquets that start at dawn and culminate in midnight feasts.

Tailor-made trips

Entertainment and activities afloat can be tailored to meet the needs of incentive clients as required. Companies can charter anything from a cabin to a full deck – whether for a sailing, a month or an entire season. Group hospitality desks and other personalized touches can be arranged as needed.

Seagoing delegates often board ship in Miami, well placed for mini-cruises in nearby Bahamian waters. Those seeking to go farther afield can fly down to the Dutch Antilles, where Dolphin Cruise Line's SS *OceanBreeze* leaves Aruba every week for cruises to the Panama Canal, and the islands of the southern Caribbean.

Refurbished in 1992, *OceanBreeze* is a fine example of what cruise ships can offer adventure-loving, but cost-conscious corporate cruisers. It has a two to one passenger/crew ratio, a choice of dining and entertainment venues, a surfeit of good food, a twin-deck casino and a non-stop programme of activities.

Upmarket choices

Designed with strictly upmarket corporate traffic in mind are ships like Majesty Cruise Line's *Royal Majesty*, based in Miami and serving the short-breaks market. Launched in 1992, the ship boasts the latest in dining and recreation amenities afloat, in addition to a choice of well-planned meeting areas. Its credentials include a Broadway-style theatre, casino, night club, high-tech gym and award-winning food.

Lines operating on the Baltic, North Sea and the Mediterranean also offer excellent facilities. P&O's new *Oriana*, due to set sail in 1995, will have a range of facilities for the corporate cruiser and be available for charter. Newer ships such as the *Royal Viking Queen* boast staterooms with luxurious 5-foot high windows and other features.

Note the following points before packing your bags and shinning up the gangplank:

- Cruise ships are a case of horses for courses. There's a huge difference between the glitzy new American ships, where it's all non-stop partying, and the more sedate liners carrying over-60s to Madeira.
- Remember you get what you pay for. Budget ships won't be ideal for incentive goers.
- Tips can be a hefty expense. Make sure you know who's paying.

CORPORATE HOSPITALITY

It's often said that for every $1 million spent on corporate entertainment, a firm can expect $20 million in new business. Usually reserved for the top 20 per cent of clients who provide 80 per cent of the business, hospitality wins greater returns than any other form of sales promotion. Not surprisingly it can gobble up company cash.

Corporate hospitality works on many levels. It can be used as a thank you to staff, a celebration of corporate milestones, or a means of engaging in some liquid lobbying with key clients. Manage it well, and you will achieve marvels of motivation and market penetration.

Top UK corporate jollies include test cricket matches and Wimbledon, together with social diary events like Ascot, Henley and Cowes. Other treats earning lashings of social kudos are Concorde flights, hot-air balloon rides, weekends at big race meetings and dinners in castles and hunting lodges. Firms often whisk clients off to the Monaco Grand Prix, the Longchamps races in Paris or the Milanese opera. Summertime day-trips might feature grouse shooting in the Highlands complete with picnic hampers, oodles of bubbly, helicopter rides or a chauffered Rolls.

Schoolboy games

Participation events are now hugely popular, since they are often cheaper than big spectator events and gourmet extravaganzas, and are more effective at getting people to bond. Rally driving, schoolboy games, clay pigeon shooting and treasure hunts can moreover be as big a hit with the female contingent as with the Action Men.

Events can also have a big fun element. One popular murder mystery features the managing director being bumped off over dinner – only to come back dressed as the devil five minutes later. Whodunnits are also popular, especially when featuring characters well known at work.

Corporate hospitality needs to be done well or not at all, since there's no second chance to impress. Busy clients are less willing to take time out these days, so make sure your invitation is impossible to refuse if you're doing the asking. Remember, too, that you won't end up pleasing everyone. For every nine people who have a wonderful time, one will probably hate every second.

Champagne sharks

Hospitality events often carry a high mark-up, and the business has more than its share of champagne sharks and caviar cowboys. Many clients have come badly unstuck after handing over large sums of money, and discovering too late they have been left holding 2,000 useless black market tickets to a major event. The moral is to check things out before handing over a cheque.

Identifying your target audience and giving them what they really want is imperative. So too is making sure your invitation doesn't look like a blatant sweetener. Evening and weekend events will generally draw bigger numbers, providing partners are invited. Top staff – not scantily-clad bimbos – should be on hand to help things go smoothly.

Assuming you are the host this time around, you'll need to answer the following questions to be certain your guests will enjoy their corporate freebie as much as you plan to:

- Is your idea of a great event shared by your clients? Will your female guests enjoy the Cup Final? Will the company chairman go bungee jumping?
- Have you issued an invitation which would be awkward to accept? No one will want to go on a three-day jolly when half the workforce has been put out of a job.
- Can you vouch for the company recruited to organize the event? You don't want to be taken for a ride by a bunch of vol-au-vent villains.
- Will there be enough scope for mixing? Watching Wimbledon may be less useful than setting off with quad bikes and rally cars.
- Have the details been thought through? Better to carry off something tried-and-tested than botch something over-ambitious.

OVER AND OUT

- When UK holiday retailer Lunn Poly asked customers who they would most like to stow away with on a cruise, Hollywood sex symbols failed to make the top grade. Most people chose their partner. Asked who they would most like to push overboard, however, most were more forthcoming. Taking indisputable top place was Saddam Hussein.

- Guest at a Four Seasons hotel: 'Say, the cheeseburgers here are great. I'd love to airship one to my cousin in Bahrain, but only if you can get it to him hot.' Concierge: (without batting an eyelid) 'Cheddar or bleu, sir?'

New Internationalist magazine

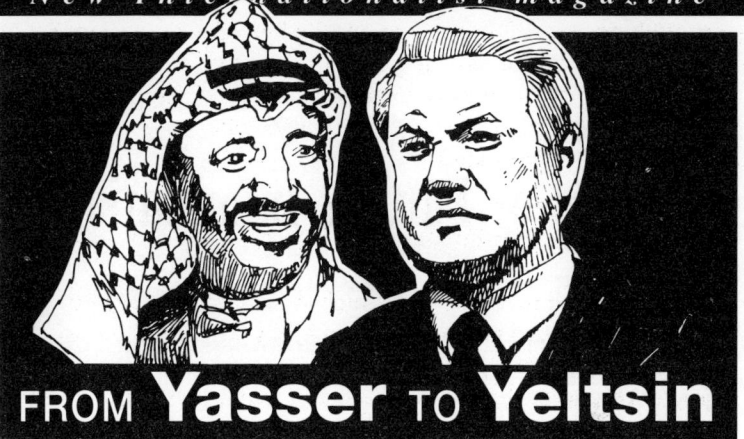

FROM **Yasser** TO **Yeltsin**

Get a grasp of the events and the ideologies that shape an ever more complex world. Read the **NI** magazine. Each month we tackle one subject in depth. It could be *Food* or the *Arms Trade*, *Africa* or the *Amazon*. The ideas, the facts and the arguments are all neatly compressed into just 36 pages of clear charts, lively articles, high quality colour photos and vivid graphics. An instant monthly briefing. Quicker to read than a book and right up-to-the-minute.

But you don't have to take our word for it. Fill in the box below and we will send you this month's issue **FREE**, yours to keep whether or not you subscribe. ■

FREE *magazine*

"I warmly recommend it."
David Bryer, Director of Oxfam

"A remarkable magazine."
John Pilger, journalist

NO-RISK TRIAL SUBSCRIPTION

YES PLEASE send me my introductory free issue. To continue receiving **NI** I need do nothing: my year's subscription will start the following month. But if I wish to cancel and receive a full refund I will write and tell you within 10 days of receiving my free issue.

Payment by UK cheque, Eurocheque, Access/Mastercard or Visa. Annual subscription rates:
UK £18.40
Overseas £25.40.

(BLOCK LETTERS please)
Name _____
Address _____
_____
_____ Postcode _____

☐ I enclose a cheque payable to **"New Internationalist."**
Please charge my ☐ Access/Mastercard ☐ Visa card

Access VISA

Signed _____ Expiry date _____
Card Number ☐☐☐☐ ☐☐☐☐ ☐☐☐☐ ☐☐☐☐

Post to: **UK NEW INTERNATIONALIST, FREEPOST CN2283 Mitcham CR4 9AR, UK**
Outside UK: **NEW INTERNATIONALIST, 120-126, Lavender Ave, Mitcham CR4 3HP, UK**

NI Publications Ltd. Reg in England No 1005239. Reg Office 55 Rectory Road, Oxford, UK. 5DNHY

Appendix
☐ Sources of Further Information

Information given here is by necessity selective, rather than exhaustive. For space reasons, contact telephone numbers are confined primarily to London or the UK.

USEFUL ADDRESSES

General

International Airline Passengers
  Association (IAPA)
PO Box 380
Croydon
Surrey CR9 4NZ
Tel: 081-681 6555

International Air Transport
  Association (IATA)
PO Box 672
CH-1215, Geneva Airport
Switzerland
Tel: 022 799 2525

Association of European Airlines
Avenue Louise 350
1050 Brussels
Belgium
Tel: 322 648 4017

The Executive Club International
520 Fulham Road
London SW6 5NJ
Tel: 071-384 1877

Guild of Business Travel Agents
  (GBTA)
Premier House
10 Greycoat Place
London SW1P 1SB
Tel: 071-222 2744

American Express Travel Management
  Services
Portland House
Stag Place
London SW1E 5BZ
Tel: 071 834 5555

Hogg Robinson Travel Ltd
Meirion House
Guildford Road
Woking
Surrey GU22 7QF
Tel: 0483 756060

Thomas Cook Travel Management
PO Box 36
Thorpe Wood
Peterborough PE3 6SB
Tel: 0733 63200

Wagonlit Travel
400 Great Cambridge Road
Enfield
Middx EN1 3FY
Tel: 081-292 7000

The Economist Intelligence Unit
40 Duke Street
London W1A 1DW
Tel: 071-493 6711

Employment Conditions Abroad Ltd
Anchor House
15 Britten Street
London SW3 3TY
Tel: 071-351 7151

The Centre for International Briefing
Farnham Castle
Farnham
Surrey GU9 OAG
Tel: 0252 721194

Health matters

British Airways Travel Clinic
156 Regent Street
London W1
Tel: 071-439 9584

Circadian Travel Technologies Inc
7315 Wisconsin Avenue
Suite 1300W
Bethesda, MD 20814-3202
Tel: (301) 961 8559

Thomas Cook Vaccination Centre
45 Berkeley Street
London W1A 1EB
Tel: 071-408 4157

MASTA (Medical Advisory Services
   for Travellers Abroad)
Keppel Street
London WC1E 7HT
Tel: 071-631 4408

Fear of flying

Relax Air
876 Eastern Avenue
Ilford
Essex IG2 7HY
Tel: 081-554 8000

Aviatours
c/o City Press Services
Chapel House
172 Chapel Street
Manchester M3 6BG
Tel: 061-832 7972

Safety

Control Risks Group
83 Victoria Street
London SW1H 0HW
Tel: 071-222 1552

Streetwise Map Company
The Lodge
Franklyn Road
Godalming
Surrey GU7 2LD
Tel: 0483 861278

The Counter Spy Shop
62 South Audley Street
London W1V 5FE
Tel: 071-408 0287

Spycatcher
25 Lowndes Street
London SW1X 9JF
Tel: 071-245 9445

FURTHER READING/REFERENCE

Official Airline Guides
Bridge House
Lyons Crescent
Tonbridge
Kent TN9 1EX
Tel: 0732 352668

ABC Executive Flight Planner
ABC International
Church Street
Dunstable LU5 4HB
Tel: 0582 600111

The Airline Passenger's Guerilla Handbook – George Albert Brown (Blakes Publishing Group)

The Tropical Traveller – John Hatt (Penguin Books)

Travellers' Health: How to Stay Healthy Abroad – Richard Dawood (Oxford University Press)

The Traveller's Handbook – Ed Sarah Gorman (Wexas Ltd)

Taking the Fear out of Flying – Maurice Yaffe (David and Charles)

USEFUL MAGAZINES

Business Traveller – Ed Gill Upton
Compass House
22 Redan Place
London W2 4SZ
Tel: 071-229 7799

Executive Travel – Ed Mike Toynbee
6 Chesterfield Gardens
London W1Y 8DN
Tel: 071-355 1600

Inside Flyer – Ed/Publ Randy Petersen
Flightplan Inc
4715-C Town Center Drive
Colorado Springs
CO 80916
USA
Tel: (719) 597 8880

AIRLINE RESERVATION TELEPHONE NUMBERS

Aer Lingus
UK: 081-899 4747
US: 800 223 6537

Aeroflot
UK: 071-355 2233

Aerolineas Argentinas
UK: 071-494 1001

Air Canada
UK: 0800 181313
US: 800 776 3000

Air France
UK: 081-742 6600
US: 800 237 2747

Air India
UK: 071-491 7979

Air Lanka
UK: 071 930 4688

Air New Zealand
UK: 081-741 2299
US: 800 262 1234

SOURCES OF FURTHER INFORMATION ■ 225

Air UK
UK: 0345 666777

Air Zimbabwe
UK: 071 499 8947

Alaska
US: 800 426 0333

Alitalia
UK: 071-602 7111
US: 212 903 3300

All Nippon Airways
UK: 071-355 1155
US: 800 235 9262

American Airlines
UK: 0345 789789
US: 800 433 7300

Ansett Airlines
UK: 0345 747767

Australian Airlines
UK: 081-897 4400

Austrian Airlines
UK: 071-434 7300

British Airways
UK: 081-897 4000
US: 800 452 1201

British Midland
UK: 071-589 5599

BWIA International
UK: 071-839 9333

Canadian Airlines Int'l
UK: 081-667 0666
US: 800 426 7007

Cathay Pacific
UK: 071-747 8888
US: 800 233 2742

Cayman Airways
UK: 071-581 9960

China Airlines
UK: 071-434 0707

Cityflyer Express
UK: 081-897 4000

Continental Airlines
UK: 0800 776464
US: 800 231 0856

Cyprus Airways
UK: 071-388 5411

Delta Airlines
UK: 0800 414 767
US: 800 221 1212

El Al Israel Airlines
UK: 071-437 9255
US: 800 223 6700

Emirates
UK: 071-930 3711
US: 800 777 3999

Egyptair
UK: 071-734 2395

Finnair
UK: 071-408 1222
US: 212 689 9300

GB Airways
UK: 081-897 4000

Garuda Indonesia
UK: 071-486 3011

Gulf Air
UK: 071-408 1717
US: 800 553 2824

Hawaiian Airlines
US: 800 367 5320

Iberia
UK: 071-830 0011
US: 800 772 4642

Icelandair
UK: 071-388 5599

Japan Airlines
UK: 071-408 1000
US: 800 525 3663

Jersey European Airways
UK: 0345 676676

Kenya Airways
UK: 071-409 0277

KLM
UK: 081-750 9000
US: 800 374 7747

Korean Air
UK: 071-930 6513
US: 800 438 5000

Kuwait Airways
UK: 071-412 0006

LOT Polish Airlines
UK: 071-580 5037

Lufthansa
UK: 0345 737747
US: 800 645 3880

Malev Hungarian Airlines
UK: 071-439 0577

Malaysia Airlines
UK: 081-862 0800

Northwest Airlines
UK: 0345 747800
US: 800 225 2525

Olympic Airways
UK: 071-409 3400
US: 800 223 1226

Pakistan Int'l Airlines
UK: 071-734 5544

Philippine Airlines
UK: 071-379 6855
US: 800 435 9725

Qantas
UK: 0345 747767
US: 800 227 4500

Royal Air Maroc
UK: 071-439 4361

Royal Brunei Airlines
UK: 071-499 9249

Royal Jordanian Airlines
UK: 071-734 2557

Ryanair
UK: 071-794 0544

SAS
UK: 071-734 6777
US: 800 221 2350

Sabena
UK: 081-780 1444
US: 800 955 2000

Saudia
UK: 081-995 7777

Singapore Airlines
UK: 081-747 0007
US: 800 742 3333

South African Airways
UK: 071-734 9841

Swissair
UK: 071-439 4144
US: 718 995 8422

Thai Airways Int'l
UK: 071-499 9113

Turkish Airlines
UK: 071-499 9249

Transavia Airlines
UK: 0293 538181

Transwede Airways
UK: 0293 568812

TWA
UK: 071-439 0707
US: 800 892 4141

Tunis Air
UK: 071-734 7644

United
UK: 081-990 9900
US: 800 538 2929

US Air
UK: 0800 777333
US: 800 428 4322

Varig Brazilian Airlines
UK: 071-629 5824

Viasa (Venezuela)
UK: 071-493 5573

Virgin Atlantic
UK: 0293 562000
US: 800 862 8621

Zambia Airways
UK: 071-491 7521

HOTEL RESERVATION NUMBERS

Best Western
UK: 0345 737373
US: 800 782 9422

Canadian Pacific
UK: 0800 898852
US: 800 828 7447

Choice Int'l
(Sleep/Comfort/Quality Inns,
  Clarion Hotels)
UK: 0800 444444
US: 800 221 2222

Ciga
UK: 071-930 4147
US: 800 221 2340

Concorde
UK: 0800 181591
US: 800 888 4747

Conrad
UK: 081-780 1155
US: 800 445 8667

Consort
UK: 0800 272829

Copthorne
UK: 0800 414741

Edwardian
UK: 081-564 8888

Flag/Friendly
UK: 0345 242400
US: 800 624 3524

Forte
UK: 0800 404040
US: 800 225 5843

Four Seasons
UK: 0800 282245
US: 800 332 3442

Golden Tulip
UK: 0800 951000
US: 800 344 1212

Hilton Worldwide
UK: 081-780 1155
US: 800 446 6677

Hilton UK
UK: 071-734 6000

Holiday Inn
UK: 0800 897121
US: 800 465 4329

Hyatt
UK: 0345 581666
US: 800 233 1234

Ibis
UK: 071-724 1000

Imperial Family of Hotels
UK: 071-584 5018

Inter-Continental
UK: 0345 581444
US: 800 327 0200

Kempinski
UK: 0800 898588
US: 800 426 3135

Leading Hotels
UK: 0800 181123
US: 800 223 6800

Loews (LRI)
UK: 0800 282811
US: 800 223 0888

Mandarin Oriental
UK: 0345 581442
US: 800 526 6566

Marriott
UK: 071-439 0281
US: 800 228 9290

Meridien
UK: 071-439 1244
US: 800 543 4300

Mount Charlotte Thistle
UK: 071-937 8033

New Otani Int'l
UK: 071-437 1002
US: 800 421 8795

Novotel
UK: 071-724 1000

Oberoi
UK: 0800 515517
US: 800 6 OBEROI

Omni International
UK: 071-937 8033
US: 800 843 3311

Orient Express
UK: 071-928 6000
US: 800 237 1236

Pan Pacific
UK: 071-491 3812
US: 800 327 8585

Peninsula
UK: 0800 181123
US: 800 223 6800

Prima
UK: 0800 181535
US: 800 447 7462

Queens-Line
UK: 0800 289330

Rafael
UK: 0800 282684
US: 800 223 1588

Ramada/Renaissance
UK: 0800 181737
US: 800 228 9898

Regent Int'l
UK: 0800 282245
US: 800 545 4000

Resort
UK: 0345 313213

Ritz-Carlton
UK: 0800 234000
US: 800 241 3333

SAS Int'l
UK: 0500 100737

Shangri-La
UK: 081-747 8485
US: 800 942 5050

Sheraton
UK: 0800 353535
US: 800 325 3535

Small Luxury Hotels
UK: 0800 282124
US: 800 525 4800

SRS
UK: 0800 898852
US: 800 223 5652

Stakis
UK: 0800 262626

Swissotel
UK: 0800 898338
US: 800 637 9477

Taj
UK: 071-828 5909

Westin
UK: 071-408 0636
US: 800 228 3000

Reservation agencies

Expotel
UK: 071-328 9841

Utell
UK: 071-413 8877
US: 800 44 UTELL

AIRLINE DESIGNATOR CODES

AA	American Airlines	CO	Continental Airlines
AC	Air Canada	CP	Canadian Airlines Int'l
AF	Air France	CU	Cubana
AH	Air Algerie	CX	Cathay Pacific
AI	Air India	CY	Cyprus Airways
AJ	Air Belgium	C9	Compagnie Aeronautique Européene
AL	Alsair		
AM	AeroMexico	DB	Brit Air
AO	Aviaco	DC	Golden Air Flyg
AP	Aliadriatica	DD	Conti-Flug
AR	Aerolineas Argentinas	DE	Condor Flugdienst
AT	Royal Air Maroc	DI	Deutsche BA
AV	Avianca	DL	Delta Air Lines
AY	Finnair	DM	Maersk Air
AZ	Alitalia	DO	Dominicana
BA	British Airways	DS	Air Senegal
BC	Brymon European Airways	DX	Danair A/S
BD	British Midland		
BG	Biman Bangladesh	EI	Aer Lingus
BI	Royal Brunei	EK	Emirates
BL	Pacific Airlines	ET	Ethiopian Airlines
BM	Aero Trasporti Italiani	EY	Europe Aero Service
BP	Air Botswana	EZ	Sun-Air
BR	Eva Airways	FA	Finnaviation
BU	Braathens SAFE	FC	Berliner Spezial Flug
BW	BWIA	FF	Tower Air
BX	Coast Air	FG	Ariana Afghan
BY	Britannia Airways	FI	Icelandair
CA	Air China	FQ	Air Aruba
CB	Suckling Airways	FR	Ryanair
CI	China Airlines	FU	Air Littoral
CK	Gambia Airways	FV	Viva Air

GA	Garuda Indonesia	LE	Airlink
GC	Lina Congo	LG	Luxair
GF	Gulf Air	LH	Lufthansa
GH	Ghana Airways	LO	LOT-Polish Airlines
GI	Air Guinee	LT	LTU Int'l Airways
GM	Flitestar	LX	Crossair
GN	Air Gabon	LY	El Al Israel Airlines
GR	Aurigny Air Services	LZ	Balkan-Bulgarian
GT	GB Airways		
		MA	Malev
HE	LGW Walter	MD	Air Madagascar
HM	Air Seychelles	ME	Middle East Airlines
HN	KLM CityHopper	MH	Malaysia Airlines
HV	Transavia	MK	Air Mauritius
HX	Hamburg Airlines	MN	Commercial Airways
HZ	Euroflight Sweden	MP	Martinair Holland
		MR	Air Mauritanie
IB	Iberia	MS	Egyptair
IC	Indian Airlines	MU	China Eastern Airlines
IG	Meridiana		
II	Business Air	NB	Sterling Airways
IJ	TAT European Airlines	NG	Lauda Air
IL	Istanbul Airlines	NH	All Nippon Airways
IQ	Interot Airways	NI	Portugalia
IR	Iran Air	NN	Air Martinique
IT	Air Inter	NQ	Orbi Georgian Airways
IV	Air Gambia	NS	Eurowings
IW	AOM French Airlines	NW	Northwest Airlines
IY	Yemenia	NX	Nationair
IZ	Arkia Israeli Airlines	NZ	Air New Zealand
JE	Manx Airlines	OA	Olympic Airways
JG	Swedair	OK	Czechoslovak Airlines
JL	Japan Air Lines	OM	Air Mongol
JM	Air Jamaica	OS	Austrian Airlines
JY	Jersey European	OU	Croatia Airlines
		OV	Estonian Air
KE	Korean Air		
KF	Air Botnia	PB	Air Burundi
KI	Air Atlantique	PK	Pakistan Int'l
KL	KLM	PR	Philippine Airlines
KM	Air Malta	PS	Air Ukraine Int'l
KQ	Kenya Airways	PT	West Air Sweden
KR	Karair	PV	Latvian Airlines
KU	Kuwait Airways	PY	Surinam Airways
LA	Lan-Chile	QC	Air Zaire
LC	Loganair	QF	Qantas

QM	Air Malawi	TQ	Transwede Airways
QS	Tatra Air	TU	Tunis Air
QU	Uganda Airlines	TW	TWA
QZ	Zambia Airways	TZ	American Trans Air
RA	Royal Nepal	UA	United Airlines
RB	Syrian Arab	UK	Air UK
RC	Atlantic Airways	UL	Air Lanka
RD	Avianova	UM	Air Zimbabwe
RG	VARIG	US	USAir
RJ	Royal Jordanian	UU	Air Austral
RK	Air Afrique	UY	Cameroon Airlines
RN	Euralair Int'l		
RO	TAROM	VA	VIASA
RY	Air Rwanda	VG	Eurowings
		VO	Tyrolean Airways
SA	South African Airways	VS	Virgin Atlantic
SD	Sudan Airways	VV	Flexair
SK	SAS		
SN	Sabena	WA	Newair
SO	Austrian Air Services	WT	Nigeria Airways
SQ	Singapore Airlines	WY	Oman Air
SR	Swissair	WZ	BASE Business Airlines
SU	Aeroflot	XV	Air Express
SV	Saudia	YK	Cyprus Turkish
SW	Air Namibia	YO	Heli Air Monaco
		ZA	ZAS Airline of Egypt
TC	Air Tanzania	ZB	Monarch Airlines
TE	Lithuanian Airlines		
TG	Thai Airways Int'l	3G	Skywings
TI	Baltic Int'l	6E	Malmo City Air
TK	Turkish Airlines	7Y	Albanian Airlines
TP	TAP Air Portugal	9U	Air Moldova

AIRPORT/CITY CODES

ABJ	Abidjan, Ivory Coast	AMS	Amsterdam, Netherlands
ABQ	Albuquerque, US	ANC	Anchorage, US
ABZ	Aberdeen, UK	ANK	Ankara, Turkey
ACA	Acapulco, Mexico	ANR	Antwerp, Belgium
ACC	Accra, Ghana	ATH	Athens, Greece
ADD	Addis Ababa, Ethiopia	ATL	Atlanta, US
AKL	Auckland, New Zealand	AUH	Abu Dhabi, UAE
ALG	Algiers		
AMM	Amman, Jordan	BAH	Bahrain

232 ■ THE HIGH FLYER'S HANDBOOK

BCN	Barcelona, Spain	GBE	Gaborone, Botswana
BER	Berlin, Germany	GIB	Gibraltar
BEY	Beirut, Lebanon	GLA	Glasgow, UK
BFS	Belfast, UK	GVA	Geneva, Switzerland
BHX	Birmingham, UK	HAM	Hamburg, Germany
BJL	Banjul, Gambia	HAN	Hanoi, Vietnam
BJS	Beijing, China	HAV	Havana, Cuba
BKK	Bangkok, Thailand	HEL	Helsinki, Finland
BNE	Brisbane, Australia	HKG	Hong Kong
BNJ	Bonn, Germany	HND	Tokyo (Haneda), Japan
BOG	Bogota, Colombia	HNL	Honolulu, US
BOM	Bombay, India	HOU	Houston, US
BOS	Boston, US	HRE	Harare, Zimbabwe
BRU	Brussels, Belgium		
BSL	Basle, Switzerland	IAD	Washington (Dulles Int'l), US
BUD	Budapest, Hungary	IST	Istanbul, Turkey
BUE	Buenos Aires, Argentina		
BUH	Bucharest, Romania	JED	Jeddah, Saudi Arabia
		JFK	New York (John F Kennedy), US
CAI	Cairo, Egypt		
CBR	Canberra, Australia	JKT	Jakarta, Indonesia
CCS	Caracas, Venezuela	JNB	Johannesburg, South Africa
CDG	Paris (Charles de Gaulle), France	JRS	Jerusalem, Israel
CHC	Christchurch, New Zealand	KHI	Karachi, Pakistan
CHI	Chicago, US	KIN	Kingston, Jamaica
CMB	Colombo, Sri Lanka	KRT	Khartoum, Sudan
CPH	Copenhagen, Denmark	KTM	Kathmandu, Nepal
CPT	Cape Town, South Africa	KUL	Kuala Lumpur, Malaysia
		KWI	Kuwait
DAM	Damascus, Syria		
DAR	Dar es Salaam, Tanzania	LAS	Las Vegas, US
DEL	Delhi, India	LAX	Los Angeles, US
DFW	Dallas/Fort Worth, US	LED	St Petersburg, Russia
DHA	Dharan, Saudi Arabia	LGA	New York (La Guardia), US
DKR	Dakar, Senegal	LGW	London (Gatwick), UK
DOH	Doha, Qatar	LHR	London (Heathrow), UK
DUB	Dublin, Ireland	LIM	Lima, Peru
DXB	Dubai, UAE	LIS	Lisbon, Portugal
		LOS	Lagos, Nigeria
EDI	Edinburgh, UK	LUN	Lusaka, Zambia
EWR	New York (Newark), US	LUX	Luxembourg
FCO	Rome (Leonardo da Vinci), Italy	MAD	Madrid, Spain
		MAN	Manchester, UK
FPO	Freeport, Bahamas	MBA	Mombasa, Kenya
FRA	Frankfurt, Germany	MCT	Muscat, Oman

SOURCES OF FURTHER INFORMATION ■ 233

MEL	Melbourne, Australia	SCL	Santiago, Chile
MEX	Mexico City	SEA	Seattle, US
MIA	Miami, US	SEL	Seoul, Korea
MIL	Milan, Italy	SFO	San Francisco, US
MNL	Manila, Philippines	SGN	Ho Chi Minh City, Vietnam
MOW	Moscow, Russia	SHA	Shanghai, China
MRS	Marseille, France	SIN	Singapore
		SOF	Sofia, Bulgaria
NAS	Nassau, Bahamas	STL	St Louis, US
NBO	Nairobi, Kenya	STN	London (Stansted), UK
NRT	Tokyo (Narita), Japan	STO	Stockholm, Sweden
NYC	New York City, US	SVO	Moscow (Sheremetyevo), Russia
ORY	Paris (Orly), France	SYD	Sydney, Australia
OSA	Osaka, Japan		
OSL	Oslo, Norway	THR	Tehran, Iran
		TIP	Tripoli, Libya
PAC	Panama City	TLV	Tel Aviv
PAR	Paris, France	TPE	Taipei, Taiwan
POS	Port of Spain, Trinidad & Tobago	TUN	Tunis, Tunisia
PRG	Prague, Czech Republic	VIE	Vienna, Austria
RAK	Marrakesh, Morocco		
RBA	Rabat, Morocco	WAS	Washington, US
REK	Reykjavik, Iceland	WAW	Warsaw, Poland
RGN	Rangoon, Burma		
RIO	Rio de Janiero, Brazil	YUL	Montreal, Canada
ROM	Rome, Italy	YVR	Vancouver, Canada
RUH	Riyadh, Saudi Arabia	YVZ	Toronto, Canada
SAO	Sao Paulo, Brazil	ZRH	Zurich, Switzerland

☐ Index

ABC World Airways Guide 54
accidents *see also* security and safety
  cars 106–8
after hours 14
  brothels 150–2
  etiquette 204–5
  meeting people 153–4
  women 196–7
AIDS and HIV 50, 53, 150–2, 180–1
air fares
  class 35–6, 41
  codes 42
  deregulation 34
  discount 38, 40–1
  promotions 37–8
  round-the-world 38
  three-day excursions 38
  tricks of the trade 39–40
air traffic control 23–4
Air Transport Users Committee 33
Air Travel Consumer Reports 24
The Airline Passenger's Guerilla Handbook (Brown) 139
airlines
  class 35–6
  complaints 32–3
  congestion 23–4
  credit cards 165–6
  deregulation 22–3
  effects of recession 11, 17–18
  hub networks 20, 22
  jargon 48
  liability 32–3
  losing tickets 29
  luggage allowance 30–1
  mega-carriers 18, 20
  mergers 18, 20
  overbooking 29–30
  performance data 24
  smoking 26–7
Airpass 37
airplanes
  cockpit mechanics 136–7
  safety 133–7
airports
  business meetings 67–8
  checking in 63–4
  city-centre 63–4
  congestion 70
  connecting flights 71–2
  customs 72–4, 76
  delays 70
  duty-free shopping 68–70
  food 65–6
  future improvements 24–6
  lounges 66–7
  meeters and greeters 80
  parking 62–3
  porters 78
  tickets and check-in 25
  transport 80–1
Airports Guide International (Thomas Cook) 80
America: A user's guide (Hoggart) 95
apartments 128
Apex 36, 37
aromatherapy 183
Association of British Travel Agents 41
ATB (automatic ticket and boarding passes) 25
Automobile Association (AA) 131

banks
  changing money 160–1, 162
  travellers' cheques 162, 164

INDEX

black market
  currencies 161–2
boarding passes 25
body language 202–3
booking 54–5
books 68
bribery 79, 170–1, 206
Brown, George Albert
  The Airline Passenger's Guerilla Handbook 139
bucket shops 46–7
bumping 48, 70–1
bureaux de change 160–1, 162, 167–8
buses 81, 111
business cards 56, 204
business class 35–6, 84–6, 88–9
Business Traveller (magazine) 54, 84, 104, 123, 124
Business Women's Travel Club 189

car parks 139
car rental 103–6
  accidents 106–8
  costs 103–6
  credit cards 169
  fly-drive 104
  insurance 103–4, 105–6, 107
  theft 140
Channel Tunnel 111
checking in 25, 63–4
cheques
  Eurocheques 164
  travellers' 160, 162, 164
children 195
Circadian Travel Technologies 184
class
  business 35–6, 84–8
  economy 92–4
  first 91–2
  mid-economy 90, 93
  upgrades 89–91
clothes
  in-flight 57, 186
  packing 57
  women 197–8
code-sharing 46
communication 201–3
  body language 202–3
  in-flight 27
complaints 60

airlines 32–3
computer reservation system (CRS) 43, 45–6
computers
  hotels 124, 125
  in-flight 27
  laptop 56
Conde Nast Traveller 135
conferences 214–15
consulates 168
Control Risks 144
conventions 214–15
corporate hospitality 218–20
Counter Spy Shop 145
credit and charge cards 165–9
  airlines 29
  hidden charges 168
  theft and fraud 166–8
crime *see* security and safety
cruises 217–18
currencies 159–60 *see also* money
  black market 161–2
  changing 79, 160
  customs 51, 73
  ticket tricks 39–40
customs 72–4, 76

Dawood, Dr Richard
  Traveller's Health 178
denied boarding compensation (DBC) 30, 48
departure taxes 65
deregulation 22–3
  air fares 34
  bucket shops 47
diarrhoea 178–80
dress *see* clothes
drinking
  driving 108, 141
  duty-free spirits 68
  etiquette 205
driving licences 107
drugs 73, 76, 180

eating
  tipping 169–70
  women 193
economy class 36, 92–4
Egon Ronay 131–2
entertaining 204–5

236 ■ INDEX

entertainment *see* after hours
etiquette 211
   after hours 204–5
   forms of address 202
   gifts 206
   punctuality 203
   taboos and superstitions 206
Eurobudget 37
Euromoney 84, 124
Europ Assistance 52
European Community
   air fares 34
   blue channels 73
   business travel industry 11–12
   deregulation 22–3
   health care 182
   travel agents and 44–5
European Currency Unit (ECU) 160
Executive Club International 105
executive jets 98–100
Executive Travel (magazine) 24, 54, 84, 123, 124, 182
Expression (magazine) 123

fares
   public transport 112
   sharing a jet 100
fatigue 141
fax machines 56
   hotels 124, 125
   in-flight 27
fear of flying 186–7
ferries 111
fifth freedom flights 48
film (photographic) 65
first class 35–6, 91–2
flights *see also* airlines; airports
   connecting 71–2
   delays 70
flying, fear of 186–7
food
   in-flight 28–9
   vegetarians 29
foreign languages 211
   chatting up in 156
   communication 201–3
   phrase books 56
frequent flyers 89–90, 94–8
   hotels 120
   lounges 88

   mileage madness 94–6
   reward options 96–7
   tax 96
   transfer options 97

GESA Assistance 52
gifts 206
Guild of Business Travel Agents 44, 47

Half Price Europe 117, 118
Hatt, John
   The Tropical Traveller 143, 178
health *see also* AIDS and HIV
   animal hazards 178
   diseases 176–8
   drugs 180
   hotel spas 125
   immunizations 175–7, 178
   in-flight fitness 185–6
   insurance 181–2
   jet lag 182–5
   medical insurance 52–4
   stomach upsets and diarrhoea 178–80
   sun 180
   women 198
Health Advice for Travellers (Dept of Health) 182
helicopters 81
Hoggart, Simon
   America: A user's guide 95
holidays 51, 213–20
Hotel Express International 118
Hotel Proprietors Act 146
hotels
   after hours 154–5
   airport 72
   all-suite 127–8
   booking agencies 118
   business apartments 128
   charges 122
   choosing 123–6
   computer reservation system 46
   credit cards 168–9
   effects of recession 11, 115–16
   executive floors 126–7, 192–3
   fires 145–6
   green travelling 128–9
   health spas 125
   keys 147

INDEX ■ 237

loyalty benefits 119–20
luxury 129–30
overbooking 122–3
problems 121–2
rates 116–19
safes 146–7
security and safety 146–8
sex 155
taxes 122
technology 124–5
tipping 169–70
townhouse 130
travel agents 42
women 191–4, 196–7

immigration channels 25
immunizations 50, 175–7, 178
Inside Flyer (magazine) 96, 97
insurance 52–4
cars 103–4, 105–6, 107
health 181–2
private craft 100
International Air Transport Association (IATA) 11, 48–9
International Airline Passengers Association (IAPA) 40, 52, 67
car rentals 105
hotels 118
insurance 182
International Civil Aviation Organization (IACO) 49
International Investor (magazine) 123, 124
itinerary 51

jargon 48–9, 55
jet lag 182–5
light therapy 184

languages *see* foreign languages
Leading Hotels of the World 130
Learmount, David 133
liability
airlines 32–3
limousines 80, 111
lockers 79–80
lounges 66–7, 88
Love Talk in Five Languages 156
luggage 58, 60
airport security 138

allowance 30–1
carry-on 31–2
compensation 32
excess 64–5
forbidden items 32
left 79–80
lost or damaged 77–8
security 77–8

Mathieu, Albert 111
maximum permitted mileage (MPM) 48
Medical Advisory Service for Travellers Abroad 178
Medical Assistance Service for Travellers Abroad 181
medical insurance 52–4
United States 53
medical safety *see* health
meetings
airports 67–8
hotels 126
mergers 17
Michelin guides 132
mid-economy class 90, 93
Mile High Club 157
Mondial Assistance 52
money *see also* currencies
begging 171
bribery 170–1
budgeting 159–60
changing 160–2
claiming expenses 173
credit and charge cards 165–9
Eurocheques 164
shopping 171–3
tipping 169–70
travellers' cheques 162, 164
motorway toll charges 108

National Association of Independent Travel Agents 44
nationality 51
nightlife *see* after hours

Official Airlines Guides (OAG) 54
offline carrier 48
open jaw tickets 42, 48
overbooking 89
airlines 29–30

hotels 122–3
Overcoming Jet Lag (Ehret and Scanlon) 183

packing *see also* luggage
　clothes 57–8
　excess 64–5
　gadgets 55–6
　phrase books 56
　safety 31
parking 108
passports 50–1
Petersen, Randy 97
Pex 37
Phillips, Perrott 205
police 143–4
private jets 98–100
public transport 111
punctuality
　airlines 24
　delays 70
　etiquette 203
　Japan 207
　travellers' priority 83–4

A Question of Class (Hogg Robinson) 54

railways 112–13
Relais and Châteaux 130
round-the-world 38
Royal Automobile Club (RAC) 131

security and safety
　air travel 133–7
　airports 137–8
　cars 139, 140–1
　at home 148–9
　hotels 145–8
　luggage 58, 60, 77–8
　near-misses 137
　packing 31
　street crime 141–4
　taxis and touts 138–40
　terrorism 137, 144–5
　women 190
sex
　AIDS and HIV 152–3, 180–1
　aphrodisiacs 155–6
　brothels 150–2
　foreign language 156
　meeting people 153–4
　Mile High Club 157
　movies 156
sexually transmitted diseases 152–3
shopping 172–3
　bargaining 171–2
　duty-free 68–70
　in-flight 27
sidetrips 213–14
Signature (magazine) 205
Small Luxury Hotels 130
smoking 26–7, 185
smuggling *see* customs
spirits 68
stereotypes 207–11
　Africa 209–210
　Arab states 209
　Eastern Europe 208–9
　Europeans 210–11
　Japan 207–8
　Latins 208
　North Americans 207
　orientals 210
stomach upsets and diarrhoea 178–80
Streetwise Map Company 140
suitcases 58 *see also* luggage

Taking the Fear out of Flying (Yaffe) 186
taxes
　frequent flyers 96
　hotels 122
taxis 81, 108–11
　fares 110–11
　safety 138–40
　women and 196
technology
　hotels 124–5
telephones
　answering machines 124
　cards 121–2
　hotels 121–2, 124–5
　in-flight 27
television 124
terrorism 137
theft
　cars 104
　credit and charge cards 166–8
　home 148–9

INDEX

hotels 146–8
luggage 77–8
tickets 25 *see also* air fares
   back-to-back 39
   cross-border 39
   discounted 40–1, 46–7
   hidden city 40
   losing 29
   open jaw 42, 48
   reading 41–2
   reconfirming 55
tipping 110, 169–70
tobacco 68
toll charges 108
tourists 12
trade fairs 214–15
trains 80–1
travel agents 42–3, 90
   bucket shops 46–7
   choosing 47–8
   code-sharing 46
   EC packages 44–5
   hotels 118
   jargon 55
   management data 43–4
travel associations 105

Travel Safe (Dept of Health) 181
Traveller's Health (Dawood) 178
The Tropical Traveller (Hatt) 143, 178

underground trains 81, 111

vaccination *see* immunization
VAT 69–70
violence 141–4
visas 50–1

Wicked French 156
Wicked Italian 156
women 188–90
   abroad 195–6, 204
   with children 195
   dress 197–8
   harassment 198–200
   health 198
   hotels 196–7
   in-flight 194–5
   on the streets 198

Yaffe, Maurice
   Taking the Fear out of Flying 186

☐ Index of Advertisers

Ballantines	19
Bank of Valletta International Ltd	15
Beaufort House Services	35
British Homes London Flats Ltd	53
Boardroom Services	3
Cashback Consultancy (UK) Ltd	59
Cheval Apartments	iii
Datum Bridge	71
Diners Club International	13
Discount Telecommunications Cards Ltd	5
Draycott House Ltd	74, 75
Dubai Duty Free	ii
First Data Corporation	outside back cover
Fitzgerald & Associates	87
Hotelink International	21
Interlink Express Parcels	93
Lambs Department	99
New Internationalist Publications	221
Sloane Apartments	3
Sprint International	Inside front cover
Targus Benelux BV	7